Positive Systemic Practice

The Crosscare Teen Counselling Model
of Intervention for
Adolescents and their Parents
(A practice manual)

Alan Carr, Jane Fry, Tom Casey,
Mary Forrest, Fidelma Beirne and Ciara Cassells

with contributions from
Crosscare Teen Counselling Staff (2010-2012)

July 2013

Published by: Crosscare Teen Counselling,
The Red House, Clonliffe Road,
Dublin 3, Ireland.
www.crosscare.ie/teencounselling

Published: July 2013

Copyright: © Crosscare Teen Counselling
Manual and Research Committee

Format and design: Margaret Agnew, Administrator
Crosscare Teen Counselling.

Printed by: Casimir Print Ltd

Contact in relation to this publication:
Tel: 00353-1-4623083   Email: tomcasey@crosscare.ie

Price: €25.00

ISBN: 978-0-9926135-0-1

Acknowledgements

The model of work set out in this manual has evolved over almost 40 years. Teen Counselling, originally Mater Dei Counselling Centre, was initiated in 1973 to support the work of Guidance Counsellors in Dublin secondary schools. The service was under the auspices of The Mater Dei Institute of Education until the end of 1989 and subsequently under the auspices of Crosscare, the social care agency of the catholic archdiocese of Dublin (formerly the Catholic Social Service Conference). Since 2007 Teen Counselling has been a programme of Crosscare.

In 1990 the first Teen Counselling outreach centre was opened in Clondalkin, followed by Teen Counselling Tallaght in 1995, Teen Counselling Finglas (originally Ballygall Schools and Family Counselling Service) in 1998 and Teen Counselling Dun Laoghaire which started out in Ballybrack in 2002. Most recently Teen Counselling Blanchardstown was set up as a two day pilot in 2010.

We acknowledge the innovative work of the early pioneers in setting up a psychological service for adolescents 12-18 years, and their parents, and for evolving the systemic model. Many clinical and administrative staff members have contributed their skills and enthusiasm to develop the model and the service since 1973, but we particularly acknowledge the contribution of the staff group during the period 2010 to 2012, not only to the contents of this manual, but to the study which followed to evaluate the effectiveness of Positive Systemic Practice.

Our special thanks are due to *Professor Alan Carr*, School of Psychology, University College Dublin, for articulating the model of Positive Systemic Practice with such clarity, initiating and supervising the research project which followed and encouraging and supporting staff throughout the endeavour. We also acknowledge the guidance of the advisors to the project, *Professor Pat Dolan*, NUI Galway and *Professor Robbie Gilligan*, Trinity College Dublin, and the sustained and systematic work of our researcher, Ciara Cassells, post graduate student in the School of Psychology, UCD.

Mary Forrest, Jane Fry, Fidelma Beirne and Tom Casey
Crosscare Teen Counselling Manual and Research Committee

Teen Counselling development has been funded by:

- *the Health Service Executive (HSE), formerly the Eastern Regional Health Authority and the Eastern Health Board*
- *the Family Support Agency*
- *the Young People's Facilities and Services Fund*
- *the Charitable Infirmary Charitable Trust*
- *voluntary donations*

Practice manual development and research has been funded by:

- *the Teen Counselling Research Trust*
- *the Charitable Infirmary Charitable Trust*

We are very grateful for this support of our work.

Authors' Notes

Professor Alan Carr is the head of the School of Psychology and director of the Doctoral training programme in clinical psychology at University College Dublin. He is also a Consultant Couple and Family Therapist at the Clanwilliam Institute in Dublin. He has published over 20 books and 200 academic papers and conference presentations in the fields of family therapy and clinical psychology. His work has been translated into a number of languages including Korean, Polish and Chinese. He has extensive experience in family therapy and clinical psychology, having worked in the field in the UK, Ireland and Canada.

Jane Fry was the Senior Psychologist in Crosscare Teen Counselling when this manual was written and she co-ordinated the subsequent evaluation of 'Positive Systemic Practice'. Jane worked in Teen Counselling for 18 years. She is a Registered Member and Associate Fellow of the Psychological Society of Ireland (PSI) and has served on PSI Council and also as chair of the Child and Adolescent Special Interest Group. Her particular interest in adolescence began whilst working in the juvenile justice system where the need for early intervention and preventative work with teenagers and their families was very evident.

Tom Casey was a Senior Social Work Practitioner in Crosscare Teen Counselling when 'Positive Systemic Practice' was developed. Tom continues to work in Teen Counselling where he has 17 years' experience as a social worker. He is also a Psychotherapist and a member of the Irish Association of Humanistic and Integrative Psychotherapy and the Irish Association of Alcohol and Addiction Counsellors (IAAAC). Tom has experience of working in Child and Adolescent Mental Health and also has a private practice. He has developed a particular interest in mentalization which he uses in his work with families.

Jane and Tom worked together as a counselling team for 17 years and articulated the stances in this manual which guided their practice with teenagers and parents.

Mary Forrest was Clinical Director of Crosscare Teen Counselling during the period that the manual was written and 'Positive Systemic Practice' was researched. She continues to work in the service where she has worked for more than 25 years. Mary is a Clinical Psychologist and Family Therapist and is a registered member of both the Psychological Society of Ireland and the Irish Association of Family Therapy. Since her early career, as a guidance counsellor, Mary has been a vocal advocate for adolescents as a marginalised group without voice and holds strong views on the need for 'adolescent shaped' services as outlined in this manual.

Fidelma Beirne was the Senior Social Worker and Child Protection Officer in Crosscare Teen Counselling when 'Positive Systemic Practice' was developed. Fidelma continues to work in the service where she has more than 20 years' experience. She is an active member of the Irish Association of Social Workers and holds a Masters in Management in the Voluntary/Community Sector. She is a social work tutor and skills facilitator on the Bachelor of Social Studies (Social Work) programme at Trinity College Dublin. Fidelma is very aware of the importance of accessible community services in the spectrum of support available to families and their role in promoting the welfare and safety of teenagers.

Ciara Cassells is a Postgraduate PhD Psychology student in her final year at University College Dublin. She has an undergraduate degree in Psychology (Hons). Ciara also works as a lab demonstrator and tutor in the School of Psychology in UCD. Her research interests include family therapy and youth mental health. In addition, Ciara volunteers as a support group facilitator with AWARE.

Contributors – Crosscare Teen Counselling Staff 2010 – 2012
Clinical Staff: *Carol Donnellan, Fina Doyle, Averil Kelleher, Patricia McGuire, Simon Molloy, Siobhan NicCoitir, Orla O'Donovan, Brian Smith.*
Administrative staff: *Margret Agnew, Ann Donnellan, Monica Ferns, Catherine Fullam, Ann O'Sullivan, Nollaig Tubbert.*

Case examples in the manual are based on the real experiences of clients and counsellors; however names and non-essential details have been changed to ensure anonymity.

Introduction

Positive Systemic Practice started its life in 1973 with ideas generated from staff of the Diploma in Career Guidance course in the Mater Dei Institute for teacher training in Dublin. Recognising adolescent needs, these early educators realised that for Dublin teenagers and their parents, the existing services of Child Guidance Clinics were not always appropriate either in the medical model of access, or the 16 age cut off which applied. These early educators envisaged a service which school guidance counsellors, social and youth workers and others could offer to teens and parents which was not medically directed, was easily accessed, and dealt with teens up to 18 years of age. These seem modest aspirations today when many services are restructuring to address these issues, but 40 years ago it was very innovative.

From its early inception the service had adolescence as it area of expertise and retains this to this day. Again this was innovative as services for young people specialised in a single problem area for example mental health, addiction, criminality or education. Positive Systemic Practice addresses all of these issues holistically, at an earlier stage of the problem cycle and in a family context, and therefore is more likely to work with the 'drivers' of the problem than with their expression. The service was refined through the 1980s with a more formal systemic focus. Parents were equally involved in describing their difficulties, rather than receiving a diagnosis for their teenager, and also in agreeing a goal for the intervention

Providing therapy to teenagers poses unique dilemmas. They are not young children so giving parents open access to the content of a session is not appropriate, nor are they young adults so keeping parents out of the process, unless there are serious child welfare concerns, is equally inappropriate. In its search for the best way to help teens, Teen Counselling has developed a way of working which is tailor-made for each family. It is a transdisciplinary team model of counselling which involves two counsellors and both individual and family sessions. Both counsellors meet the parents and teens together for the first session to establish their perspectives on the presenting problems, their willingness to address them and to plan future work. Separate sessions are then planned, with one counsellor working with the teen and one with the parents. Both parents and teen are told that these sessions are confidential and what a teen says to Counsellor A is not told to their parents, and what parents say to Counsellor B is not told to the teen, but both counsellors discuss progress and problems together.

Trust and safety are the biggest benefits of this way of working, particularly when conflict is high, but even when a family are able to agree on the problem, it is usually understood differently by teens and their parents. Sometimes sharing these differences is useful and then conjoint sessions allow productive and therapeutic interactions without the need for separate sessions. More often with families seeking counselling for teens, mutual understanding and conversation are problematic. In these cases separate sessions are effective to process misunderstandings, hurts, complaints and secrets and to discuss family life. As the counselling team share information, the possibility of change is 'speeded up' and the risk of change being unacknowledged within the family is minimised. Using this model, when conjoint sessions are arranged there is a high likelihood of a constructive discussion which may be the first time in years that parents and teens have had such an experience.

During the 1990s the service started to expand to outreach centres and now has 6 locations around Dublin. In the mid-2000s it became increasingly evident that interventions with young people and their families needed to be evaluated. At conferences and in the literature I explored evidence based models, most usually from the US, and I was struck by the similarities to our Teen Counselling model of work, even though there were some significant differences. I was excited by the possibility of bringing an evidence based model to Dublin and a small group convened to explore this. However, it soon became clear that the economic climate was deteriorating and development funding would be a problem.

At one of these meetings Professor Carr said that he would be interested in evaluating the Teen Counselling model for two reasons; his belief in the value of a 'home-grown' treatment model which was attuned to the culture and values of its community, and also his knowledge and regard for the service acquired as a student, and through supervision of trainees. Over the years many social work and psychology students have chosen to do placements in the service and gain adolescent experience.

The work involved in producing this manual and setting up the research was considerable and was spearheaded by the clinical staff in our Tallaght branch, Tom Casey and Jane Fry. All staff members were unstinting in doing what was required to contribute to the manual and to the complex task of evaluation. The commitment of the clinical administrative secretaries was crucial to the success of the project, as was the creative and sustained work of our administrator in producing the manual. This was a very intensive team effort and I much appreciated the support of all staff, a reflection I think of their belief in the value of the model. The research steering committee met regularly to address the many challenges that arose and the advice of Professor Robbie Gilligan and Professor Pat Dolan was most generous.

The final mention has to be of the more than 6,000 families with teens who have attended the service and allowed us to join with them in their struggle, and witness their success, as they found solutions to their problems. Daily we are privileged to see the courage of teens and the fortitude and care of their parents during the wonderful transformation that is adolescence.

Mary Forrest

Mary Forrest

Clinical Director - Crosscare Teen Counselling 2000 - 2012

Contents

Introduction

Contents

Contents

Contents

Contents

CHAPTER 1

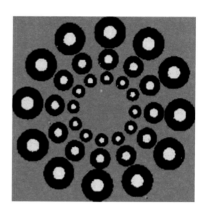

Positive Systemic Practice

This manual describes a model of counselling for adolescents and their parents (or those *in loco parentis* including foster parents, step parents, other family carers or residential service key workers). The model was developed within the Teen Counselling service in Dublin, Ireland. In this manual the approach is referred to as Positive Systemic Practice (PSP), because it emphasises strengths rather than deficits and focuses on the adolescent's social system, rather than the adolescent as an isolated individual.

1.1. Crosscare Teen Counselling Service

Positive Systemic Practice has evolved over 40 years within a community-based counselling service at centres which are now in six areas of Dublin. The Teen Counselling service is a programme of Crosscare, the social care agency of the Catholic Archdiocese of Dublin, and the Health Service Executive is the primary funder. Each of the six centres was founded and developed in response to community demand and most are located in disadvantaged areas. The service is offered free of charge and accepts self-referrals directly from parents as well as from schools, community agencies and family doctors. The service receives about 500 referrals per year, of which about half become clients and engage in counselling. The service is for adolescents aged 12-18 years, with approximately 60% of teen clients being under 16 years, and 15 year olds being the most usual referrals.

Teen Counselling was developed to provide a professional counselling service for adolescents struggling with behavioural and emotional problems and their parents, and also to inform, support and complement the role of the state sector and other voluntary organisations. In practice Teen Counselling meets the needs of adolescents and families who may be unwilling to engage with statutory mental health and child protection services, and those whose needs would not be prioritised within those services. A central policy of Teen Counselling is to be *'adolescent-friendly'* and to value, welcome, respect and protect all young people who attend the service. So while Teen Counselling primarily offers counselling services to its clients, where appropriate it also serves a child protection function. Addressing child protection issues is a critical aspect of this approach and will be addressed later in this manual. Counsellors in Teen Counselling have varied professional training e.g. psychology and social work, and a psychiatrist is available to the service on a consultation basis. The service offers a counselling service to clients, and also offers training and support to students and other agencies, as well as contributing to policy development on adolescent issues.

In the Teen Counselling Annual Report 2011 the following statistics were noted. The average waiting time was eighteen weeks. For cases closed during the year families engaged, on average, in 9 sessions over 9 months. This involved, on average, 24 hours of clinical time (counselling plus case management and administration), but there was considerable variability with a range from 2-144 hours. On the Children's Global Assessment Scale (CGAS[1]) which assesses adolescent adjustment, the average improvement was 17 points. On the Global Assessment of Relational Functioning (GARF[2]) which assesses family adjustment, the average improvement was 13 points. Both the CGAS and the GARF are 100-point scales. Over a 12 month period, a full-time team of two counsellors (with administrative support) manage about 80 cases, and usually intake two new cases per week.

Teamwork and supervision

Within Teen Counselling, clinical staff members work in teams comprising two counsellors. Parents and adolescents attend an initial conjoint session with the counselling team, and this is usually followed by parallel parent and adolescent sessions, where one counsellor works with the parents and the other with the adolescent. These parallel sessions typically occur over the same broad time period, but specific appointments do not usually occur during the same hour. There may also be periodic conjoint family sessions, in addition to parallel concurrent parent and adolescent sessions, according to a flexible counselling protocol. The confidentiality boundaries of individual and conjoint sessions are clearly explained. While this is the basic approach to practice, there are variations and the counselling team may decide that conjoint sessions only are most appropriate for a particular family or that for some older teenagers a more individual approach is indicated. Counselling teams receive regular supervision from a senior clinician. The counselling protocol and approach to supervision are described in detail in later chapters.

Professional ethics and professional indemnity insurance

At Teen Counselling, counsellors adhere to the ethical guidelines of their professions which include psychology and social work. The service has a Clinical Handbook and a Child Protection Policy. These well-developed policies and protocols underpin clinical practice. The service holds professional indemnity insurance.

Common adolescent problems

The most common reasons for referral to Teen Counselling are adolescent behavioural and emotional problems, and so it is these that PSP has been developed to address. Behavioural problems include disruptive behaviour, aggression, theft, substance misuse and rule-breaking at home and in school. Emotional problems include depression, anxiety, eating problems, self-harm, adjustment to illness and sexuality concerns.

Four domains – home, school, friends and self

Adolescents' behavioural and emotional problems are typically subserved by problematic relationships within the home, school or peer group contexts and are also affected by personal characteristics of adolescents themselves. However, these four domains of the adolescent's home, school, friends and self also contain protective factors and strengths which are potential resources for resolving presenting problems.

The transition to adolescence

Problematic relationships within the family, school and peer group may be associated with difficulties in adjusting to the transition to adolescence. This global transition involves a number of subsidiary transitions such as the gradual move from dependence to independence; from directed thinking to self-directed thinking; from parent-dictated rules to parent-adolescent negotiated rules; from primary to secondary education; and from being a school child to being an adult contributor to society. These transitions are challenging for adolescents themselves, but may also be challenging for their parents, their schools and their friends.

Family stresses

In some families, adolescent transitional problems are exacerbated by other significant family stresses such as intergenerational factors, social disadvantage, violence, trauma, parental separation, bereavement, or parental physical and mental health problems, including substance misuse. PSP helps families with these stresses by focusing on both the adolescents' and the parents' contribution to the difficulties and their strengths in finding solutions to presenting problems. Where appropriate, PSP also helps young people draw on strengths within the school and peer group contexts.

Aims and objectives

PSP aims to support the normal systems that support adolescents, such as the family, school and friends, so as to maintain adolescents within their families, schools and pro-social peer groups. It aims to help adolescents develop into well-rounded adults by reducing the negative impact of adolescent problems on later development.

These aims are best achieved through early intervention. When considering referral enquires, early engagement in counselling is encouraged, so that problems are *nipped in the bud*. Waiting for problems to escalate to crisis levels before starting counselling is actively discouraged when networking with potential referrers and Teen Counselling cannot provide a crisis intervention service.

PSP also achieves its aims through providing adolescents and parents with time and space, apart from their normal routines, in which to work out or resolve the issues that contribute to their distress.

In addition PSP achieves its aims by fostering strong therapeutic alliances, focusing on individual and family strengths, normalising adolescent problems, advocating for adolescents, and avoiding stigmatising and pathologising practices. Engaging in counselling is made as welcoming, user-friendly and attractive to adolescents and parents as possible. The Teen Counselling centres have been set up to look informal, yet professional, and counselling is provided free of charge. The establishment of a strong therapeutic alliance between counsellors and clients is prioritised from the outset. The development of a strong alliance between parents and adolescents is promoted by encouraging mutual understanding and respect. To normalise problems, wherever feasible, adolescents' difficulties are reframed so that they can be understood as part of the adolescent's and family's way of dealing with normal individual and family developmental challenges and processes.

1.2. Structure of the manual

This manual provides a detailed description of the Positive Systemic Practice approach to counselling developed at Teen Counselling centres over the past 40 years. The approach is an evolving one, and so this manual is a snapshot in time of what the approach looked like in 2012. We expect that it will continue to evolve. This manual is intended for flexible use. Like any clinical protocol, counsellors should use it in a way that fits with their clinical style and the needs of their clients. The manual is structured as follows:

Chapter 2. Principles of Positive Systemic Practice In chapter 2 the principles

of PSP are given. These are the overarching considerations which guide the management of any individual case.

Chapter 3. Stances in Positive Systemic Practice In chapter 3 the specific

stances that counsellors adopt to translate the principles set out in chapter 2 into clinical practice are described. Adopting these stances enhances engagement, facilitates child protection, promotes insight and understanding, fosters behavioural change, facilitates the transition to adulthood and facilitates closure in the counselling process. A description of stances within each of these areas is presented in this chapter.

Chapter 4. The referral process The referral process is described in chapter 4.

This covers managing referral enquiries, explaining the child protection policy and the limits of confidentiality, recording referral details, waiting list management, explaining the importance of parental involvement and addressing issues concerning consent to treatment.

Chapter 5. The first session The process of engaging with families is described in

chapter 5. This covers the aims of the first session which are forming an alliance, naming issues and developing a shared understanding. The therapeutic style of the first session is also addressed with reference to the importance of adopting a conversational approach; valuing all viewpoints; adopting a curious, respectful, invitational approach; being empathic; assuming normal developmental tensions; reframing conflict; and highlighting key issues. There is also a consideration of pre-session planning; the format of the first session with reference to the agenda for the first session; the session break taken after much of the interview has been completed; giving feedback of the preliminary formulation and counselling plan to clients; the team's post-session debriefing; and record keeping. The agenda for the first session includes the reasons for referral and the main concerns, and explorations of relevant factors from the four domains of home, school, friends, and self which are covered in detail in chapter 5.

Chapter 6. Middle and closing phases
The middle and closing phases of counselling are described in chapter 6. For the middle phase of counselling there is a discussion of using stances described in chapter 3 to work with adolescents and parents separately and in joint sessions. With respect to adolescents, there is focus on stances that help to strengthen the alliance; promote insight and understanding; and behaviour change. With respect to parents, stances appropriate for addressing both parenting issues and personal or couple issues are considered. In regard to family sessions, there is a focus on stances relevant to respecting all viewpoints; facilitating communication, negotiation and joint problem-solving; and making space for critical processes such as apology and forgiveness. For the closing phase there is a consideration of stances that facilitate a review of progress and setbacks; lessons learned during counselling; and future plans for relapse management.

Chapter 7. Teamwork, team development and supervision
With regard to teamwork, team development and supervision, there is a discussion of how members of counselling teams use information about the content and process of individual work with parents and adolescents to inform the overall counselling process, and of how supervisors match their supervision style to the developmental stage of a counselling team.

Chapters 8-12. Case studies
In chapters 8 to 12, five cases are described to illustrate what PSP is in practice. Working with a family with alcohol and drug use, sexual promiscuity and adolescent depression issues is described in chapter 8. Chapter 9 describes working with a violent father-son relationship. A case of mother-daughter conflict is outlined in chapter 10. In chapter 11 working with bullying, sexual abuse and

family violence is outlined. The main concerns in the final case study in chapter 12 are school expulsion, cannabis use, attention deficit hyperactivity disorder and family conflict.

Chapter 13. Evaluation of PSP The way counsellors routinely evaluate progress is described in this chapter. An archival study of PSP and the preliminary results from a controlled trial are also presented.

References

Appendices 1-4. The appendices contain a summary of the ten principles of PSP and the stances used to translate them into therapeutic interventions. They also contain responses to frequently asked questions about the Teen Counselling service, referral forms and assessment instruments used in routine practice.

SUMMARY

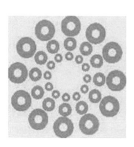

This manual describes Positive Systemic Practice, a strengths oriented model of counselling for adolescents who have behavioural and emotional problems, and their parents.

This approach was developed over 40 years within the Teen Counselling service in Dublin, Ireland.

The Teen Counselling service, which has six centres in various parts of Dublin, complements the statutory mental health and child protection services.

Clinical staff work in teams comprising two counsellors, and receive regular supervision from a senior clinician.

It is assumed that adolescent emotional and behavioural problems are affected by risk and protective factors within the four domains of home, school, friends and self, and are associated with difficulties in adjustment during the transitions of adolescence.

The aim is, through early intervention, to support the normal systems that support adolescents, such as the family, school and friends, so as to maintain adolescents within their families, schools and pro-social peer groups.

This manual includes 13 chapters and offers detailed guidance on how to conduct PSP.

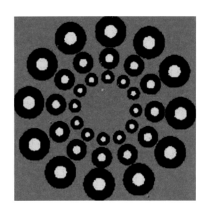

CHAPTER 2

Principles of Positive Systemic Practice

PSP is based on ten principles which are elaborated in this chapter[1]. The principles are:

1. A positive perspective

2. A systemic perspective

3. A normal developmental perspective

4. A preventative and therapeutic perspective

5. Counselling as phasic

6. Therapeutic alliance as central

7. Problem-solving in counselling as evidence-based

8. Motivation and resistance

9. Counselling team development

10. Evaluation

2.1. A positive perspective

Counsellors adopt a positive, optimistic, hopeful perspective[2]. While adolescents and their families present with distressing and complex problems, counsellors work from the optimistic premise that the level of distress clients experience can be reduced by working with them to find solutions to those aspects of their difficulties that are solvable (such as nightmares following trauma), or by supporting them in accepting and coping with unsolvable problems (such as grief following bereavement). Counsellors also assume that adolescents and parents have a degree of resilience and possess strengths and competencies that they may use to work out their difficulties. That is, there is an assumption that while adolescents and their families are referred because they have problems and associated risk factors, they also have strengths and protective factors.

Counsellors avail of opportunities to draw clients' attention to their strengths, competencies and resilience in the face of adversity. They encourage clients to mobilise these protective factors to address their difficulties. They also encourage clients to creatively use normal positive life events and challenges (such as birthdays, holidays, illnesses, or exams) to contribute to the resolution of the presenting problems. Finally, it is assumed that over the course of counselling in which counsellors have adopted a positive perspective, adolescents and parents will gradually embrace a more positive, optimistic and hopeful outlook on life.

2.2. A systemic perspective

Counsellors adopt a systemic perspective[3]. They view adolescents, not as isolated individuals, but as people embedded in multiple social systems including the family, the school and community, and the peer group. Problematic relationships (involving repetitive patterns of interaction, belief systems, narratives and emotional attachments) between adolescents and their parents, family members, school staff, community agencies and peers may contribute to, and maintain, adolescents' presenting problems. These problematic relationships may be exacerbated by family stresses including poverty, violence, trauma, parental separation, bereavement, parental physical and mental health problems or substance misuse. On the positive side, parents, family members, school staff, friends and other involved professionals may also be able to help with presenting problems, especially by changing problematic aspects of the way they conduct their relationships with referred adolescents.

Counselling teams organise counselling sessions to take account of the fact that adolescents are members of complex social systems. Counselling involves family sessions, sessions with the adolescent alone and the parents alone, and phone contact or meetings with other relevant members of the adolescent's social system, particularly school staff. Counsellors reframe the problems for which families seek help as family problems, rather than as problems intrinsic to the adolescent. This reframing is particularly important where parents take a very negative view of their adolescent's behaviour and deny or minimise their own roles in contributing to these problems through their own behaviour. Counsellors also reframe solutions as involving positive changes in the family rather than just positive changes in the adolescent. Counsellors also refrain from entering into alliances with parents, often displayed as knowing looks between adults which give the covert message that the adolescent is the problem.

Finally, counsellors assume that over the course of counselling they temporarily become members of the adolescents' and parents' social system, and by becoming members of this system can help families resolve problems, reduce distress and move from problematic to supportive ways of conducting their relationships. The degree to which this is possible depends upon the quality of the alliance counsellors develop with adolescents and parents, the counsellors' individual skills, the counselling team's effectiveness and the family's readiness for change.

2.3. A normal developmental perspective

Counsellors adopt a normal developmental perspective[4]. That is, they view individuals and families as progressing through a series of normal developmental stages over the course of the life cycle. Stages are characterized by relative stability, while transitions from one stage to the next are marked by significant changes in family's routines, rules and roles and individuals' personal characteristics. Adolescence is a transitional period. This global transition involves a number of subsidiary transitions such as the gradual move from having the physique of a child to that of an adult; from dependence to independence; from directed thinking to self-directed thinking; from parent-dictated rules to parent-adolescent negotiated rules; from primary to secondary education; and from being a school child to being an adult contributor to society. These transitions are challenging for adolescents themselves, but may also be challenging for their parents, their schools and their friends. For example the transition from directed to self-directed thinking is particularly challenging for some adolescents, whereas the transition from parent-dictated rules to parent-adolescent negotiated rules is particularly challenging for some parents. Adolescent behavioural and emotional problems and problematic relationships within the family, school and peer group may be viewed as difficulties in adjusting to the normal transitions of adolescence. However, these difficulties may be grounded in longer standing problems within the family system.

Counsellors match interventions to the developmental stage of the adolescent and family. Thus, interventions for younger adolescents (aged 12-14) making the transition from childhood to early adolescence are different to those for older adolescents who are making the transition from late adolescence to adulthood (aged 17-18). For parents of younger adolescents, psycho-education about parenting is an important component. For parents of older adolescents there is a focus on enhancing parents' and adolescent's capacity to negotiate with each other.

Counsellors normalise adolescent problems by reframing them as problems that can be understood as part of the adolescent's and family's way of dealing with normal individual and family developmental challenges and processes as opposed to using clinical diagnostic terminology to describe the presenting symptoms. Counsellors support the normal systems that support adolescents, such as the family, school and friends, so as to maintain adolescents within their families, schools, and pro-social peer groups. This enables them to develop into well-rounded adults by reducing the negative impact of adolescent problems on later development.

2.4. A preventative and therapeutic perspective

Counsellors attempt to prevent minor problems from developing into chronic, complex problems by encouraging early engagement in counselling. Counselling provides adolescents and parents with time and space, apart from their normal routines, in which to work out or resolve the issues that contribute to their distress. In an initial conjoint session the parents' and adolescents' views of the main problems are explored. If parents and adolescents have different concerns, an attempt is made to reframe these in terms of a common goal.

2.5. Counselling as phasic

Counselling evolves through phases[5]. It has engagement, middle and closing phases. The initial phase is concerned with engaging with adolescents and their parents, building an alliance with and between family members, exploring their main concerns, agreeing a focus or goals for counselling and generating hope that the family's goals can be achieved. In the middle phase, the emphasis is on therapeutic problem-solving. Counsellors draw on the available evidence-base about interventions that are effective for achieving the family's goals and individualise these interventions to fit with the family's unique needs. Helping the family to re-conceptualise their difficulties in a normative developmental way, where possible, and to understand how they drew on their strengths to overcome their difficulties, and developing plans for anticipating and managing future situations where there may be a risk of relapse is the main focus in the closing phase of counselling.

In each phase, key tasks must be completed before progressing to the next phase. Failure to do so may jeopardise the counselling process. For example, attempting to engage in therapeutic problem-solving without first having fully explored the main concerns may lead to conflict between clients and counsellors. In the early phase, parents and adolescents attend an initial conjoint session with the counselling team. Then most usually parallel parent and adolescent sessions are conducted where one counsellor works with the parents and the other with the adolescent. Usually much of the middle phase of counselling is conducted this way, with periodic joint family sessions according to a flexible counselling protocol. The concluding phase of counselling may involve parallel adolescent and parent sessions and most usually a closing joint family session.

2.6. Counselling alliance as central

Counsellors form therapeutic relationships in which they value, welcome, respect, protect and advocate for the adolescents and parents with whom they work[6]. Central to this is explaining and maintaining clear boundaries and confidentiality within parallel sessions for parents and teenagers. Engaging in counselling is made as welcoming, user-friendly and attractive as possible. Counsellors prioritise building a strong working alliance, since without it families drop out of counselling or fail to make progress. The only exception to this rule is where the safety of an adolescent or family member is at risk, and in such cases protection takes priority over alliance building. A respectful, invitational approach is adopted in which adolescents and parents are invited (not directed) to participate in counselling. Counselling is only conducted with client consent. Warmth, empathy and genuineness characterise the counsellors' communication style. Counsellors form collaborative partnerships in which family members are experts on their own families and lives, and counsellors are experts on adolescent problems and the counselling process.

Counsellors attempt to match the way counselling is conducted to clients' readiness to change, since to do otherwise may jeopardise the therapeutic alliance. For example, if a counsellor focuses on offering technical assistance with problem-solving to clients who are still only contemplating change and needing help exploring the pros and cons of change, conflict will arise. Clients will feel coerced into action by the counsellor and probably not follow through on therapeutic tasks, and the counsellor may feel disappointed that the clients are showing resistance. Counsellors avoid blaming clients even for unreasonable behaviour and take the initiative in resolving any difficulties or misunderstandings that occur which weaken the therapeutic alliance. As well as fostering strong alliances between themselves and family members, counsellors also promote positive and mutually respectful relationships between adolescents and parents; between families and schools; and between adolescents and pro-social peers. They continually reframe conflict and *'blaming'* between members of the adolescent's social system in positive terms. Conflict and blaming may be reframed, for example as, a reflection of the good intentions of those involved, a side effect of the adolescent's move towards increasing independence, personal hurt or disappointment being expressed as anger, or genuine misunderstanding. Counsellors also highlight the shared goal of all members of the adolescent's social system: to help the adolescent make the transition to adulthood and to grow up to be a well-adjusted adult.

2.7. Problem-solving is evidence-based and customised

In addressing adolescent and family problems, counsellors draw on the available evidence base about *'what works?'* but customise these interventions to clients' unique individual needs[7]. In the following three paragraphs, for illustrative purposes, conclusions from the evidence-base for the effective treatment of adolescent behavioural problems, depression and anxiety are summarised. Counsellors draw on this type of information, but customise it to the unique needs of specific cases.

For adolescent behavioural problems, effective evidence-based approaches involve empowering parents (teachers and those *in loco parentis*) to negotiate clear rules and consequences for rule keeping and rule breaking, and following through consistently in implementing such agreements; promoting mutually respectful communication and problem-solving between parents and adolescents, helping adolescents develop self-control, pro-social peer relationships and competence in school work; and helping parents manage personal vulnerabilities, such as mental health problems, that compromise their capacity to parent effectively. These interventions disrupt coercive and chaotic patterns of interaction between parents and adolescents, and destructive belief systems and narratives that maintain behavioural problems.

For adolescent depression, evidence-based systemic work includes facilitating parents' understanding and support of depressed adolescents and organising home-school liaison to help the teenager re-establish normal home and school routines, and a normal lifestyle. Adolescents often need a great deal of reassurance that they are not *'going mad'* and that their reactions can be seen as a reasonable reaction to the situation. Adolescent-focused interventions include exploration of contributing factors; facilitating mood-monitoring; increasing physical exercise, social activity and pleasant events; modification of depression-maintaining thinking styles, defence mechanisms and patterns of social interaction; the development and use of social problem-solving skills; and the development of relapse prevention skills. Where parents manage personal vulnerabilities, such as depression, that compromise their capacity to support their adolescents, these need to be addressed with evidence-based interventions. For adolescent depression there is also evidence that counselling may be offered as part of a multimodal programme of which antidepressants are one element. A psychiatric assessment is arranged when appropriate. Collectively, these interventions disrupt lifestyles, belief systems and unsupportive family interaction patterns that maintain depression.

For anxiety disorders in adolescents, evidence-based counselling involves helping adolescents and parents understand and monitor anxiety and avoidance behaviour; facilitating the development of relaxation and coping skills; and facilitating using these skills during gradual exposure to feared stimuli and situations. Parents may be helped to implement reward programmes to reinforce their adolescent's successful completion of exposure exercises and to avoid inadvertent reinforcement of avoidant behaviour. In cases of school refusal, home-school liaison is also required. Where parents have personal vulnerabilities, such as anxiety, that compromise their capacity to support their adolescents, these need to be addressed also. These interventions disrupt patterns of family interaction in which parents inadvertently reinforce adolescents' anxiety-related avoidant behaviour and empower adolescents to develop coping skills and courage.

When counsellors work with families of adolescents who have behavioural problems, depression or anxiety, they draw on this type of information and also on their knowledge of families' risk and protective factors. Counselling is therefore, evidence-based, but not evidence driven. It is customised to clients needs' and conducted in a *'seamless'* and subtle conversational style.

2.8. Motivation and resistance

From the start, setbacks in counselling are common. Families often have difficulty collectively agreeing to engage in counselling, and when they do they often take two steps forward and one step back. In these situations, counsellors acknowledge and address attitudes, expectations, emotional responses and interactional routines that clients and counsellors inadvertently bring to the working alliance from other contexts and relationships which interfere with therapeutic progress[8]. For example, demoralised clients with a history of many failed attempts to resolve their problems may believe that there is no point in following through on therapeutic tasks. Clients, who have had conflictual relationships with their parents, may inadvertently engage in similar conflictual relationships with their counsellors. These *'resistance issues'* are openly and respectfully discussed as they arise.

2.9. Counselling team development

Counsellors work in teams of two and engage in regular team consultation and supervision to develop their teams[9]. The quality of the alliance or relationship between team members is important for the success of counselling. In a team one member works with the adolescent and the other works with the parents. Team members meet regularly, initially to discuss how to conceptualise the difficulties the adolescent and parents are articulating, how to bridge the gap between those descriptions and then to develop a way of understanding the difficulties which honours both the adolescent's and parents' perspectives. Further on-going consultations focus on how to progress this developed understanding and decide the frequency, function and way of conducting joint family sessions. Within these conjoint sessions, it is essential for the counselling team members to have a strong alliance with each other, if they are to help adolescents and parents strengthen their relationship. For this reason, frequent case discussions between team members about the progress of specific cases are essential. Regular team supervision offers team members an opportunity to reflect on the process of team development, and also to think creatively about cases where progress is slow or difficult. In addition to team discussions and team supervision, counsellors attend individual supervision for personal and professional development, and administrative staff meetings which focus on referrals, service management and professional issues.

2.10. Evaluation

Counselling outcome is evaluated and counsellors take responsibility for helping families achieve positive outcomes. At the outset of each session, counsellors review progress. Families who make slow progress, or who have frequent setbacks, are not blamed for this. Rather the counsellor takes responsibility for exploring issues that make progress difficult. Before and after a course of counselling, adolescents and parents complete evaluation forms to assess the degree to which counselling has helped them address their problems and achieve their therapeutic goals. Counsellors also make a range of assessments before and after counselling.

SUMMARY

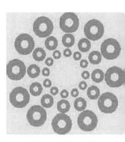

In this chapter the ten principles on which Positive Systemic Practice is based were presented.

1. A positive perspective Counsellors adopt a positive perspective in which they are hopeful that counselling can make a difference; where they are sensitive to family strengths; and where families may become more optimistic.

2. A systemic perspective Counsellors adopt a systemic perspective where adolescents are viewed as embedded in multiple social systems including the family, the school and community, and the peer group.

3. A normal developmental perspective Counsellors adopt a normal developmental perspective, seeing individuals and families as progressing through a series of normal developmental stages over the course of the life cycle, and viewing adolescence as a transitional period.

4. A preventative and therapeutic perspective Counsellors adopt a preventative and therapeutic perspective by encouraging early engagement in counselling, and where following an initial joint family session, adolescents and parents most usually engage in parallel confidential sessions, and periodic joint family sessions. In some instances only conjoint sessions are offered if counsellors judge this to be appropriate.

5. Counselling as phasic Counselling evolves through phases of engagement, a middle phase and a closing phase.

6. Therapeutic alliance as central Counsellors prioritise building a strong working alliance with clients and promote positive and mutually respectful relationships between adolescents and parents; between families and schools; and between adolescents and pro-social peers.

7. Problem-solving in counselling as evidence-based Counsellors draw on the available evidence-base about *'what works?'*, but customise these interventions to clients' unique individual needs; they conduct counselling in a conversational style.

8. Motivation and resistance Counsellors accept that setbacks in counselling are common and these *'resistance issues'* are openly and respectfully discussed as they arise.

9. Counselling team development Counsellors work in teams and two and engage in regular team consultation and supervision to develop their teams.

10. Evaluation Counselling outcome is evaluated and counsellors take responsibility for helping families achieve positive outcomes.

In light of these ten principles, PSP may be described, paradoxically, by contradictory characteristics. It is a *manualised* approach, but requires counsellors to be *creative* and individualise interventions to the needs of each family. It is deceptively *simple*, but in practice requires the use of *complex* and subtle clinical skills. It is a distinct and *well-defined* approach to systemic practice and yet it is *continually evolving*.

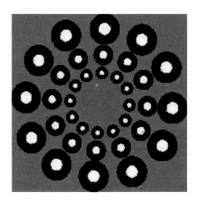

CHAPTER 3

Stances in Positive Systemic Practice

The principles which underpin PSP were set out in chapter 2. In this chapter, the specific stances that counsellors adopt to translate these principles into clinical practice are described. Stances have been developed to enhance engagement, to facilitate child protection, to promote insight and understanding, to foster behavioural change, to facilitate the transition to adulthood and to facilitate closing the counselling process. There is also a central fundamental stance which permeates all of PSP. A description of stances within each of these areas is presented in this chapter.

3.1. The Fundamental Stance

There are four stable elements in the fundamental stance of PSP:

- genuineness of relating

- understanding of the defensive

- recognising the underlying validity of differing perspectives

- only adopting an *'expert'* position where there are clear benefits

Be genuine in your relationship with adolescents and parents

The relationship between counsellor and client is at a human level[1]. It is a relationship in which one human being is *with* another, as distinct from a relationship in which there is an emphasis on one person being an expert and the other being a patient. The expert-patient model of the therapeutic relationship may create a boundary which distances the counsellor and client by stressing the differences between the two. This distancing process may weaken the therapeutic alliance. Thus, counsellors are known by their first names and no emphasis is placed on their disciplinary backgrounds. This facilitates a closer relationship and a stronger alliance between clients and counsellors. Where clients ask, it is appropriate for counsellors to indicate their clinical backgrounds, but not appropriate to put counsellors' disciplinary training at the centre of their relationships with clients.

Understand the defensive function of much problematic behaviour

Counsellors engage with each family from a position of curiosity and a belief that the intentions of family members are good, despite the fact that their behaviour may be challenging or hurtful. Thus, where adolescents are disrespectful, or parents say that they have had enough and are threatening to give up on their teenagers, counsellors are curious about the defensive function of this challenging or hurtful behaviour[2]. Such acting out is conceptualised as the defensive positions which adolescents and parents adopt because they have not been able to connect with each other and are defending themselves from the inherent disappointment of not being able to do so. Counsellors assume that this is not how family members want to be with each other and interpret their attendance at counselling as indicative of that, even if it is well disguised. Counsellors are curious about the disappointments, frustrations and fears that have prevented them from being able to listen to each other and express their need to be attached to each other in positive ways.

Recognise the underlying validity of differing perspectives of adolescents, parents and others in their social networks

Counsellors try hard to recognise the validity of the individual viewpoints of parents and adlescents[3]. This is difficult to do, because often these viewpoints are presented in highly defensive, negative ways. Adolescents who feel misunderstood and unsupported by their parents may express this as monosyllabic belligerence towards both parents and counsellors. Parents who feel helpless and disrespected by their adolescents may express this by criticising and blaming them. Counsellors actively avoid responding negatively to these defensive positions. They attempt to grasp the genuineness of adolescents' and parents' arguments. They attempt to empathise with the conflicting viewpoints of both parents and teenagers. Sometimes this is quite difficult, particularly with a belligerent or monosyllabic teenager. However, it is none the less possible to gain an appreciation of the genuineness of such a teenager's position, despite believing it to be based on a false premise. Similarly counsellors attempt to empathise with parents, even if they are inappropriately blaming of their adolescents.

Only adopt an 'expert clinical position' where there are clear benefits for clients

It is useful to make a distinction between a *'normalising position'*, where difficulties are conceptualised and discussed in normal developmental terms, and an *'expert clinical position'* where problems are conceptualised and described using diagnoses and other mental health constructs. Counsellors adopt a *'normalising position'*, unless there are clear benefits to adopting an *'expert clinical position'*. With a *'normalising position'* counsellors conceptualise the way teenagers and parents present the symptoms with which they come to counselling, and the way in which they talk about clients' concerns, in normal developmental terms. When this position is adopted, counsellors talk to clients in language that normalises rather than pathologises the young person's complaints.

Here is a description of a girl given from a *'normalising position'*:

Jennifer (age 13) presented with a lot of worry about general issues, but particularly about her mother to whom she felt <u>very</u> close. Her father seemingly was a distant figure for her. She had experienced an episode of self-harm (cutting) and now complained of feeling nothing and not being able to remember things at school. She seemed to sleep excessively and she had lost interest in some of her usual activities. She felt very fragile.

This example given from a *'normalising position'* is quite different to the following description of the same case given from an *'expert clinical position'*.

A 13 year old girl with possible enmeshment to her mother, depressive symptoms and possible alexithymia.

With the description given from the *'normalising position'*, everyday terms were intentionally used because they reflect how family members might talk to a counsellor and how the counsellor would talk to them about these issues. Grounding conceptualisations of families' difficulties in the descriptive language typically used by clients has important therapeutic advantages. Clients understand this sort of language better than that used when an *'expert clinical position'* is adopted. Clients experience counsellors who adopt a *'normalising position'* as more accessible. Everyday language also normalises, rather than pathologises client's complaints. When clients experience themselves being pathologised - viewed primarily as troublesome clinical entities rather than as normal human beings - this imposes a boundary between them and their counsellors. When counsellors adopt a *'normalising position'*, they avoid triggering those defences which client's may deploy when they hear a counsellor say that there is *'something wrong'* with them and their family. Everyone wants to be *'normal'* and to be perceived as such. All parents, without exception, want to believe that they have done a good job of bringing up their children, even when they acknowledge their family is having difficulties. Consequently, adopting an *'expert clinical position'* and the use of expert clinical or diagnostic language, such as that contained in DSM IV[4] or ICD 10[5], only aids engagement under very specific circumstances.

Counsellors must distinguish clearly between *'normalising'* and *'expert clinical'* positions and judge when it is appropriate to use each position. For reading clinical literature and communicating with certain professional colleagues, adopting the *'expert clinical position'* is appropriate. Clinical literature on evidence-based practices is inherently linked to clinical diagnoses, risk and protective factors and so forth. Counsellors must ground their practice in this literature, so adopting the *'expert clinical position'* is appropriate in this context. So too, is adopting this position when communicating with certain colleagues in medicine, psychiatry and other mental health professions. It is appropriate to adopt an *'expert clinical position'* in conversations with clients and members of their networks when this leads to clear benefits for referred teenagers[6]. Where parents, carers or schools have not recognised the presence of severe clinical conditions and the significant implications of these for the young person's well-being, future development and entitlement to health or educational resources, then adopting an *'expert clinical position'* may be justified. For example, where parents have not grasped the intensity of a teenager's depressive symptoms and how these impact on school attendance and academic performance, and are inappropriately blaming the young person for being lazy, then there are clear benefits to explaining that depression rather than laziness, accounts for their adolescent's school problems. Where young people meet the diagnostic criteria for conditions such as Attention Deficit Hyperactivity Disorder, Asperger's Syndrome, Obsessive Compulsive Disorders, Tourette's Disorder and so forth, a clinical diagnosis and *'label'* may be very important to teenagers and their families. The provision of a diagnosis may facilitate understanding and acceptance of challenging or problematic behaviours which have been the focus of concern; it may provide prognostic information which can help the family plan how to manage the condition in the future; it may suggest that referral to other mental health or educational professionals is appropriate; and it may enable resources to be allocated for support in school. Within PSP, adopting an *'expert clinical position'* is an intervention in and of itself, but one that is used only when there are clear benefits to doing so, that outweigh the costs of pathologising clients through *'labelling'* and running the risk of alienating them.

3.2.1. Stances to enhance engagement

The following 10 stances may be used to build therapeutic alliances and enhance engagement in the counselling process:

- Accept that a teenager's perspective is valid

- Respect teenagers and their struggle, and have a sense of humour

- Accept that teenagers are not a homogeneous group

- Do not over-react to teenagers' narratives (as this inhibits further communication)

- Accept that conflict between teenagers and parents is inevitable

- Normalise teenagers' occasional challenging behaviours

- Accept that good family relationships promote well-being

- Accept that parents really want to love and do the best for their teenagers

- Accept that parents really matter to teenagers

- Accept that counsellors working with teenagers and their parents have multiple roles.

Accept that a teenager's perspective is valid

When parents complain about their teenagers' behaviour they often expect other adults to agree that the young person is indeed unreasonable, selfish, out of order and so forth. Such parents may discuss their teenagers' behaviour with their relatives and friends in these negative terms. These conversations may result in a teenager becoming *'persona non-gratis'* with adults in their families and with their parents' friends. To express their disapproval of the young person's behaviour, and their solidarity with the parents, adults in the extended family and the parents' social circle may stop speaking to the teenager. Parents may expect counsellors, because they are adults, to join with them in criticising teenagers. They may expect counsellors to deal with teenagers as they do, by requiring them to conform to parental wishes.   Unfortunately teenagers often share these expectations prior to their first counselling session. This may sometimes account for their reluctance to attend.

For counselling to be effective, the counsellor always respects the teenager's perspective and accepts that it is valid[1]. Counsellors ask teenagers about their views of the difficulties which have brought them to counselling. They listen attentively and respectfully to their accounts, probing for missing details until as full and coherent an account as can be made has been given. It may be challenging for parents to listen to their teenagers talking, often at great length, about their views of the problems that have led to them coming for counselling. It may be particularly challenging for parents to see counsellors giving teenagers sustained attention and treating their views with respect and importance. In these conversations, it usually becomes clear that teenagers' problematic behaviour is an understandable reaction to some aspect of their lives. Validating teenagers' perspectives is central to engaging them in counselling.

Respect teenagers and their struggle, and have a sense of humour

It is a normal part of a teenager's individuation to test out different values and attitudes on their parents, teachers and authority figures - including their counsellor. The strength of this testing is often in direct proportion to the strength of a teenager's experience or expectation of resistance. An important aspect of working therapeutically with teenagers is to facilitate an exploration of their values and attitudes. Teenagers need to explore their values and how others respond to them. Facilitating this exploration involves respecting teenagers, respecting their struggle to find and articulate their values and attitudes, and having a sense of humour about the fact that they will inevitably challenge the values of adult authority figures. They may do this, by for example, pointing out inconsistencies between what we say others should do and what we ourselves actually do. If a counsellor adopts a stance which sends the message *'I know better'*, or lectures from an authoritarian position, this undermines the teenager's quest to discover their own values. If a counsellor adopts an expert, authoritarian position, or acts with condescension and without genuineness, young people are unlikely to use counselling in an explorative way.

The challenge for counsellors is not to be precious about their views and values. Their views are not absolutely right. They are the best they could find up to the current point in their lives, but are open to revision. There are multiple other possible points of view and values. Counsellors are tolerant of these and open to exploring them. This stance offers young people a good role model. It shows them how to be flexible. It also helps them to explore and find their own values. Such a stance also helps them to regulate their anxiety about growing up, clarify their own values and take charge of their lives. Parents and other authority figures of young people referred for counselling have often failed to adopt this stance, or been unable to maintain it in response to the young person's problematic behaviour. Rather, they have taken things *'very seriously'*, worried unduly, or become excessively critical. This flexible stance, that adult values are not always absolutely right, not only is empowering for teenagers, but also models a position for their parents that may help them to regulate the anxiety they may have about their teenagers' problematic behaviour.

Accept that teenagers are not a homogeneous group

'Well, you know what teenagers are like' is a commonly used phrase when parents are describing their teenager's behaviour. This phrase can refer to a multitude of behaviours from the relatively innocuous listening to loud music, to behaviours which are extremely oppositional, anti-social or life threatening. Simple single factor theories, like *'just hormones',* or *'video games'* or *'modern schooling'* or *'being bone idle'* may be suggested as the cause of all teenagers' problems such as mood disturbance, self-harm, aggressive or sexual behaviour. Parents may validate their simple single-factor theories from stories in the media or through accounts given by friends and neighbours who *'know what teenagers are like'*. The reality is that in thousands of ways, all teenagers are not alike and any teenager's problems are not due to one simple single factor, but to a complex constellation of multiple factors[7]. Teenagers know this. When they perceive adults to be taking the position that all teenagers are alike, their need to be respected and understood as unique individuals becomes frustrated. They feel misunderstood and offended, and this may exacerbate rather than resolve problems such as aggression, sexual acting out or self-harm. It is important for counsellors to help parents and other authority figures treat teenagers as individuals, and not to be distracted by stereotypes of what *'all teenagers are like'*. Parents feel misunderstood and hurt when their teenagers say things like *'all parents are alike: bossy, mean and clueless'*. Well this sense of *'not being seen'* and the hurt that goes with it is very similar to what young people experience when their parents say *'You know what teenagers are like. They are all the same: nothing but trouble'*.

Do not over-react to teenagers' narratives (this inhibits further communication)

If counsellors want to be allowed into a teenager's world and be told what is happening, they have to be able to handle the information teenagers tell them in a calm manner. If they over-react by becoming angry, anxious or agitated, teenagers will conclude that it is not safe to confide in them. They will not be seen as a secure base from which to explore their problems and concerns. In counselling, teenagers often recount experiences that they know would shock their parents or other adults. The role of the counsellor is to listen attentively to these narratives, come to a clear understanding of the teenager's point of view and empathise with their position so that the young person feels understood and respected. This does not mean that counsellors have to agree with, or condone rule-breaking or risky behaviour. Rather, they should give the teenager an invitation to recount their experiences and explore their reflections on these, so that they can come to their own conclusions about whether or not they did the right thing or made a mistake, and what they would like to do in similar circumstances in future.

This process often crystallises teenagers' sense of having made a mistake and strengthens their resolve not to repeat this mistake in future. If counsellors (and parents) are to be a resource to young people in making good decisions they need to allow them time to talk through their reflections on episodes of problem behaviour, before offering their own opinions or guidance. This can be challenging because it may require counsellors (and parents) to regulate their own strong reactions of anxiety, anger or agitation. Clearly there are occasions when there can be little debate about the inappropriateness of teenagers' rule-breaking or risk-taking behaviour, but prematurely offering an opinion does little to foster a teenagers' sense of accountability, responsibility and autonomy.

Accept that conflict between teenagers and parents is inevitable

During adolescence there are many influences on young people, apart from their parents and teachers. Teenagers are influenced by their peers, the TV, popular music, the internet, fashion, magazines, papers and other media. It is not surprising that on many issues they develop ideas and opinions which differ from those of their parents. Compared with pre-adolescent children, teenagers express their own opinions, which differ from those of their parents, more forcefully. This is because their drive for independence and autonomy becomes more powerful with the transition into the teenage years. Consequently conflict between parents and teenagers is inevitable[7]. However, the degree to which this conflict escalates into destructive battles or constructive conversation depends upon the way parents and teenagers manage conflict.

To manage conflict constructively, parents and teenagers need to learn to respect differences – to agree to disagree – and to work out compromises and accommodations which both can live with. Conflict resolution is an essential skill for all family members to learn. From a parent's perspective, there are so many potential issues to fight and argue with teenagers over, that parents need to carefully select issues where they go against their teenagers' wishes and preferences, and only take a stand when absolutely necessary. For example, differences of opinions about clothing, hairstyles and body piercings are probably not worth having a major row about. However, substance misuse, theft and promiscuity are serious issues, and parents taking a stand is vital for the young person's well-being. Sometimes parents become so tired of conflict that they actively avoid challenges and agree to all their teenager's demands, however inappropriate, *'for peace sake'*.

Normalise teenagers' occasional challenging behaviours

Teenagers are meant to be challenging. Survival of our species necessitates that young people grow up to become independent individuals in their own right. This transition to independence begins in adolescence. During the teenage years there is a strong drive to have greater freedom and to have more privacy. Teenagers occasionally do risky things to express this drive for freedom and privacy. They may stay out late at night. They may go to weekend-long rock concerts. They may get drunk or stoned. Most teenagers are far more secretive about their relationships and activities than pre-adolescent children. During the teenage years, in their struggle to become individuals, they try out different styles of outward appearance (clothes, make up, etc.), different behaviours and different values, attitudes, and opinions before settling on a relatively stable sense of identity.

For parents of young people referred to counselling, the way their teenagers try to express their need for freedom and privacy and the way they experiment with different styles, behaviours and values may be anxiety provoking. This can lead to angry confrontations between parents and teenagers, which may result in parents and teenagers becoming estranged from each other. In situations where teenagers' experimental behaviours have not become chronic behaviour problems, counsellors encourage parents not to react strongly to these new behaviours and to view them as a normal part of the individuation process. Such behaviours are often transitory. Unfortunately parents may jump to the conclusion that for example, a teenager's drunken night is the beginning of alcoholism as opposed to a bad mistake. Parents benefit from being reminded that they too made mistakes when they were teenagers.

Accept that good family relationships promote well-being

To protect teenagers and parents from distress associated with episodes of normal conflict, they need to regularly share positive non-conflictual time together so that their relationships can thrive[7]. If parents and teenagers do not know how to talk together about ordinary everyday matters in a way that makes them feel respected and understood, it will be very challenging for them to talk about difficult conflictual issues in a way that does not make them feel distressed. It is useful for counsellors assessing family communication, to ask about the amount of time parents and teenagers spend together doing activities or jobs, watching TV and eating meals. It is also useful to ask about the amount of time teenagers spend away from their parents, for example in their bedrooms, on their computers, or eating alone. Developing good communication between parents and teenagers is a focus for counselling in most cases, so that teenagers' relationships with their parents become a resource they can draw on when they need support.

Accept that parents really want to love and do the best for their teenagers

When there has been sustained conflict between parents and teenagers, both parents and teenagers may become deeply hurt. Unfortunately this hurt feeling can lead both parents and teenagers to adopt defensive postures that obscure the fact that parents really love their teenagers and want to do the best for them[3]. For example, after sustained conflict that has led to estrangement, parents may present with a victim-like, helpless and almost fatalistic attitude towards their errant teenagers. They may say things like: *'He doesn't care about us anymore. He only uses the place like a hotel. We have made sacrifices for him. But now he has no respect for us. We don't know what to do, but we want the best for him'.* In response teenagers may say *'You don't care about anyone but yourselves. You stopped me doing what I wanted. I hate you!'* Unfortunately this type of angry defensive posture taken up by teenagers may make it very difficult for them to hear the essential genuineness of their parents' message: that they really do care.

Counsellors must recognize these defensive postures as ways of coping with the underlying hurt and estrangement. The parents' victim-like helplessness and the young person's aggression are both their way of dealing with the fact that they have each temporarily lost a highly valued relationship and that this loss has caused each of them a deep sense of hurt. It is important for counsellors to be hopeful that eventually parents and teenagers will be able to connect with this underlying sense of hurt and loss; that parents will express their care for their teenagers from a strong protective position rather than a victim-like helpless one; and that their teenagers will be able to say they hear this, rather than hide behind a wall of anger. To hold the hope in this way involves distinguishing clearly between the underlying primary emotions of hurt, loss and love (or attachment) on the one hand, and the secondary defensive emotions of helplessness and anger on the other.

A useful distinction may be made between primary emotions, such as hurt and disappointment, which are often masked by secondary emotions such as anger or helplessness. Counsellors may acknowledge that parents and teenagers feel secondary emotions such as helplessness or anger. However, it is important for them also to suggest that under the anger and helplessness may be feelings of being hurt, disappointed or misunderstood. If the secondary emotions of helplessness and anger are given credibility as all that clients feel, then parents and teenagers may lose hope for recovery of their relationship. Counsellors must actively move to hold the hope for parents and teenagers until they connect with their feelings of hurt, loss and love and can hold the hope for themselves.

N B.

Accept that parents really matter to teenagers

Teenagers referred for counselling often state very vociferously that they hate one or other, or both, of their parents. They may also add that they do not care about their parents' behaviour towards them. The *'not caring'* may be about behaviour that, on the face of it, would clearly be hurtful to any son or daughter. For example, it may be about a separated father with whom there is little or no contact, or about a mother who is constantly finding fault and criticising the young person. The teenager's statements about hating parents and not caring about their behaviour may be accompanied by barely concealed tears. This is not surprising because, as was explained in the previous section, anger is frequently used as a defensive posture when young people experience a deep sense of hurt.

Parents really matter to young people. Teenagers need to be loved by, and attached to their parents[8]. They need to be cared for, understood and respected by them. When parents do not meet these very legitimate needs over a protracted period, young people become deeply hurt. They come to believe that they are not worth a great deal because their parents do not care about them. Rather than express these needs and risk further rejection or frustration, they adopt a defensive, angry posture. They say they hate their parents and they don't care about their parents' hurtful behaviour. When counsellors hear such statements, they may acknowledge that they represent part of what the young person feels, but not all of it. There is a duty for counsellors to invite young people to explore the underlying sense of hurt and loss that is concealed by the angry defensive posture and then to explore ways to re-connect the young person with their parents.

Parents of young people referred for counselling rarely wilfully frustrate their teenagers' needs to be cared for, understood and respected by them. Often this occurs inadvertently. For example, non-resident parents may have difficulty meeting regularly with their teenagers due to the high level of conflict with their ex-partners, the demands and responsibilities of their new living arrangements, or other problems such as addiction or imprisonment. Other parents who do not understand teenagers' needs for increased independence, freedom and privacy may interpret their teenagers' spending much time with their peers and little time with the family as rejection. In response they may become deeply hurt and resentful when their teenagers *'only want them for money'* or *'only want them for lifts'* as they see it. To cope with this hurt and resentment, such parents may adopt critical or punitive defensive postures, or withdraw from their parenting role. This on-going criticism or withdrawal may lead teenagers to feel hurt, uncared for and misunderstood. In these circumstances, counsellors help parents understand that what parents think about their teenagers is always of fundamental importance and a major factor in promoting self-esteem and self-worth. Counsellors promote appropriate contact between teenagers and estranged or non-resident parents. They also help parents to respond to a teenager's increasing needs for independence, freedom and privacy in a mature way that allows for increasing autonomy, but encourages a sustained caring connection with parents.

Accept that counsellors working with teenagers and their parents have multiple roles

Counsellors' roles include maintaining a therapeutic alliance, being non-directive and supportive in some circumstances, but being directive in others and being protective.

Counsellors have a central role in developing a therapeutic alliance with teenagers and maintaining this over time. With articulate young people this is straightforward. However, where teenagers cannot express themselves or give monosyllabic answers, but still make it clear that they want to engage in counselling, maintaining a therapeutic alliance is challenging. Considerable creativity may be required to help such teenagers express their views. Art, self-help workbooks, therapy computer programmes, diary writing, readings and other methods may be used to maintain therapeutic momentum. There is a greater amount of responsibility on counsellors working with such teenagers to maintain the alliance compared to those engaged in work with parents or more articulate young people.

Where a clear focus for counselling has been established that involves dealing with feelings of depression or personal distress, the role of counsellor is to *'accompany'* the young person on their therapeutic journey. The role entails helping them overcome their depression or process the trauma that caused the distress and move on. In such cases, the counsellor working with the teenager also has a responsibility to keep the parents and their counsellor informed about the pacing and impact of this sort of work, with the consent of the young person, so parents can appropriately support teenagers as they recover. Where parents have problems with low mood or unresolved issues, their counsellor also adopts the role of accompanying them on their therapeutic journey.

In contrast to the relatively non-directive role appropriate where the main concern is supporting the young person or the parents through distress, counsellors adopt a directive role where young people are engaged in on-going rule-breaking or risk-taking behaviour. For example, with young teenagers it's appropriate for a counsellor to state that it's not OK to drink 8 pints of beer at 14 years of age. It's also appropriate to be directive about unsafe driving, drug misuse, sexual promiscuity and criminality. A directive role is also necessary when working with parents whose judgements regarding the appropriateness of drink, drugs or sexual relationships are significantly different from societal or legislative norms. Taking a directive stance is particularly useful when parents treat teenagers as *'special'*, and adopt a very permissive stance towards them, rarely sanctioning rule-breaking or risk-taking behaviour, and not acknowledging the seriousness of their teenager's problematic behaviour. Parents may treat a teenager as *'special'* if he or she is an only child, a child who survived a life-threatening illness, or a child born after a stillbirth or cot death. The issue of *'special'* children is discussed later in the chapter in the section on stances that foster behaviour change. The stance deals with accepting that experiencing the consequences of their actions is essential for teenagers to learn to be responsible for their behaviour.

A final role that counsellors adopt entails child protection. A protective role is appropriate in cases where suicidality, domestic violence, child abuse, or physical aggression are central concerns. It is to stances associated with this role that we now turn.

3.2.2.   Stances to facilitate child protection

The following 5 stances facilitate child protection (in the broadest sense of the term):

- Make it clear from the outset that violence is not tolerated

- Make it clear that usually the longer young people stay in the education system the better

- Help families prevent destructive repetitive behaviour patterns

- Accept that parents are not always right, a positive influence or a resource

- Advocate for teenagers.

Make it clear from the outset that violence is not tolerated

Families are informed in the first session of counsellors' child protection responsibilities and the limits of confidentiality within counselling sessions, before any discussion takes place. If families then choose to disclose any significant abusive or violent incidents they know that counsellors will be obliged to report these to the relevant statutory agency (which in Ireland is the Health Service Executive or HSE). This will then lead to an assessment by the statutory child protection agency.

Where occasional episodes of escalating family conflict occur, and parents are violent to their teenagers, they are usually very ashamed about their loss of control. They may feel particularly ashamed about their inability to remain calm in response to their teenagers' provocative gestures or statements such as *'Go on then, hit me, you big f****** bully!'* In these situations, parents who have successfully relied on their greater size or volume of shouting to assert their authority in the past may find that they are unable to resolve these parent-child conflicts because their teenagers are as big as they are and can shout just as loud. When teenagers feel misunderstood, intimidated, hurt and frustrated by their parents in these sorts of situations, they can express their anger, attempt to protect themselves and obtain a sense of victory by taking the high moral ground, or ringing a help-line or the police to report their abusive parents. In other situations, where teenagers are bigger and stronger than their parents, teenagers may be the perpetrators. In these situations, teenagers may use the threat of violence or actual violence to get their own way and intimidate their weaker parents and siblings.

From a counsellor's perspective, these families are challenging to work with. No-violence contracts are essential to prevent, or reduce, the frequency and intensity of occasional violent incidents. Conflict in these families typically escalates very quickly. Parents and teenagers may have disagreements that lead to frustration, verbal abuse, aggressive gestures such as banging doors or throwing objects and then ultimately to physical violence. The task of the counsellor is to first stop the violence and then help families develop other skills for managing conflict. Counsellors also have to facilitate the processes of apology and forgiveness which are important for helping families move on from past violence and abuse.

Make it clear that usually the longer young people stay in the education system the better

Dropping out of school has a profoundly negative impact on the development of many young people[7]. It prevents, or seriously compromises, further academic achievement and this in turn limits employment and career opportunities. However, it also has a detrimental effect on social development. Daily school attendance provides young people with routine, structure, peer support and opportunities to learn about how to respond appropriately to authority figures. When teenagers stop regular school attendance, they lose all this. They often find that they have no reason to get out of bed before 3 p.m. and have nothing to do except watch television and *'hang out'*. This is a dreary and depressing way to live. Where young people have stopped regular school attendance, a priority is understanding why they *'can't hack school'* and then helping them to find a way to return to education. This will usually involve working closely with their parents and finding an appropriate educational setting.

There are many reasons why teenagers stop attending school. Some have learning difficulties which were not identified at an earlier stage and the repeated experience of academic failure eventually leads to dropping out of school. Others have separation anxiety and suffer abdominal pains or panic attacks when they attempt to leave the safety of their homes. They may also fear that something catastrophic will happen to their parents if they leave home and attend school. Bullying may prevent some teenagers from attending school. Teenagers from disorganised families may have difficulty conforming to the structure and authority inherent in schools and become engaged in escalating conflict with their teachers, culminating in suspension or expulsion.

When counsellors identify the key factors that have led to school non-attendance, then they can work with the school staff and the family to explore ways of helping the young person return to school. Schools are often prepared to work with counsellors to support young people and reduce the number of suspensions or the constant threat of expulsion. Where a return to the school previously attended is not possible, counsellors may help families explore possibilities for enrolment in another school or an alternative programme for young people who have dropped out of school.

Certain approaches have limited impact on school non-attendance. Teenagers who have dropped out of school rarely respond to advice about the negative impact lack of education will have on their future career, because they often have unrealistic ideas about getting work without any qualifications or training. A few hours individual home tuition, as an alternative to school attendance, does not provide sufficient structure or opportunities for learning to respond appropriately to authority to meet the needs of most young school non-attenders. When a young person is over 16 years old, there is sometimes a case to be made for them leaving school if other training or work opportunities are available. Some teenagers having struggled with school flourish in the world of work.

Help families prevent destructive repetitive behaviour patterns

Families of teenagers referred for counselling typically repeat the same destructive behaviour patterns over and over again, for months or years[3]. For example, a day may start with rows about the young person not getting out of bed; being too long in the bathroom; not eating a breakfast; wanting money for the bus, food, *'smokes'* or phone credit; wanting a lift, but not being ready; and being verbally abusive in their interactions with their parents about these issues, as their parents try unsuccessfully to help the teenager organise themselves for school. Everyone leaves home in a bad mood. The teenager may be late for school and rude with teachers. The school staff may ring the teenager's parents to complain about their behaviour. When the teenager returns home, the parents may be angry about the school's phone call, especially if it has happened previously. Conflict between the parent and young person may escalate. The teenager may storm out of the house without eating dinner (which the parents have prepared) and upset younger siblings in the process. The young person may ignore or object to any attempts parents make to discuss the situation or arrangements such as what time to return home, when to do homework or household chores. While out of the house the teenager may *'hang out'* with peers, ignore parental phone calls or texts, before arriving home late to stomp upstairs to bed. The next day the whole destructive cycle may repeat again!

Such parents and teenagers may become very angry and distressed as a result of engaging in these repetitive destructive behaviour patterns. Their distress may be compounded by the belief that the behaviour patterns are uncontrollable and will repeat again and again. Not knowing how to break out of such destructive patterns and knowing that each school day will be a disaster before it even begins can be very distressing. Counsellors should help families to understand these patterns and to identify ways to prevent them from repeating again and again.

Accept that parents are not always right, a positive influence or a resource

Most parents want what is best for their children. However, some parents have limitations that prevent them from meeting their children's needs in a sustained way[3, 6]. Parental addictions, abusive relationships, health problems and financial difficulties may all prevent parents from adequately caring for their children. As youngsters move from childhood into adolescence, they may become more judgemental of their parents and be able, and willing, to challenge them. It is essential for counsellors to acknowledge the validity of teenagers' concerns, consider the long-term impact of parental behaviour on adolescent development and explore ways for young people to have their parenting needs more adequately met. However, the process of addressing parental limitations is complex. While teenagers may be highly critical of their parents' shortcomings, if their counsellor also becomes critical of their parents, teenagers' loyalty to their parents may lead them to retract previous statements about their parents behaving badly. They may also minimise or deny the negative impact of their parents' neglectful or abusive behaviour.

Teenagers usually value the opportunity to let their parents know how their problematic behaviour affects them. They also may find it difficult to understand why parents do not take account of their criticisms and change immediately, by for example, giving up drug taking, alcohol misuse or gambling. When parents do acknowledge the impact of their problematic behaviour on their teenagers and apologise or make efforts to change, young people can be very forgiving. Counsellors have an important role in helping parents to access services to help them address problems that compromise their parenting capacity. They also have a critical role in facilitating the process of apology and forgiveness in these types of families and in helping young people to cope when parents are unable to change.

Advocate for teenagers

In families where teenagers are not adequately listened to or respected by their parents, counsellors may be advocates for them so that their voices are heard. For example, in joint family sessions counsellors who have conducted individual work with teenagers may help them present their views to their parents, so that their parents acknowledge their views and respond to them with respect. Where teenagers have inadequate resources at school to meet their special educational needs, counsellors can liaise with schools and explore ways for securing the required additional educational resources to meet the teenager's educational needs. Teenagers in care often value the advocacy role of a professional who is not part of the care system.

3.2.3. Stances to promote insight and understanding

The following 8 stances help parents and adolescents understand each other and gain insight into the impact of the family on the adolescent's development:

- Help parents and teenagers understand each other's perspective (even if they do not agree with it)

- Provide psycho-education to give parents and teenagers information relevant to their problems

- Help parents update their teenagers on how family history has affected their current lives

- Help parents address family of origin issues

- Accept that what is not said (and kept secret) is often as important as what is

- Help parents accept that they cannot re-live their own adolescence through their teenagers

- Help teenagers and parents explore the pros and cons of changing their behaviour

- Help parents and teenagers acknowledge and re-appraise negative thoughts.

Help parents and teenagers understand each other's perspective (even if they do not agree with it)

When teenagers and their parents come for counselling, often a central organising idea is *'who is right and who is wrong'*. This *'right and wrong'* frame of reference leads parents and teenagers to attack each other's views and defend their own. For families to resolve problems through counselling, this idea that there is one right viewpoint and all other viewpoints are wrong, must be replaced by a frame of reference in which it is normal for people to have different viewpoints on the same issue and where it is very useful for solving problems to be able to understand many of these viewpoints[3]. This frame of reference leads family members to try to understand each other, rather than prove that their viewpoint is right and other viewpoints are wrong.

Counsellors help families make this shift from the *'right and wrong'* frame of reference to *'understanding all viewpoints'* frame of reference by inviting each family member to explore their own views and those of other family members in detail. This gives them insight into their own positions and allows them to gain an understanding of positions held by other family members. This process may be used for facilitating understanding of mundane issues such as *'Why didn't you get up in the morning for school?'* to more complicated issues such as parental separations and family conflict. The emphasis is on exploring multiple perspectives and seeking to understand them, rather than immediately judging the correctness of each viewpoint. When counsellors invite parents and teenagers to understand each other's viewpoints they learn that it's possible to fully understand another person's position without having to agree with them. The experience of *'agreeing to disagree'* without having to engage in attacking and defending can reduce the frequency and intensity of destructive conflictual behaviour patterns. Conflicts between parents and teenagers are more likely to be resolved, and compromises reached, when the emphasis changes from who is right or wrong, to how well parents and teenagers can understand each other and empathise with each other's positions.

Provide psycho-education to give parents and teenagers information relevant to their problems

Where teenagers and parents lack necessary relevant information to deal effectively with their problems, counsellors can provide this. It may be provided in conversation, by suggesting or lending self-help books, or directing them to web-based or other material. Psycho-education may be provided on a range of topics including sexual issues, pregnancy, educational difficulties, the effects of drug misuse or specific syndromes such as ADHD. A critical aspect of psycho-education is discussing with clients the implications of the information for their specific problems.

Help parents update their teenagers on how family history has affected their current lives

The problems of teenagers referred to counselling are sometimes associated with significant historical events that happened within the family many years ago[3]. These include parental separations, imprisonments, family bereavements, accidents and serious illnesses. Teenagers sometimes have limited knowledge about these important events and may be very reluctant to broach the subject at home for fear of causing upset. Often it is important for teenagers to know about these events to be able to understand the impact of them on their current life situation. This need for information about significant family events increases as children mature into teenagers. A four year old may accept that dad is working in England. However, when that four year old becomes a teenager, he will be confused if his mother tells him his father is in England and his peers or other family members tell him his dad is actually in prison. Parents may not have told their teenagers about these significant historical family events recently for various reasons. In some cases it is because they thought their youngsters already knew about them because they explained the situation previously. In others it may be because parents did not want to cause distress to themselves or their children by remembering stressful family situations. For example, talking about absent parents who are not in contact with the young person is a particular challenge for teenagers, and the resident parent may find it very difficult to talk about their past partners. As young people develop they may need more regular and detailed discussions about these sorts of issues and counsellors can facilitate such conversations between young people and their parents so that the level of information shared is appropriate to the person's age and stage.

Help parents address family of origin issues

Some parents of teenagers referred to counselling have difficulties in meeting their young person's needs because of past challenges they faced in their families of origin, or because of on-going problematic relationships within their families of origin[3]. Parents who were abused, neglected, harshly treated or overprotected in their families of origin may re-enact the problematic parenting they received, or try desperately to avoid doing so, and as a consequence overcompensate. For example, those who were harshly treated may treat their own children harshly, or too leniently. Where parents are in on-going problematic relationships with their own parents, they may find that this interferes with their own capacity to parent teenagers. For example, a mother who continues to have an over involved relationship with her mother may find that she cannot work co-operatively with her husband to develop an agreed joint approach to parenting, because her own mother continues to influence her parenting style. In these situations, counsellors help parents acknowledge the effects of family of origin issues on the way they parent their teenagers, and explore ways of reducing negative effects of family of origin issues on current parenting.

Accept that what is not said (and kept secret) is often as important as what is

The problems of teenagers referred to counselling are sometimes affected by family secrets, or topics which are taboo and never talked about[9]. These include paternity issues, bereavements, domestic violence and child abuse. These family secrets may involve a great deal of hurt or shame and may have a significant impact on the family dynamics and relationships which in turn may affect the wellbeing of teenagers. Parents may feel that they are issues from the past and that their teenagers do not know anything about them and do not need to know anything about them. It is sometimes these issues which teenagers are most interested in discussing and yet it is not possible for them to raise these issues with their parents at home. In these situations, teenagers can benefit from having time to consider their parents' experience of being parented, abused, subjected to domestic violence, or separated and may then come to see why parents may be so *'hung up'* on a particular issue. This type of insight may help parents and teenagers understand each other and communicate better. This is a special instance of helping parents and teenagers understand each other's perspective, mentioned in the opening paragraph of this section.

Help parents accept that they cannot re-live their own adolescence through their teenagers

Parents of young people referred for counselling may want their teenagers to have the life that they themselves would have liked, but did not have. This is often an aspiration of parents who had children in their teens and for parents who did not have good educational opportunities, or did not avail of the opportunities available. Unfortunately a great deal of tension and conflict can build up between parents and their teenagers if they attempt to coerce their teenagers into avoiding making the same mistakes that they did. Parents' efforts in this regard often have a paradoxical effect. Teenagers whose parents coercively direct or nag them to avoid early pregnancy and do well in school may react by behaving promiscuously and underachieving academically. The problem is that to avoid remaking parental mistakes, teenagers need to be listened to and understood by their parents and given information so that they can make informed decisions about how to live their own lives. Coercion and nagging, in contrast, are likely to compromise their capacity for mature decision making[3].

Help teenagers and parents explore the pros and cons of changing their behaviour

Where parents or teenagers are ambivalent about changing their behaviour, or show resistance to making positive therapeutic changes, counsellors help clients explore the advantages and disadvantages of their problem behaviour or of making significant therapeutic changes[10]. For example, teenagers involved in drug misuse, may be invited to explore the pros and cons of drug use. Parents of teenagers with behaviour problems, who have not followed through on suggested new parenting plans, may be invited to explore the pros and cons of effective limit setting.

Help parents and teenagers acknowledge and re-appraise negative thoughts

Where depressed clients have pessimistic beliefs, anxious clients have threat-sensitive thoughts, or angry clients have hostile thoughts, counsellors may help clients acknowledge and challenge or reappraise them, using techniques from the cognitive behaviour therapy tradition[11]. For example, a teenager who believes she has been a failure may be invited to collect evidence to show that she has had some successes.

3.2.4.   Stances to foster behaviour change

The following 10 stances may inform interventions that foster therapeutic changes in parenting behaviour and adolescent behaviour problems:

- Help family members communicate, negotiate and jointly problem-solve

- Facilitate the processes of apology and forgiveness

- Help parents and teenagers develop clarity about acceptable and unacceptable behaviour (because *'everybody does not do stuff'*)

- Accept that parental over control and under control can lead to adolescent problems

- Respect family and community norms (unless they are too permissive or oppressive)

- Accept that experiencing the consequences of their actions is essential for teenagers to learn to be responsible for their behaviour

- Accept that mistakes are learning opportunities

- Help anxious teenagers develop courageous behaviour

- Help teenagers develop assertive behaviour

- Help family members develop self-care routines.

Help family members communicate, negotiate and jointly problem-solve

In joint family sessions, and in sessions attended by both parents, counsellors use opportunities to facilitate communication, negotiation and joint problem-solving[3]. Poor communication is a common problem in families of teenagers referred for counselling. Families may have difficulty with fair turn-taking. Family members may talk over each other, shout each other down, or remain silent. Family members may have difficulty actively listening to each other and empathising with each other's viewpoints, using the time when others are speaking to think up what they will say next rather than actively listening. There may also be difficulties with expressing views clearly and respectfully, with views being expressed vaguely, or in disrespectful or aggressive ways. Mind-reading may also occur where family members say things like *'You said X, but I know you really meant Y'*. When facilitating clearer communication, counsellors help family members to become better at fair turn-taking; active listening and checking that what was heard was what was intended; and speaking in a clear respectful way.

As teenagers mature, they need to negotiate with their parents about being permitted to have more freedom, privacy and autonomy. Parents also need to negotiate with each other about the shared approach they will take to parenting their maturing adolescents. Negotiation difficulties are common in families of teenagers referred for counselling. In some families, negotiations are problematic because family members misunderstand each other. They have difficulty communicating clearly (as outlined in the previous paragraph). Negotiation problems may also occur when family members take rigid inflexible positions, leading to angry standoffs, or where parents or teenagers do not follow through on their side of negotiated agreements. Counsellors help family members engage in these negotiations, by facilitating clear communication, flexibility, controlling the expression of strong negative emotions while negotiating, and following through on negotiated agreements.

On a daily basis families have to solve dozens of problems, like how everyone will get up on time and get to school or work, how the household jobs will be done, how people will get to sports or leisure events, how meals will be organized, how homework will be done, how different people in the house will get access to bathrooms, TVs or computers and how everyone will get a good night's sleep to be ready for the next day. There are also problems that families resolve on weekly, monthly and annual cycles, like how to get to and from outings at the weekend, organising holidays, arranging to go to rock concerts and so forth. Jointly solving some of these problems effectively may be challenging for families of teenagers referred for counselling. In some such families joint problem-solving is problematic because family members have difficulty communicating clearly (as outlined earlier). Difficulties may also occur when family members let negative feelings interfere with creatively looking for the best solutions and implementing them. Counsellors help family members engage in effective joint problem-solving, by facilitating clear communication, encouraging the exploration of multiple creative solutions, and then settling on the one with the most advantages and the fewest disadvantages, while preventing the expression of strong negative emotions from interfering with this process.

Facilitate the processes of apology and forgiveness

In some families referred for counselling, one family member has been hurt by another. Teenagers may be hurt by their parents. For example, parents may have neglected, mistreated, failed to protect, abused or disappointed their children. These sorts of difficulties may arise where parents have addiction problems, mental health difficulties, where parents are separated, or where adverse family of origin experiences compromise their capacity to parent adequately. Parents too may be hurt by their teenagers through engaging in on-going conflict with them or through behaviour problems such as violence, theft, drug misuse, promiscuity and so forth. In families where one family member has been hurt by another, counsellors may need to facilitate the processes of apology and forgiveness[12]. Counsellors help those who have hurt others acknowledge, and accept responsibility for, the hurt they have caused, and then express this to the person they have hurt. Concurrently counsellors help those who have been hurt listen to the apology, be open to the possibility of forgiveness and eventually, if possible, express this forgiveness. Facilitating apology and forgiveness can be a slow process and counsellors pace this work to suit the rate at which clients can progress.

Help parents and teenagers develop clarity about acceptable and unacceptable behaviour (because 'everybody does not do stuff')

Parents of teenagers referred for counselling, particularly where the young person is their first teenager, may be uncertain about what constitutes normal or acceptable adolescent behaviour. This uncertainty may be compounded by their teenager forcefully insisting that their parents are unfair because other parents treat their teenagers much more permissively. For example, such teenagers may argue that 'everybody does stuff' such as getting €50 at the weekend from their parents, staying out until 2 in the morning and drinking 8 cans of beer. They may then name half a dozen friends who they claim are permitted these privileges and argue that this proves that their parents are being unfair. The certainty with which teenagers make the assertion that 'everybody does stuff', the anger they direct at their parents for being unfair and parents' lack of information about what is normal or acceptable, all may make it very challenging for parents to confidently set clear limits; that is, to say what behaviour is acceptable and unacceptable. Counsellors have the advantage of working with many teenagers and their parents and being exposed to a very broad range of parenting ideas and styles and an equally broad range of teenage behaviours, both positive and negative. They can therefore confidently support parents in these arguments by saying that they know that 'everybody does not do stuff', (meaning all other teenagers of the same age do not behave in unacceptable ways). They can also point out that just because six of the teenager's closest peers *'do stuff'* does not mean that it is acceptable. This then may pave the way for parents and teenagers to negotiate a fair set of limits in a joint session.

Accept that parental over control and under control can lead to adolescent problems

The problems of teenagers referred for counselling may arise from parental over control or under control[6, 7]. Providing an appropriate amount of parental control, supervision and guidance is important for healthy adolescent development. As children mature and become teenagers the amount of control they need gradually decreases. During adolescence teenagers need to be supported so that they can develop their own judgement and the ability to make good decisions and take responsibility for them. Parents may find this challenging and err on the side of being over controlling or under controlling.

When parents exert too much control over their adolescents, this can lead to excessive conflict, because teenagers may see excessive control as unreasonable and unfair. Teenagers may become very frustrated and give up trying to negotiate reasonably with their parents about achieving a fair degree of freedom, privacy and autonomy. In some instances this frustration of the need for autonomy can lead to low self-esteem, low mood and social withdrawal. Teenagers may come to view themselves as helpless and unable to control their own lives. In other instances, teenagers may cope with overly strict limits set by their parents by becoming very secretive and telling their parents lies about where they have been and what they have been doing to avoid further conflict with their parents. They may spend a lot of time out of home with peers, to avoid their parents' restrictive limit setting. They may also engage in more risky behaviour involving drugs, sex or dangerous activities to assert their need for more autonomy, which in turn may lead to further difficulties such as drug dependency, teenage pregnancy or injury.

At the other extreme, parents may overestimate their teenager's ability to be autonomous and allow them too much freedom setting no clear limits or boundaries and providing too little supervision and guidance. They may have expectations of their teenagers which are much too *'adult'* and make statements such as *'Sure, they're reared'* or *'We're like mates now'*. Lack of parental control can lead to antisocial behaviour. Young people whose parents are too permissive and do not provide them with age-appropriate limits, supervision and guidance often have great difficulty controlling their behaviour. They may become uncontrollably aggressive to peers and authority figures such as teachers, sports referees, police officers and employers. They may also lie and steal outside the home because at home there may have been no adverse consequences for such antisocial behaviour, so they have no expectation of negative consequences when they do so in the community. Parental under control also leads teenagers to experience a distressing feeling of insecurity. They may experience a sense of loss that their parents are no longer prepared to supervise them. They may be upset by the fact that no one cares enough, or is strong enough, to guide them in an authoritative and benevolent way. Periodically they may be ashamed at the consequences of not being able to control their impulses, for example if they badly injure someone in a fight, or get suspended from playing sports for hitting the referee.

Counsellors should help parents and adolescents negotiate age-appropriate limits; that is, a fair set of rules about acceptable and unacceptable behaviour, with clear and reasonable consequences for adhering to or breaking rules. Where parents have difficulties engaging with this process, counsellors may explore parental issues, especially their experiences of being parented, that may be compromising their capacity to provide their teenagers with an age-appropriate level of control.

Respect family and community norms (unless they are too permissive or oppressive)

When young people referred for counselling have difficulties such as excessive drinking, drug misuse and sexually promiscuous behaviour, in the first instance it is important for counsellors to respond to these sorts of problems with non-judgmental curiosity to explore the circumstances that led to their development. There is also a requirement for counsellors to respect family and community norms when setting goals with teenagers and their parents about changes in drug and alcohol use, sexual behaviour and other risky behaviours. In some instances it may be appropriate for counsellors to challenge family norms if they are too permissive or too rigid; if they are significantly different from societal norms; or behaviours prohibited by legislation.

Accept that experiencing the consequences of their actions is essential for teenagers to learn to be responsible for their behaviour

Much of our behaviour is shaped and influenced by the consequences to which it leads[13]. We tend to engage in behaviour that is rewarding or fulfilling. In contrast, we tend to control impulses to engage in aggressive and destructive behaviours because these usually lead to negative consequences, such as being reprimanded, punished, injuring ourselves or feeling ashamed. Problems for some teenagers referred for counselling arise because their parents have protected them from experiencing the negative consequences of their problem behaviours. These young people do not learn to control their aggressive and destructive impulses and to take personal responsibility for their actions. Consequently, their behaviour becomes increasingly out of control. This is because their parents protect them from the consequences of their problem behaviours by, for example, paying their debts or for property they have vandalised; by complaining to school teachers who reprimand them for treating them unfairly; or by blaming peer pressure for leading them astray.

Such teenagers may have a *'special'* or privileged place in the family that underpins the protective way their parents treat them. For example, they may have been born after a stillbirth or cot death; they may be an only child; they may be an unexpected *'miracle'* baby born to a previously infertile couple; they may have been born following parental separation and given meaning and direction to the single mother's post-separation life; or they may have attained their privileged status after recovering from a serious illness.

Where parents have protected young people from the negative consequences of their problem behaviours, they may report a catalogue of their teenager's misdemeanours which had no meaningful consequences until the youngster came to the attention of the police for carrying out a seriously aggressive or destructive behaviour outside the home or school environments. Counsellors help parents to understand the importance of allowing their teenagers to experience the negative consequences of their problem behaviours, explore obstacles to them doing so and circumstances that have led them to protect their teenagers from such consequences.

Accept that mistakes are learning opportunities

We all make mistakes and if these mistakes lead to negative consequences, we learn not to repeat them[13]. Teenagers tend to make more mistakes than children or adults because developmentally they take greater risks and behave more impulsively, especially when they are with groups of friends. Teenagers referred for counselling may make more mistakes or larger mistakes than their parents can comfortably cope with. They may be repeatedly stoned or drunk or overdosed. They may crash a car or be injured in a fight. They may contract sexually transmitted diseases. They may be apprehended by the police for unlawful behaviour. Some families come for counselling after one very significant mistake for which their teenagers have been grounded *'forever'*. Others come for counselling after a big mistake which occurred following a history of many previous mistakes. These many previous mistakes may have arisen as a result of parents protecting young people from the consequences of their problem behaviour, as described in the previous section.

When parents view big mistakes as indicators that their teenagers will never again be trustworthy, they may review teenagers past mistakes each time the young person requests an extra privilege, more freedom or greater privacy. They may then use this review of past mistakes to justify not granting their teenager their current request. In this way, past mistakes are repeatedly revisited and never done with, forgiven or forgotten. They are viewed by parents as reliable indicators of how the young person will behave now and in the future. They are not viewed as important learning experiences which are now over, and from which the young person and the parents must move on. When parents repeatedly revisit past mistakes in this negative way, teenagers may point out that they have learned from their past mistakes, that these occurred long ago and that its time to look to the future. However, a teenager's time perspective is different from that of parents. What seems a long time ago to teenagers, may seem very recent to parents. When young people say *'that was ages ago'*, their parents may still be reeling from the night they spent in the hospital's accident and emergency department while their teenager's stomach was pumped following an overdose, or a night spent in the police station where the teenager was interviewed after a serious misdemeanour. It is important for counsellors to be sensitive to the differing time perspectives of teenagers and parent, and to help them understand each other's time perspectives. However, it is also important for counsellors to help parents and teenagers agree that to learn from past mistakes it is essential that at some stage the slate must be wiped clean and a fresh start made. This usually involves an agreed plan to make restitution, minimise risk and re-build trust.

Help anxious teenagers develop courageous behaviour

Where teenagers are scared or anxious in particular situations, counsellors help them develop courageous behaviour so they can deal with these situations more confidently[14]. This involves exploring ways to cope with anxiety in counselling and then using these coping skills to deal with a series of graded challenges in which they enter increasingly anxiety-provoking situations. Counsellors may involve parents in this process, inviting them to encourage their teenagers to follow through on graded challenges and providing praise and rewards if they are successful.

Help teenagers develop assertive behaviour

Where teenagers have become involved with antisocial friends who entice them to engage in antisocial behaviour, then counsellors may help them plan ways of assertively refusing to be involved with these sorts of peer groups[15]. Some teenagers become involved in romantic relationships and feel uncomfortable about the way their boy or girl friends treat them, but are unable to say so. In these instances, counsellors can help them plan assertive responses to make to their partners.

Help family members develop self-care routines

Where family members have been putting the needs of others before their own to an excessive degree, counsellors invite clients to consider increasing their level of self-care. This is appropriate, for example, where single parents devote most of their energy to parenting, or teenagers spend a lot of time caring for parents who have addictions, disabilities or other problems.

3.2.5.   Stances to facilitate the transition to adulthood

The following 7 stances may facilitate adolescents' transition to adulthood:

- Help parents let go of directive parenting and adopt a style based on negotiation – because when primary school is over parenting must change

- Help parents to manage their anxiety so as to promote their teenager's independence

- Help parents provide teenagers with age-appropriate jobs to do at home

- Help parents allow their teenagers opportunities to develop strategies for protecting themselves in their social environment

- Help non-authoritative parents to be parents (not friends) to their teenagers

- Ask teenagers to take responsibility for their attendance at counselling

- Help parents and teenagers accept that a parent's job is to become redundant.

Help parents let go of directive parenting and adopt a style based on negotiation – because when primary school is over parenting must change

During the pre-adolescent, primary school years, a directive approach to parenting is appropriate and parents arrange almost all aspects of a child's life. The life of the pre-adolescent is generally well structured and centred within the family, the school and the local community. Before adolescence parents organise their child's life and know almost everything about it and everyone involved in it. Once the transition to adolescence and secondary school is made, the situation changes dramatically. Teenagers' needs for increased autonomy, freedom and privacy are far greater than those of pre-adolescents[7]. They want to have an increasingly greater say in how they organise their lives. Therefore, parents should replace the directive parenting style they have been used to during the young person's pre-adolescent years with a style based on negotiation where they take account of their teenager's wishes and preferences. They must allow their teenagers increasing responsibility for organising their own lives, and accept that the teenager's horizons are broader than those of a pre-adolescent. When children mature into adolescents their lives expand beyond the family, school and immediate locality. Their peer groups change and expand, often including people who their parents do not know. In adolescence, opportunities for recreational activities increase dramatically and in many instances parents may not be fully familiar with all of their teenagers' activities.

This transition from rearing a child to rearing an adolescent may leave parents feeling out of control and worried. They have less control over their teenagers, less knowledge about their lives, they spend less time with them and there is less certainty about how each day will work out. They may feel as if parenting an adolescent is a journey into the unknown with a young person who no longer needs their constant companionship.

Parents of teenagers referred for counselling may be stuck in *'primary school parenting mode'.* They may be having difficulty making the transition from a directive parenting style to one based on negotiation. This can lead to distressing conflict. Teenagers may complain that their parents are overly strict and intrusive, giving them insufficient freedom and privacy. Teenagers may find it oppressive when their parents interrogate them, or their friends, about their activities; are inflexible about curfew times or giving permission to go to entertainment or recreational events; and check their school bags, bedrooms, diaries, and phones in an attempt to know *'everything'* about this new stage of life and about everyone in it. Parents may view their curiosity and concerns as perfectly reasonable. With these families, the counsellor's role is to help families make the transition from a directive parenting style to one based on negotiation.

Help parents to manage their anxiety so as to promote their teenager's independence

A key concern for some teenagers referred for counselling is the anxiety their parents experience in response to their growing autonomy. As teenagers mature and become more autonomous, they spend less time with the family and more time at school or work, or with their peers engaged in recreational activities outside the home[7]. In response to this increasing independence some parents worry unduly about their teenagers' safety and their ability to cope with the all of the new situations they encounter. To control this anxiety, some parents curtail their teenagers' activities or repeatedly check on their whereabouts (most often by mobile phone). Their anxiety prevents them from appreciating how important it is for their teenagers to expand their world and learn to take responsibility for keeping themselves safe outside the home. Some parents are so anxious that their teenagers cannot stop them worrying by reassuring them in the normal way; that is by discussing where they are going, who they are with, when they will be back and agreeing to contact home if difficulties arise and they need support.

Young people referred for counselling may cope with high levels of parental anxiety in ways that compromise their healthy development. For example they may stay at home to stop their parents worrying. In doing so they are deprived of essential opportunities for developing autonomy and parental trust in their ability to cope with the challenges of increasing independence. Other teenagers cope with excessive parental anxiety by keeping their life outside home a secret from their parents. They don't tell their parents about their friends or activities outside the home to prevent their parents from worrying, nagging, arguing or becoming ill. Unfortunately this type of secrecy may lead teenagers to become involved in risky behaviours, including substance misuse and sexual promiscuity. If parents find out about these risky behaviours, it reinforces their belief that the teenager cannot cope with greater independence and requires continual parental supervision and guidance. In counselling it is essential that such parents are helped to manage their anxiety more effectively so that their teenagers can enjoy an appropriate level of freedom and privacy and also feel comfortable discussing the important issues in their lives with their parents.

Help parents provide teenagers with age-appropriate jobs to do at home

Where teenagers referred for counselling don't have age-appropriate jobs to do in their homes, it is useful to help their parents provide them with such jobs, because these sorts of responsibilities can promote the development of autonomy[7]. It is not unusual to meet families in which one member, most usually the mother, does all the housework including the cleaning, washing, shopping, cooking, caring for the pets and so forth. In some such families, teenagers may be discouraged from helping around the house, because their parents expect that they will not do housework properly. This approach sends young people messages such as: *'Don't help because you'll do it wrong and make a mess'*. These messages do little to build young people's self-confidence. When parents in these families feel stressed by the amount of housework they have to do and aggrieved that their teenagers do not help, they may complain that their youngsters are lazy. This approach sends young people conflicting message such as: *'Be good and leave the house work to your mother, because you will mess it up'* and *'You're lazy for leaving all the housework to your mother'.* These conflicting messages are confusing to deal with and can lead young people to feel helpless and sad or angry. Counsellors should help parents arrange for their teenagers to take on jobs in the home which are appropriate to their age and stage of development. This may involve supporting parents to have positive expectations that their teenagers can help with housework; carefully negotiating with their teenagers about what jobs they will take on; teaching their teenagers the skills to do the jobs well; refraining from criticising the results of their teenagers' performance; and praising their positive efforts.

Help parents allow their teenagers opportunities to develop strategies for protecting themselves in their social environment

For shy or anxious teenagers who live in neighbourhoods with high rates of anti-social behaviour, it can be very challenging to walk to the shop or school and deal with the taunts or threats of aggressive peers. In Dublin, tough young people who engage in this kind of bullying when confronted deny or minimise its impact by saying *'Sure I was only messing; I was only slagging him'.* However, this kind of bullying can be very intimidating. It is, therefore, tempting for parents to be protective of their shy or anxious teenagers and perhaps accompany them out of the house or drive them everywhere to allay their own and their teenager's fears. Unfortunately this protective parental behaviour can have paradoxically negative effects. It may lead to protected young people developing a reputation of being unable to stand up for themselves. It also deprives them of opportunities to develop social skills, such as humour and assertiveness, essential for dealing with taunts or threats from antisocial peers. Counsellors should help parents to accept that, except in extreme situations, it is important for a teenager's self-confidence and their street credibility to learn strategies which enable them to move freely in their community and avoid intimidation[7].

Help non-authoritative parents to be parents (not friends) to their teenagers

For families of some young people referred for counselling the usual boundary between parents and teenagers does not exist, and parents have very limited authority over their teenagers. This non-hierarchical structure can occur in single-parent families; in single parent-families where a partner of the parent has recently moved in; in two parent families with a single child; or in families in which a son is protecting his mother from his abusive father. In these types of families, sometimes teenagers are treated as equals by their parents. They may be described by parents as best friends and may be deferred to in inappropriate ways. For example, by being encouraged to sit in the most comfortable chair in the counselling room! In non-hierarchical families, teenagers, on the one hand, enjoy many privileges and seem to have a great deal of freedom. However, on the other hand, they are deprived of the security offered by authoritative parents who maintain a boundary between themselves and their teenagers. They may feel trapped within the family, since their parents come to rely on them inappropriately. They are deprived of normal parental supervision and guidance, and gradual encouragement to become independent. They may become over involved in their parents' lives and find themselves monitoring their parents' relationships, drinking, drug misuse and financial worries. They may feel obligated to provide physical and emotional support for their parents rather than receive it. To help young people develop autonomy, counsellors must help parents in these non-hierarchical families to develop supportive relationships with people other than their teenagers, and then to make a clear boundary between themselves and their teenagers[3, 7].

Where a teenager has been fulfilling the role of their single parent's *'best friend'*, particular difficulties may arise if the parent finds a new partner. The young person may feel sad at losing the special relationship with their parent and angry with the new partner for displacing them and expecting them to respect their authority. Helping these families become reorganised so that there is a clearer boundary between the single parent and their partner on the one hand, and the young person on the other, can be challenging.

Commonly teenagers resist losing their privileged position. However, the feeling of security and the freedom from adult concerns that accompanies the introduction of a boundary between adults and teenagers in these families can be a great relief. This is because it allows young people who have been trapped in these types of non-hierarchical families to develop autonomy and get on with their own lives.

Ask teenagers to take responsibility for their attendance at counselling

Although some teenagers ask for counselling themselves, most are referred by parents or other adults who think it would be useful for them. Many teenagers, therefore, are at best neutral, if not ambivalent about attending counselling. It is common for young people to agree to come to counselling just once to get their parents *'off their case'*. A minority of teenagers are extremely reluctant to attend even once. Their parents may use threats or bribery to coerce them into attending. It is the counsellor's responsibility to build an alliance with teenagers; engage them in the counselling process, especially during the first session; and develop a therapeutic contract with them. Following the initial appointment, teenagers are encouraged to take responsibility for attending their own counselling appointments. This involves remembering the appointment dates, informing the school (unless their school has a protocol involving parents when time off is needed), finding their way to the counselling centre and ringing to cancel appointments if they are unable or unwilling to attend. This is made clear to teenagers who agree to a counselling contract at the conclusion of the first session. Attendance at counselling is voluntary and encouraging teenagers to take responsibility for their own counselling appointments is an integral part of the therapeutic process. It allows young people to experience a degree of autonomy.

In some exceptional circumstances parents may need to be involved in assisting young people with appointment attendance by providing transport. For example, very young teenagers or those who cannot make their way by public transport, walking or cycling may need parental assistance. However, the emphasis is on young people being responsible for attending their own appointments. Parents who complain that their teenager is immature or childish and then offer to take responsibility for their appointments, send an implicit message that the young person is incapable of doing so. Therefore, parents are discouraged from taking appointment cards on behalf of the teenagers, phoning to cancel appointments for them, or apologising when the young person's appointments are missed.

If at the conclusion of the first session, a teenager immediately hands the appointment card to a parent, or the parent becomes involved in the appointment making, the expectation that the young person is responsible for attending their own appointments is clarified. Relating to young people in a way which expects them to be capable and responsible for their own appointments is appreciated by them. Even the most immature young person can make a point of living up to this expectation and in so doing gain self-belief and self-esteem.

For teenagers to be motivated to continue attending counselling regularly, counsellors have to work hard at maintaining a strong therapeutic alliance. This is quite different from some forms of adult counselling, where much of the responsibility for engaging rests with the client rather than the counsellor.

Help parents and teenagers accept that a parent's job is to become redundant

A parent's role is to prepare their teenagers to live as autonomous independent adults[7]. When they have successfully fulfilled this role, they become redundant as parents. Parents of some teenagers referred for counselling have difficulty accepting this way of viewing their parenting role. Rather than encouraging their teenagers towards autonomy, they restrain their development of independence. This can occur for a variety of reasons. Some parents experience intense anxiety and worry that their teenagers will be harmed if they are not constantly supervising them and so they repeatedly check on their whereabouts. Socially isolated parents may find the company of their teenagers eases their sense of loneliness and so encourage their teenagers to stay home and keep them company. Parents from conflictual marriages may become overinvested in the life of their teenagers to distract them from marital disharmony. In all of these circumstances, counsellors may invite parents to accept that their role is to make themselves redundant by fostering their teenagers' autonomy. However, it is important for them to also explore in an empathic way with parents the factors that are inhibiting them from doing so.

3.2.6.   Stances that facilitate closing the counselling process

The following 3 stances facilitate closing the counselling process:

- Review progress and setbacks

- Help families discover what they have learned

- Help families plan for lapses and relapses.

Review progress and setbacks

In the closing phase of counselling, counsellors help clients remember and review how their problems were when they started, the progress they made over the course of counselling, and the pattern of improvements and setbacks they experienced[3,7]. This gives clients a sense of the extent to which they were able to use counselling to address their problems. Most forms of counselling lead to improvements for about two thirds of clients. At the end of counselling, the counselling team routinely complete the 100 point CGAS[16] and GARF.[17] In 2011 at Teen Counselling on the CGAS, which assesses adolescent adjustment, the average improvement was 17 points and on the GARF, which assesses family adjustment, the average improvement was 13 points. For families that did not improve it may be useful to distinguish between those who derived no benefit from counselling, and those for whom counselling prevented significant deterioration in functioning. For example, in some families where counselling may not lead to measurable improvements in behavioural and emotional problems, it may prevent school drop-out, incarceration for antisocial behaviour, teenage pregnancy and so forth.

Help families discover what they have learned

Counsellors help families articulate their understanding of how active participation in the counselling process led them to resolve their difficulties, or prevent them from deteriorating[3,7]. Counsellors are careful to invite clients to reflect on their role in contributing to improvement, so clients can acknowledge that they have learned how to solve certain types of problems. Counsellors help clients attribute at least some of their gains to their own efforts.

Help families plan for lapses and relapses

Counsellors help clients anticipate future situations in which brief lapses or longer relapses may occur[3,7]. These guesses about situations in which the problems are likely to recur may be based on an understanding of the circumstances which led to the problems that brought the family to counselling. Typically such situations involve an accumulation of significant demands, stresses, changes in routines, changes within the family such as separations, birth or deaths, changes in school life, and changes in friends, such as loss of good friends, loss of important romantic relationships or engaging with antisocial peers. Counsellors then invite family members to make plans for managing these situations using the lessons they have learned during counselling.

SUMMARY

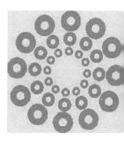

The specific stances that counsellors may adopt to translate the principles of Positive Systemic Practice into therapeutic interventions were described in this chapter.

The four elements of the fundamental stance of Positive Systemic Practice are:

- Be genuine in your relationship with adolescents and parents

- Understand the defensive function of much problematic behaviour

- Recognise the underlying validity of differing perspectives of adolescents, parents and others in their social networks

- Only adopt an *'expert clinical position'* where there are clear benefits for clients.

1. The 10 stances which enhance engagement are:

- Accept that a teenager's perspective is valid

- Respect teenagers and their struggle, and have a sense of humour

- Accept that teenagers are not a homogeneous group

- Do not over-react to teenagers' narratives (as this inhibits further communication)

- Accept that conflict between teenagers and parents is inevitable

- Normalise teenagers' occasional challenging behaviours

- Accept that good family relationships promote well-being

- Accept that parents really want to love and do the best for their teenagers

- Accept that parents really matter to teenagers

- Accept that counsellors working with teenagers and their parents have multiple roles.

2. **The 5 stances which facilitate child protection are:**

- Make it clear from the outset that violence is not tolerated

- Make it clear that usually the longer young people stay in the education system the better

- Help families prevent destructive repetitive behaviour patterns

- Accept that parents are not always right, a positive influence or a resource

- Advocate for teenagers.

3. **The 8 stances which promote insight and understanding are:**

- Help parents and teenagers understand each other's perspective (even if they do not agree with it)

- Provide psycho-education to give parents and teenagers information relevant to their problems

- Help parents update their teenagers on how family history has affected their current lives

- Help parents address family of origin issues

- Accept that what is not said (and kept secret) is often as important as what is

- Help parents accept that they cannot re-live their own adolescence through their teenagers

- Help teenagers and parents explore the pros and cons of changing their behaviour

- Help parents and teenagers acknowledge and re-appraise negative thoughts.

4. **The 10 stances that foster behaviour change are:**

- Help family members communicate, negotiate and jointly problem-solve

- Facilitate the processes of apology and forgiveness

- Help parents and teenagers develop clarity about acceptable and unacceptable behaviour (because *'everybody does not do stuff'*)

- Accept that parental over control and under control can lead to adolescent problems

- Respect family and community norms (unless they are too permissive or oppressive)

- Accept that experiencing the consequences of their actions is essential for teenagers to learn to be responsible for their behaviour

- Accept that mistakes are learning opportunities

- Help anxious teenagers develop courageous behaviour

- Help teenagers develop assertive behaviour

- Help family members develop self-care routines.

5. The 7 stances that facilitate the transition to adulthood are:

- Help parents let go of directive parenting and adopt a style based on negotiation – because when primary school is over parenting must change

- Help parents to manage their anxiety, so as to promote their teenager's independence

- Help parents provide teenagers with age-appropriate jobs to do at home

- Help parents allow their teenagers opportunities to develop strategies for protecting themselves in their social environment

- Help non-authoritative parents to be parents (not friends) to their teenagers

- Ask teenagers to take responsibility for their attendance at counselling

- Help parents and teenagers accept that a parent's job is to become redundant.

6. The 3 stances that facilitate closing the counselling process are:

- Review progress and setbacks

- Help families discover what they have learned

- Help families plan for lapses and relapses.

CHAPTER 4

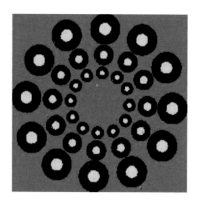

The referral process

In this chapter the referral process is described. This includes discussing referral enquires with parents or other referrers, consent and waiting list management. The procedures that are described for managing the referral process have all been designed to maximise attendance of teenagers and both of their parents at first appointments, while taking due account of important ethical issues such as consent to attendance and client confidentiality. The clinical administrative secretary in each Teen Counselling centre is usually the first point of contact for referrers and is responsible for the management of referrals.

4.1. Managing referral enquiries

Cases may be referred by family members (most usually mothers), schools, family doctors or community agencies. Each year about two thirds of referrals to Teen Counselling are made by parents. When referrals are not made directly by family members, referrers are asked to encourage parents to make contact with the service as soon as possible. Involving parents in the referral process greatly increases the chance of families engaging in counselling. When parents phone Teen Counselling centres, the secretaries may confirm details of the referral, provide information about the service and help parents to feel positive about the referral process.

The most common reasons for referral are adolescent behavioural and emotional problems. Behavioural problems include disruptive behaviour, aggression, theft, substance misuse and rule-breaking at home and in school. Emotional problems include depression, anxiety, eating problems, self-harm, adjustment to illness and sexuality concerns. As it has been developed at Teen Counselling, PSP, is not suitable for chronic eating disorders with medical complications, psychosis, severe mood disorders, chronic drug addiction, or high-risk child protection cases in which sexual abuse has been disclosed, but has not been investigated by statutory services.

At Teen Counselling, telephone referrals and enquires are generally taken and managed by a clinical administrative secretary using standardised forms. The age of the young person being referred and whether their home or school is in the Centre's catchment area is first established. Where young people do not meet these requirements, callers are advised of alternative services in their localities where such services exist. These *'advice calls'* are logged and monitored to provide information on service demands and gaps in service availability. When the enquiry is about a young person who is between 12 and 18 years old and living in the Centre's catchment area, callers are then advised of the requirements of the Teen Counselling child protection policy before they give any further information.

4.2. Child protection policy and the limits of confidentiality

Before taking any referral details such as clients' names and presenting problems, the Teen Counselling child protection policy is explained to referrers. This practice of interrupting referrers and informing them of these policies allows them to make an informed decision about whether or not they wish to proceed with a referral. Before taking a referral the secretary (or counsellor when the secretary is not available) will say:

> *To take a referral, I have to ask you some details about the problem. The information you give me is confidential, except where there is concern that a young person may be at risk. We have policies to deal with this which I can explain if necessary. OK?*

If the referrer requests clarification of this *'interrupt statement'*, or if the secretary feels it is necessary, the following is used:

> *If we receive information which causes us concern about the safety or well-being of a young person, for example where there is violence or abuse, either now or in the past, it is our responsibility to contact the local social workers. If you have any further questions about this, I can ask a counsellor to speak with you.*

If a secretary has concerns about child protection issues, a counsellor may be asked for advice or support.

4.3. Taking referral details

Once the confidentiality and child protection policies have been explained to referrers, the following details are recorded on a referral form (which is in the Appendices): the referrer's name and contact details; the agency or person who suggested the referral and their contact details (e.g. school, family doctor, social services, juvenile justice agency); the teenager and parents' names, nationalities, languages, and contact details (with separate details where parents are separated); the teenager's age and date of birth; details of the main problems; the length of time the problem has existed; and whether and when the teenager has been seen at another agency or by another professional (child guidance clinic, social worker, special school, counsellor, psychologist, psychiatrist).

Referrers are advised that their referral will be discussed by the clinical team and that they will be contacted if further information is needed. If referrers are extremely concerned about a teenager's low mood or self-harm, they are advised to attend their family doctor.

Taking referrals is an important process as it is the start of Teen Counselling's engagement with clients. Referrers, particularly parents, may be distressed when giving details of their family's difficulties and as such it is essential that the person taking the referral, most usually the secretary, has good listening skills and the ability to guide parents through the often difficult process of asking for help. Counsellors must be available to support or debrief the secretary when necessary.

The secretary presents the referrals to the clinical team at their regular intake meetings. Referrals are discussed by counsellors and decisions made about their suitability for the service. If the family is engaged with another service the possibility of inter-agency liaison is established and consent to share information is sought. If it is unclear whether the referral is suitable, then the referrer is recontacted to discuss the details of the referral further. If the counsellors judge the referral to be unsuitable, the reason is made clear to the referrer and an alternative service and sources of support are recommended where appropriate. The service is unsuitable for families of teenagers with chronic eating disorders with medical complications, psychosis, severe mood disorders, chronic addictions or high-risk child protection cases in which sexual or physical abuse is occurring. A referral to a child and adolescent psychiatric service with access to inpatient facilities is more appropriate for chronic eating disorders with medical complications, psychosis, and severe mood disorders. A referral to a specialist addiction service is more appropriate for chronic drug or alcohol addiction. For families in which sexual abuse has just been disclosed, a referral to child protection services for assessment is the course of action.

4.4. Waiting list management

At Teen Counselling, there are well established administrative procedures for waiting list management and enhancing the probability that clients attend first appointments. All new referrals accepted at the intake meetings are evaluated using a system of prioritisation and are put on a waiting list. Referrals which may be prioritised are re-referrals of past clients and/or their siblings and students prior to their Junior or Leaving Certificate exams. Referral issues which take priority are:

- Self-harm/suicide

- Teens at risk of being out of home

- Teens who request counselling themselves

- Teens who are at risk of dropping out of school

However, Teen Counselling is not a crisis intervention service and always has a waiting list.

Close to the time when a first appointment will be offered, clients are sent a letter to confirm that the family are still interested in attending the service. Here is an example of such a letter:

Dear Mr and Mrs Courtney,

On 11th November 2008 we were contacted by Mr Moriarty about counselling for your son Michael. We would hope to offer you an appointment soon.

Please ring and confirm that you are still interested in counselling for Michael so that we can arrange an appointment for you.

Our office is open 9.30 – 5.00, Monday to Friday.

Yours sincerely,

Secretary

When parents respond to such letters indicating that they are still interested in a referral, an appointment letter is sent with a request for phone confirmation that the appointment will be attended. This lets the parents know the time and place of the appointment; the fact that this first meeting will be with two counsellors, themselves and their teenager; and that the service follows national child protection guidelines. A leaflet of Frequently Asked Questions is sent with the letter to give information about the service and this is contained in the Appendices. Here is an example of such a letter:

Dear Mr and Mrs Courtney,

On 11th November 2008 we were contacted by Mr Moriarty about counselling for your son. You recently phoned and said you were still interested in counselling for Michael. We can now offer you an appointment at 10.00 a.m. on 2nd February 2009.

Please ring and confirm that you will attend this appointment. If this time is not convenient for you, we will arrange an alternative. If we do not hear from you by 25th January 2009 we will assume that you are not interested in attending and this appointment time will be offered to another family.

The initial appointment is for both of you and Michael with a counselling team. Our counsellors usually work in teams of two. Parents and teenagers often meet separately with a counsellor, but the counsellors are in regular consultation so that the needs of each family member are considered. Our primary consideration is for the safety and well-being of your teenager and in this regard we observe the National Guidelines for the Protection and Welfare of Children. Enclosed is a leaflet 'Frequently Asked Questions' which you may like to read before your appointment.

Our office is open 9.30 – 5.00, Monday to Friday. We look forward to hearing from you.

Yours sincerely,

Secretary

Where there is no response or a negative response to these letters, the referrer is contacted when relevant and informed that the family has been taken off the waiting list. These referrals are classified as not followed up (NFU). Families who are classified as NFU have typically been on the waiting list a long time. They may have sought alternative sources of support; their presenting problems may have resolved; or they may have sought services for problems which were more pressing than their adolescent's difficulties.

Where families do not attend or cancel an initial appointment, a follow-up letter is sent offering to re-schedule the appointment. Where families indicate that they no longer require a service, or indeed fail to respond to the letter, the referrer is again contacted when relevant and informed that the family has been taken off the waiting list.

When the waiting list becomes six months long, serious consideration is given to closing it, because for families with adolescents, waiting for over six months for a service to address adolescent problems is counterproductive.

4.5. Importance of parental involvement

In some instances, during the referral process, parents or referrers ask about the necessity of parental involvement in the counselling process. The key point to make in response is that parents are invited to counselling because they are central to their teenagers' lives, and in this sense the young person's problem is a family problem[1]. Both mothers and fathers, even when separated, have an important role to play in helping their teenagers resolve difficulties that arise as they make the transition from childhood to adulthood. Each parent, whether resident or non-resident, can offer an important perspective on their teenager's problems, and may contribute in important ways to supporting their teenagers as they resolve their difficulties.

Here is how these ideas may be expressed to parents or referrers:

Parents have a very important role to play in the lives of their teenagers. It therefore makes sense that we would involve you, as a parent, in the counselling process with your son or daughter.

We see adolescence as a transition from childhood to adulthood. Teenagers make this transition in the context of the family. There are often difficult patches during this transition. The young person's view of these difficulties is important, but it is also important to have an informed adult view of the situation. That's why it is critical for you, as parents to be involved.

Where parents are separated, the following type of statement may be made to give a rationale for including the non-resident parent:

Your teenager needs support from both parents. We find that a parent who does not live with their teenager often has a powerful role to play in their life, especially when they are trying to sort out their problems. The involvement of both parents in counselling is important, whether they are living together or are separated or divorced. This is why it's in your teen's best interests for us to involve both of you.

4.6. Consent

For intact families, teenagers and both of their parents are invited to attend initial appointments and to consent verbally to counselling. However, there are a number of circumstances where the issue of clients giving consent to counselling is not straightforward. These include cases in which the teenager is unwilling to attend, the teenager is living with one parent and the other parent lives elsewhere, the adolescent is in voluntary or statutory care and cases in which a coercive referral is made by a school, court or statutory agency. All of these situations require careful management to ensure ethical practice and to optimise the chances of families engaging in counselling and benefiting from it. Practice guidelines for each of these situations are given below.

Teenagers unwilling to consent

If teenagers do not wish to attend an initial appointment, parents are invited to attend without their teenagers and to meet with one counsellor. In these cases, part of the initial meeting is devoted to considering why the teenager is unwilling to attend and strategies for motivating them to attend a subsequent appointment are explored. Teenagers may not wish to attend because they are worried that counselling sessions will not be confidential, will be highly conflictual, or will lead to a variety of negative outcomes for them such as punishment, stigmatisation, hospitalisation, placement in care, court proceedings and so forth. Counsellors may suggest to parents that they let their teenagers know that attending the service involves an initial family meeting to clarify what their main concerns are and then the young person is invited to attend a series of confidential individual appointments with their own counsellor. These meetings give the young person a time and space apart from the normal routines of their lives to work out their problems. Parents may be encouraged to give a leaflet which describes the service in these terms to their teenagers. However, a critical point is that young people are not coerced into attending counselling. Young people are only engaged in counselling if they give their consent.

Non-resident parents and consent

Where parents are separated, the person taking the referral lets the referrer know that for an appointment to be given to a young person, both parents must give consent when practicable. The resident parent is asked to inform the non-resident parent about the referral and to supply an address and phone number. Teen Counselling then assume responsibility for contacting them and including them in the counselling process when appropriate. The practice at Teen Counselling centres is to accept referrals of teenagers living with one parent, except in cases where the non-resident parent explicitly refuses to consent to their teenager attending the service. Where non-resident parents have no contact with the teenager, or where non-resident parents do not reply to an invitation and do not explicitly refuse consent, then consent is assumed.

Adolescents in care and consent

Where adolescents are in statutory care, the referring social worker is assumed to be giving consent. Referrals from foster parents are processed once confirmation of agreement from the statutory social worker is received. Where adolescents are in voluntary care, before counselling can be offered, the referring social worker is asked to obtain consent from the adolescent's parents.

4.7. Coercive referrals

Referrals from schools, juvenile justice or statutory agencies which involve coercion into counselling are not accepted on coercive terms. Coercion reduces parents' and teenagers' experience of choosing to voluntarily engage in counselling, and this in turn makes it difficult to establish positive therapeutic alliances and a productive counselling process. Rather, these referrals are re-negotiated so that the parents and teenager are given the option of voluntarily engaging in counselling to achieve goals that are consistent with, but not dictated by, the statutory agency. For example, if a young person who has been suspended from school is referred by the school, with attendance at counselling as a condition for re-admittance to school, the referral is not accepted on these terms. The school is informed that it is more useful if the disciplinary procedures and attendance at counselling are kept separate. The school may indicate to the teenager and his parents the sort of behaviour that is acceptable and unacceptable at school, and require the teenager to conform to the school's standards as a condition of re-admittance. The school may also inform the parents about the availability of counselling services. If the parents and the teenager want to refer themselves for counselling to help the teenager meet the school's standards, then it is preferable that the parents and teenager refer themselves for counselling. Another problem with coercive school referrals is that counselling service waiting lists may prevent teenagers from engaging in counselling for months, and if counselling attendance is a condition for re-entry to school, the counselling service becomes partly responsible for teenagers missing months of school. Here is a sample letter to a school principal to renegotiate a coercive referral:

Dear Mr O'Brien,

On 11th November 2008 Michael Courtney was referred to our service by Mr Moriarty and we have placed his name on our waiting list.

We understand that Michael is currently suspended from school and that counselling was advised for him prior to re-admission. Our waiting list time varies, but is usually 2-4 months. As we consider this length of time too long for a youngster to be out of school we ask all schools in our catchment area to deal with disciplinary issues separately from our counselling service.

We are very happy to accept referrals for behaviour problems in school, from parents or directly for schools, but quite apart from the waiting list time, we find that youngsters and their parents engage much better in counselling when it is separate from disciplinary procedures.

Yours sincerely,

Clinical Staff Member using professional title

SUMMARY

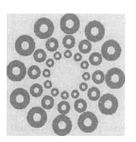

Cases may be referred by family members, schools, family doctors or community agencies for a range of adolescent problems. The approach, as practiced at Teen Counselling, is not suitable for chronic addictions, severe psychiatric presentations or high-risk child protection cases.

Referrals, most usually made by telephone, are managed by a clinical administrative secretary and presented at regular intake meetings. If it is unclear whether the referral is suitable, then a counsellor may discuss suitability with the referrer.

During some referral enquires it is appropriate to explain that family involvement is essential because parents (including non-resident parents) can offer an important perspective on their teenagers' problems and may contribute in important ways to supporting them.

To specific enquires about confidentiality, parents may be told that confidentiality is only breached where clients are a danger to themselves or to others, or where they have been harmed in the past or are at risk of being harmed at present, in line with child protection guidelines.

Waiting list management procedures are used to maximise attendance at first appointments. New referrals are discussed, prioritised and put on a waiting list when suitable. In order to minimise appointments where clients do not attend (DNA) parents are contacted to confirm they are still interested close to the time when a first appointment will be offered. They must respond by phone to receive an appointment time. Parents are sent a first appointment after which they also must respond by phone to confirm their attendance.

Parents and adolescents must consent to attend counselling.

If adolescents do not give consent, parents may be invited to attend without their teenagers and strategies for motivating teenagers to attend subsequent appointments may be explored.

Where parents are separated, non-resident parents are always contacted and invited to be involved where an address or phone number for them is available. Where non-resident parents are non-contactable or do not wish to be involved in the counselling process, the practice at Teen Counselling is to accept referrals of teenagers living with one parent, except in cases where the non-resident parent explicitly refuses to consent to their teenager attending the service.

Where adolescents are in statutory care, the referring social worker is asked to give consent, and where adolescents are in voluntary care, the referring social worker is asked to obtain parental consent.

Referrals from schools or statutory agencies which involve coercion into counselling are re-negotiated so that parents and teenagers are given the option of voluntarily engaging in counselling to achieve goals that are consistent with, but not dictated by, the statutory agency.

CHAPTER 5

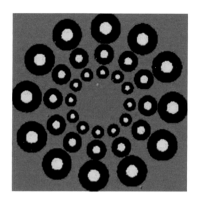

The first session

The process of engaging with families in the first session is described in this chapter. The chapter covers planning and conducting intake interviews with families, formulation and contracting for counselling. Contracts are flexible, but typically involve concurrent parallel individual sessions for teenagers and parents, with periodic joint family sessions (or in some instances all joint sessions).

5.1. Aims of the first session

The aims of the first session are to lay the foundation for a good therapeutic alliance, to name the issues to be addressed in counselling, acknowledging different goals for teenagers and parents if necessary, and to develop an understanding of family difficulties which both the counsellors and family can share.

Forming an alliance

Forming a therapeutic alliance with teenagers and parents and beginning to help them establish a more positive relationship with each other is essential[1]. Unless teenagers and parents leave the first session with a feeling that they have formed a positive relationship with the counselling team, then the chances that they will return and engage in on-going counselling are greatly reduced. If teenagers and parents leave the first session feeling that they have had their points of view heard and respected and begun to re-establish their relationships with each other, then this offers families a reason to be hopeful that counselling may be helpful for them.

Usually the most significant challenge in the first session is engaging teenagers and forming a therapeutic alliance with them. Most parents are motivated to attend counselling to help their child. In contrast, most teenagers are at best neutral about attending counselling and some may be highly anxious, defensive, or defiant if they feel blamed or have been bribed or coerced to attend. It is sometimes evident at first sessions that there has been considerable conflict between parents and teenagers during the journey to the centre and the teenager is seething with frustration. It is not unusual for parents to collect their teenager from school, tell them to get in the car and bring them to the centre without any previous discussion or warning. In other instances, teenagers may have agreed to attend counselling only once. These sorts of situations provide a difficult start to the counselling process, especially for teenagers.

Where teenagers are nervous, distressed or angry and find engaging in the counselling process very difficult, counsellors persevere and provide them with whatever support is necessary to establish a conversation. This may involve acknowledging that it is difficult for them and ignoring displays of a defiant *'attitude'* such as slumping in the chair, responding rudely, blowing bubble-gum, not answering, pulling a hat or hair over their face, and so forth until they relax and participate more spontaneously. Despite such support and encouragement some teenagers make it evident that they cannot, or will not, co-operate. Very occasionally a teenager leaves the room. When this happens a parent may be invited to check that their teenager is O.K. When parents are unable or unwilling to do this, counsellors check on the situation, particularly with younger teenagers. Most teenagers who leave the counselling room hang around outside and may engage with a counsellor when approached. Others make their way home. Teenagers who remain silent, but stay in the room listening to their parent's views, almost inevitably want to talk about their view of the situation as the session proceeds. Counsellors may invite them back into the conversation quite seamlessly without any reference to their earlier reticence to participate.

There are other hurdles to overcome to form an alliance and these need to be addressed at the outset. The team needs to keep in mind how the family was referred. If the school or health service initiated the referral process, the young person or the parents may feel as if they were *'sent'* to counselling and this can cause significant antipathy to the process. Another regular challenge is engaging parents in the counselling process as active participants. Some may prefer to drop off their errant teenager *'to be fixed'* and come back and pick them up after their first session. On occasion there is also a need to clarify for both teenagers and parents that being in counselling does not indicate that someone is *'mad'*.

Naming issues and developing a shared understanding

Naming the issues to be addressed in counselling and developing a way of understanding the family difficulty which both the counsellors and family can share is the basis for a therapeutic contract. The team aim through their interviewing to identify important issues that need to be addressed, explore each issue from the teenager's and parents' perspectives and formulate a new way for the family to understand the issues[2]. Naming the issues and developing an understanding of them in this way provides the basis for offering a therapeutic contract at the end of the first session. The emphasis placed on both the collection of clinically relevant information and developing a shared understanding of the problem is critical in truly engaging the family and forming an alliance with them.

A shared understanding (or formulation) of the problem allows family members to move from stuck or rigid positions towards a new position which encompasses the different perspectives of the teenager and parent and offers greater possibilities for improving family relationships. Achieving this is not just an assessment, but an intervention in and of itself.

Sometimes there are sensitive issues which either parents, teenagers or both do not want to name or talk about in the first session. In some cases this may be made explicit. For example a family member may say *"There is something else, but we don't want to talk about it just now."* In other cases the counselling team may wonder if there are sensitive or *'secret'* issues that family members do not wish to name until a stronger therapeutic alliance has been established. Counsellors respect this cautious approach taken by some clients and allow time for trust to develop and the therapeutic alliance to strengthen before addressing these issues. It is always important to leave space for the *'not yet said'*.

5.2. Style of the first session

Conversational style

An informal, conversational style is adopted in the first and subsequent sessions. That is, the team engage teenagers and parents in conversations about their views of their current concerns and the difficulties that precipitated the referral for counselling. The team respectfully invite each person to elaborate on their unique view of how these difficulties evolved, how they affect everyone in the family, what sorts of things have been done or might be done to resolve them and what obstacles they see to resolving problems or reducing distress. Counsellors also ask about the four domains of the adolescent's life - home, school, friends and self (as elaborated later in this chapter). However, these areas are covered in a way that is partly led by family members' accounts of their situation. That is, the session is not completely counsellor led, like a structured interview or a psychological assessment. It is more conversational than that, with the counsellor asking some questions, which open up opportunities for family members to talk fluently about their situation.

Valuing all viewpoints

Counsellors let clients know that they are aware that each person in the family may have a different view of the situation and that they are interested in each person's view, because all views of the situation are important[3]. Counsellors convey that in addressing family problems it is more useful for parents and adolescents to come to an understanding of their differing viewpoints, than it is to find out the *'truth'* of the matter, or which viewpoint is right and which is wrong.

Counsellors take a position of *'not knowing'* about the different viewpoints family members may hold. They help families move from accounts of the objective facts and events that have happened to subjective narratives which reflect each member's experience or interpretation of these facts and events. These subjective stories are more important than the objective facts, because it is these narratives that determine how families understand and try to resolve their problems. Counsellors may elicit not just each family member's viewpoint of the problem or situation, but also family members' understanding of each other's narratives. For example, teenagers may be asked what their understanding is of their parent's concerns about a particularly contentious issue with questions such as *"What sense do you think your mum and dad made of that situation?"* If teenagers respond with *"I dunno, why you don't ask them?"*, counsellors persist with responses such as *"I will in a few minutes, but I'm interested in your opinion"*. This interviewing style helps teenagers consider the way their parents see the situation. Teenagers generally respond well to this, and often with more insight than their parents thought they had.

When parents are asked to give their understanding of the young person's perceptions of some aspect of the problem, they have an invitation to share their insights into what it's like to take the perspective of their teenager and see the world from the young person's point of view (without necessarily agreeing with it). Counsellors may ask parents questions such as *"What do you think was going on for your son/daughter?"* This interviewing style helps parents consider the way their teenagers see the situation.

Curious, respectful, invitational approach

Therapeutic conversations are marked by a curious[4], respectful[5], invitational[6] approach. Often parents and teenagers have said and done things of which they are deeply ashamed. They may have hurt each other and been hurt. They may be blaming each other and expecting to be blamed by counsellors, or they may want the counsellors to blame someone else in the family rather than them. Therefore from a client's perspective, it is a relief when counsellors treat them with respect, and invite them (not direct them) to give their own account of the challenges the family has been struggling with. This respectful invitational approach may create a context within which family members have the courage to speak about difficult matters including the family's taboos. In adopting this curious, respectful, invitational approach, counsellors may invite family members to talk about the *'fall-out'* from a fight or a difficult event without discussing the details of it, since discussing the details of who said what to whom, may lead to further hurt and blaming. This kind of invitation may be offered by asking for family members' permission to talk about the *'fall-out'* with such questions as *"Is it OK to talk about what happened after or as a result of the fight?"*.

Empathy

Counsellors show empathy, warmth and genuineness, by listening carefully to clients and summarising the main themes they express periodically in a way that lets clients know that they have been understood by someone who has their best interests at heart[5]. This approach has a positive effect on both parents and teenagers. Teenagers are often surprised that they are not blamed or treated as *'the problem'* by counsellors. Parents are relieved that they are not being blamed for being *'bad parents'*. When counsellors show empathy for the positions of both the teenager and the parents, and issues are reframed as complex family difficulties, rather than a simple case of the teenager being *'the problem'*, teenagers are often empowered and become more engaged in the counselling process.

Assume normal developmental tensions

Counsellors assume that in most families there are tensions between parents and adolescents about autonomy, individuation, independence, freedom, privacy and responsibility[7]. This may find expression through parent-adolescent conflict over a wide range of issues such as school, homework, house chores, house rules, untidiness, curfew times, pocket money, clothing, drug and alcohol use, problematic peer relationships, sexual behaviour, theft, violence and so forth.

Re-framing conflict

Where adolescents and their parents hold very different or opposing views on these sorts of issues, and their relationships have become negative and conflictual, counsellors use reframing and other interventions to begin to promote positive and mutually respectful relationships between adolescents and parents[3]. For example, a mother was upset because she felt she had a poor relationship with her son. To illustrate this she mentioned an incident in which she and her son had a row because she refused to give him a lift to the local cinema. When she refused, her son became angry and said to her *"You don't care. You mustn't love me anymore"*. The counsellor reframed this by saying that the son was making inappropriate demands on the mother and then trying to get these demands met by making his mother feel bad. This behaviour typical of a pre-adolescent boy, the counsellor suggested, led to conflict between the mother and son. This reframing allowed the counsellor to explore the mother and son's views on a range of issues including how fair the demand for a lift the local cinema had been; the impact of the son accusing the mother of not loving him; why the son might believe it was OK to make such demands; if his mother had responded to such demands when he was a pre-adolescent; and if his siblings made similar demands and he had learned this from them. This process provided an opportunity for the mother and son to see that the issue was not that they had a poor relationship, but that there was a need for them and others within the family to clearly distinguish between inappropriate demands and the sorts of things it is appropriate for a teenager to ask his mother for, and how this can be done respectfully.

Highlighting the issues

During the course of the first session counsellors highlight areas of difficulty that become apparent, explore them and generate new understandings of them. This demonstrates to the family the sort of *'work'* that will occur in counselling. In the first session this process allows families to see that the emotional and behavioural problems, for which their adolescents were referred, are associated with wider family issues such as communication and relationship difficulties, and problematic parenting styles.

5.3. Pre-session planning

Hypotheses

Prior to the first session the counselling team meet and review available information on the clients[2,3]. This referral information is used to make initial tentative hypotheses about factors contributing to the family's difficulties.

Hypotheses are informed guesses that counselling teams make about factors that contribute to the development and maintenance of a family's difficulties. Hypotheses are informed by referral information, previous clinical experience with similar cases and the relevant research literature on such issues. For example, where teenagers are referred with behavioural problems, a plausible hypothesis may be that within the family there may be an inconsistent approach to parenting and limit setting, which in turn may be due to other family stresses such as parental separation or mental health problems. Where the main issue is low mood, the hypothesis may be that the young person has experienced a significant loss or failure in their lives.

The team plan broad lines of questioning that may be used within the interview structure of the first session to check out these hypotheses and to provide information about risk and protective factors in the domains of home, school, friends and self.

Counselling team roles

Prior to the first session the counselling team also plan the roles they will adopt during the session. Teams vary in the roles they take during joint sessions depending on the experience of the team members, their familiarity with the model and the length of time that they have worked together.

Typically during the first session, one counsellor takes the role of interviewer and does most of the talking, while the other takes the role of the observer and note-taker and is either invited into the conversation by their partner or intervenes occasionally.

A range of issues are factored into the decision making process about which role each member of the counselling team take in the first session. For example, if there are gender sensitive presenting difficulties (and a mixed gender counselling team), this may lead the team to decide, for example, that a female counsellor will take the interviewer role in the case of a sexually abused teenage girl, or a male counsellor will take the interviewer role in the case of an adolescent boy with behavioural problems.

The format for subsequent joint sessions is for counsellors to alternate between the roles of interviewer and observer in a fluid fashion. This format is more natural and conversational, but requires careful planning and good team work. As members of counselling teams gain experience in working together, and team members develop rapport with each other, they develop skill in alternating between the roles of interviewer and observer, and may use this skill to achieve particular therapeutic goals within joint sessions.

5.4. Introduction to the first session

Meeting and greeting

Contact between Teen Counselling and families prior to the first session, is usually through the clinical administrative secretary in the Centre as referrals are made and clarified and appointments arranged. The secretary greets the family on arrival at the Centre and shows them to the waiting room. In the first session the counselling team always meet a teenager with at least one of their parents or caregivers for a joint session.

One member of the counselling team meets the family in the waiting room and welcomes them to the counselling centre. Beginning with the teenager (in most, but not all cases), the counsellor introduces themself and establishes how clients prefer to be addressed and their relationship with each other.

Counsellor: "Hello, I'm Gerry, you must be Jonathon".

Jonathon: "It's JJ. Nobody calls me Jonathon, except me Ma when she's mad at me".

Counsellor: "Is this your Ma?"

Mother: "Yes, I'm Alice and this is my partner, Tom".

Counsellor: "Hello, it's good to meet you both".

After a brief informal chat about the weather, how easy it was to find the Centre and so forth, to help family members feel at ease, the counsellor accompanies them to the counselling room and introduces them to their counselling team partner. If a postgraduate on training placement at the Centre, or a new member of staff is observing the session, this is fully explained to family members before the session begins.

At Teen Counselling, staff members introduce themselves to clients by their first names. This normalises rather than pathologises the counselling process. If clients ask for information regarding the professional training or experience of clinical staff, they are given the details.

Sometimes a family has attended for counselling previously and this is acknowledged and they are welcomed back. Occasionally a counsellor and parent may have talked on the phone before the first session, perhaps to clarify a referral or to offer support until an appointment was available. If so, counsellors refer to that, so that the conversation in the Centre is framed as a continuation of that which they had on the phone. For example, a counsellor may say: *"Hello Alice, I think we spoke on the phone a few weeks ago, it's good to meet you."*

Service information

A brief outline of the service, its Centres and staff is given to clients at the outset. Clients are then aware that the Centre is part of a bigger organisation and that there are other staff available should the counselling team choose to involve them. For example, in some cases it may be appropriate to involve the consultant psychiatrist.

Consent and confidentiality

Counsellors also let families know the non-statutory status of the service, that attendance is voluntary and that both teenagers and parents must consent to attend. They also explain that the service is confidential, but that there are limits to confidentiality as counsellors have a child protection responsibility. Here is an example of how this is explained:

'Teen Counselling is a voluntary service – separate from other services for young people in the area like the health services or schools. We like to think of it as 'a space apart' – separate from the rest of your life – and you only come here if you want to.

Another important point is that the service is confidential – which means that what you tell us is not discussed with anyone outside Teen Counselling unless you ask us to, or

we all agree that it would be useful.

However, there are some important limitations to confidentiality which we tell everyone about before we start talking, as we never know what information families will give us.

- *When we hear that either adults or children are at risk of harming themselves or others*

- *When we hear that anyone is currently being abused or has been abused in the past*

we have to do something about it, but if we need to contact another agency we would discuss it with you first.

If after today we all agree that counselling would be useful and we arrange individual sessions, one of us will work with (name of teen) and the other will work with (name of parents) and we will meet separately as well as together like today.

We have separate sessions which are confidential and we do not:

- *Tell a teenager what a parent has said in a session*

- *Tell a parent what a teenager has said in a session*

- *Carry messages from parent to teenager or vice versa – unless there is concern about risk or we decide with you that it is a useful thing to do.*

Counsellors of course share information to make sure that the support you get is relevant.'

A confidentiality form is completed contemporaneously by the note taker and kept on file as a record that these four important points are explained to families. For families who continue with counselling, the limits of confidentiality are re-iterated at the beginning of the first individual sessions for both teenagers and parents.

Addressing clients' misconceptions about counselling

Counsellors are sensitive to the fact that teenagers and parents may have misconceptions about the counselling process. A common misconception that parents have is that the counsellor will see the teenager individually for some procedure that will either, change the teenager's behaviour, alleviate their symptoms or yield a diagnosis. Such procedures may be imagined to include scolding the youngster, being sympathetic to them, hypnotising them, giving medication or conducting a psychometric assessment. Common misconceptions that teenagers have are that the counsellor will ask them to lie on a couch and talk about their dreams, put them into care or admit them to hospital.

Misconceptions are addressed through explaining the format of the first session and the voluntary, confidential nature of the service.

Explaining the format of the first session

The format of the first session is carefully outlined so that the family know exactly what to expect. Some parents will have read the Frequently Asked Questions service leaflet, which is sent to families along with their first appointment, but most teenagers will not have. They are usually apprehensive about attending and allaying anxiety as much as possible is a priority to facilitate their engagement in the counselling process. Families are informed that:

- the counselling team always meet with the parents and teenager together at the first appointment

- the first session usually lasts about an hour and a half

- the first part of the session involves being asked a lot of questions so that the counselling team can learn as much as possible about the difficulties the family are having

- about three quarters way through the session there is a break during which the counsellors leave the room to review what the family has told them and to plan how best to support the family

- this break gives the family an opportunity to talk about their experience and discuss whether or not they would like to return for further counselling sessions

The roles of the counsellors and the function of note-taking are also explained.

Here is an example of how to explain the first session format and counsellor roles:

"We will meet for about an hour and a half this morning, so there will be an opportunity for each of you to let us know your views of the situation. After a while we will take a break. This gives us a chance to think about what you have told us and decide how we might help. Perhaps more importantly it gives you a chance to talk about whether you found the session useful and would like to return. I'll be asking most of the questions this morning and Sheila will be taking notes so that we don't forget anything important. Do you have any questions? We usually start by talking with the teenager, OK JJ?"

5.5. Framework for the first session

The reason for the referral and the four domains of home, school, friends and self are the principal areas covered in the first session. Families' views of issues within the areas usually provide sufficient information to develop a formulation of the presenting problem.

Counsellors usually start by asking teenagers for their views of the difficulties that led to them coming to counselling before asking for their parents' views. This practice helps counsellors to build an alliance with teenagers who are usually more ambivalent about engaging in the counselling process than their parents. Teenagers are often pleasantly surprised that their views are sought first and parents are often surprised at how well their children express themselves.

Reason for referral and presenting problem

In talking to teenagers it is useful to ask some of the following questions to find out the degree to which they wanted to attend counselling and their expectations.

"Why have you come here today?"

"Did you want to come?"

"Who wanted you to come?"

"How did you find out you were coming and when was this?"

"How do you feel about being here?"

"What's it like to be here?"

Whilst some teenagers (typically older girls) initiate the referral for counselling, most teenagers do not and they attend to oblige an adult, most usually their mother. Often the response to *'Why have you come here today?'* is *"Me ma made me"* which provides an opportunity for some humour: *'How did she do that?'*.

When asked about the reason they came to counselling some teenagers take ownership of their problem behaviour and others suggest that they have no idea! As counsellors tease out this issue with the teenager, parents can become quite frustrated and interrupt with the *'correct answers'*. Counsellors clarify that each person in the family may have a different view of the situation and that they are interested in each person's view, because all views of the situation are important. Here is an example of how to conduct this part of the interview:

> *"Everybody has their own view of the problem. What we are interested in finding out is each person's view. These may all be quite different. That's, OK. So I'll be checking in with you Alice when JJ has given me his view."*

Four domains – home, school, friends and self

The home, school, peer group and self constitute four important domains of adolescents' social systems[7]. In the first session, these four domains are explored to determine the relationship between the presenting problems and factors within these domains. Adolescent problems are influenced by risk and protective factors within the four domains of home, school, friends and self. In particular adolescent problems are influenced by the quality of their relationships in these four areas and their ability to repair disruptions which occur within these relationships. This ability encompasses skills in negotiation, compromise, establishing developmentally appropriate boundaries and the ability to respect boundaries. People within these domains (family members, teachers, and friends) are affected by adolescents' problems and also have varying levels of ability to repair disrupted relationships with the adolescent when these occur.

Home

The family and the home contain risk and protective factors which affect adolescent behavioural and emotional problems. Within an adolescent's family, protective factors include supportive family relationships; predictable and flexible routines, roles and rules; and good parental adjustment. These factors facilitate adolescents overcoming their problems. Risk factors include conflictual family relationships; unpredictable or inflexible routines; inappropriate roles and rules; poor parental adjustment; and a high level of family stress. These factors maintain or exacerbate adolescent behavioural and emotional problems.

In the first session, enquires about the home cover family composition, family routines, family roles, family rules, parental adjustment, family relationships and family stresses, with a view to identifying home-based risk and protective factors.

Enquiries are made about the house where the teenager lives and other residences where they stay if the parents are separated, or teenagers are in care. It is also useful to ask about the extended family including grandparents, aunts, uncles, cousins and stepfamilies.

In asking about family relationships, the most important ones to cover are those between the teenager and parent; the relationship between the two parents; the relationship between others in the parenting system including step-parents, grandparents and foster-parents; and the relationship between the teenager and siblings. Counsellors sometimes find it helpful to draw a genogram and fill in relevant information about family relationships and individual members. This can be further developed in subsequent sessions with the parents.

The key concerns in enquiring about the family domain are listed below, but these are not questions that can be directly put to family members. Rather, these concerns inform lines of questioning and the therapeutic conversations about the family domain.

- What is the normal daily routine for each person within the adolescent's house, from morning until night-time including times for getting up and going to bed, where people sleep and spend the day, mealtimes and eating arrangements, and leisure activities?

- What are family members' home, work and school roles?

- What are the family rules about seeing friends, doing homework and housework, curfew times, pocket-money?

- Are there times in the day when there are few problems and times which are particularly problematic?

- Are there family routines, roles and rules which involve few problems and others which are particularly problematic?

- How are the adolescent's problems affecting family routines, roles, rules and relationships?

- Within the family and social network which relationships are supportive and which are conflictual?

- How are the conflictual relationships contributing to the adolescent's difficulties?

- Are the parents and those within the parenting system working co-operatively together to support the adolescent and provide age-appropriate rules, responsibilities and limits?

- If they are not co-operating, how is this contributing to the adolescent's difficulties?

- Is the adolescent being asked to take sides with one parent against another and is this contributing to their problems?

- Are family and parental stresses such as bereavement, illnesses, major family changes, unemployment, parental depression, parental substance use, family violence contributing to the problems?

- Is the adolescent or anyone in the family a significant danger to themselves or others?

- Are there extended family members who have a particularly significant role in the family?

Responses to lines of questioning based on these concerns throw light on family strengths and protective factors that may be useful in addressing the presenting problems. They may also suggest the role family factors may be playing in maintaining the adolescents' problems and point to family issues to be addressed in later counselling sessions. Where there is evidence that anyone in the family is a significant danger to themselves or others, child protection interventions are considered.

School

A number of risk and protective factors are associated with school placements which affect adolescent behavioural and emotional problems. Protective factors include an authoritative, supportive relationship between school staff and adolescents; a collaborative relationship between school staff and parents; a matching of the school curriculum and resources to pupils educational needs; a balance of emphasis on academic attainment and excellence in non-academic activities; an ethos in which there is an expectation of success and good behaviour supported by clear rules, fair discipline, regular homework which is promptly graded and support for non-academic activities. The absence of these factors increases the risk that the school environment will maintain problems.

In talking with adolescents and their families about the school domain, counsellors enquire about the following areas and in doing so assess school-related risk and protective factors.

- Current and previous school placements

- Family-school relationships

- Special educational needs

- Bullying

- Educational goals and expectations

Current and previous school placements Enquiries about a teenager's school and education may cover details of their current and previous school placements. With regard to details of their current school situation, information is sought on their current stage in secondary school; the subjects, sports and activities they like and dislike; their academic grades and non-academic achievements; the subjects they are studying; their extracurricular activities; and sports in which they are involved. These enquires throw light on teenagers' perceptions of the balance of emphasis on academic attainment and excellence in non-academic activities at their school; and whether the ethos entails an expectation of success and good behaviour supported by clear rules, fair discipline, regularly graded homework and support for non-academic activities.

Family-school relationships In asking about the school, enquiries are made about the quality of the teenagers' and parents' relationships with relevant teachers and the school principal, and the view that the family believe the school have of their problems. An important concern is whether the school staff have a strong co-operative relationship with the parents and teenager and are viewed as supportive, or if they are in conflict with the teenager and/or the parents. Where there is a positive relationship, this may be drawn upon in looking for a solution to the difficulties. Where the relationship is conflictual, this may become an important focus for intervention with the school or with the family.

Special educational needs Where it is clear that teenagers are having achievement difficulties, counsellors ask if they have been assessed for special educational needs and if such needs are present, how these are being resourced and met within the school placement. These enquires indicate the degree to which there is a matching of the curriculum and resources to the teenager's educational needs. If a young person's special educational needs are not being adequately met, the counsellors may have an advocacy role in supporting the acquisition of appropriate resources.

Bullying Questions are also asked about the degree to which the teenager is supported or bullied by others within their current school class and whether the teenager is bullying others. Where young people are being bullied, or bullying others, and this is not being addressed adequately within the school, this may become an important focus for intervention with the school and family.

Educational goals and expectations Teenagers are asked about their educational goals and their perception of their parents' expectations of them. The parents are also asked about their educational expectations of the teenager. Perceived high expectations may be associated with depression and suicidality in perfectionistic adolescents. In this context it may be appropriate to ask whether teenagers are having extra tuition outside school hours (grinds) and the impact of this. In some instances grinds are supportive and useful in helping young people achieve their educational goals. In other cases, grinds and high perceived parental expectations are pressurising and cause significant stress and depression.

Very bright teenagers who are not sufficiently challenged at school, or who feel that they don't fit in with their less bright peers, may become bored, underachieve and develop school-based behaviour problems. Teenagers from disorganised families in which parents do not expect regular school attendance, good behaviour at school or homework completion may underachieve, develop school-based behaviour problems or drop out of school.

Friends

Peer group membership can be both a risk and a protective factor. Strong friendships provide teenagers with social support, which is important for good mental health. Membership of an antisocial peer group is a risk factor for behaviour problems, substance use, school drop-out, sexually transmitted diseases including HIV/AIDS, teenage pregnancy, involvement in risky and dangerous behaviour and the breakdown of parent–teen relationships. For these reasons it is important to enquire about peer relationships. The capacities to make and maintain positive friendships, and to avoid or disengage from antisocial peers, are important skills to consider in this context. Enquiries about friends may cover the following four areas:

- Number and quality of friendships

- After school activities

- Substance use, sexual behaviour and antisocial peer-group activity

- Peer pressure towards antisocial peer group activity

Number and quality of friendships In enquiring about friendships, counsellors ask about friends at home, school and in part-time work; the number and quality of these peer relationships; if there are best friends, special friends, girl or boy friends; the times when teenagers meet with friends (weekends, evenings, holidays etc.); and the ease with which they can make and maintain long-term friendships.

After school activities Enquires are made about the sorts of leisure activities, sports and other pro-social pursuits teenagers engage in with friends. Their use and experience of the internet and social media is explored.

Substance use, sexual behaviour and antisocial peer group activity Enquires are made about the sensitive issues of cigarettes, drink and drug use with friends; whether the teenager puts themselves at risk regarding sexual behaviour; and whether they are involved in antisocial gang behaviour such as harming other's property, theft, or violence. Assuming that certain behaviours are occurring and putting them on the table can be useful e.g. asking *"How many cigarettes do you smoke?"* and *"How often do you drink?"* produces fuller responses than *"Do you smoke?"* and *"Do you drink?"*, but counsellors are sensitive to the fact that teenagers may not wish to provide a great deal of information on these issues with their parents present and they are explored in greater depth in future individual sessions if appropriate.

Peer pressure towards antisocial peer group activity Counsellors ask about similarities and differences between the teenager and their friends in terms of parental rules about curfew times, substance use, sexual behaviour and pocket money. This may throw light on the degree to which they are experiencing a wish to conform with the antisocial activities in which their peers engage. Counsellors may also ask about times when they resisted the wish to participate in antisocial activities so as to be liked and accepted by friends who do not engage in such activities. For example this can involve a boyfriend or girlfriend who is not interested in a relationship if drug using is involved.

Self

A great deal of information about the adolescent's *'self'* will have been noted whilst exploring the domains of home, school and friends. However, the following areas are routinely covered:

- Physical health

- Eating, sleeping and exercise routines

- Mood, self-harm and suicidality

Physical health Enquiries about disabilities, illnesses, injuries and use of medication will indicate the degree to which physical health problems are affecting the young person's adjustment. Coping with chronic conditions like asthma, diabetes or epilepsy and dealing with the aftermath of injuries which have led to permanent problems, such as brain damage, may contribute to emotional and behavioural problems. These enquires will also indicate if youngsters have developed psychosomatic symptoms such as stomach aches and headaches in response to stress.

Eating, sleeping and exercise routines Enquiries about these routines may indicate if teenagers are at risk for developing eating disorders, particularly bulimia and anorexia, or depression. Bulimia involves binging and purging. Those at risk of anorexia, diet and exercise excessively. Sleep problems (including early morning waking, or sleeping too much or too little), appetite problems (including loss of appetite or excessive comfort eating) and taking little exercise are all associated with depression.

Mood, self-harm and suicidality Enquiries about these issues throw light on the degree to which a young person is at risk, because they are a danger to themselves[2]. To enquire about mood, it is useful to ask teenagers to rate their mood on a scale from 1 to 10 now, in the past week and at times when they have felt very low, and to note situations, relationships and thoughts that are associated with low mood. To enquire about non-suicidal self-harm, teenagers may be asked if they have ever harmed themselves, by for example cutting their skin, to achieve a sense of relief. This may be followed up with questions about the circumstances in which this occurred and the frequency and severity of this. To enquire about suicidality, it is useful to distinguish between suicidal ideation (thoughts of killing oneself), and suicidal intent (making concrete plans to kill oneself). If teenagers indicate that they have recently had frequent thoughts of killing themselves and have made a plan to do so, they are at high risk and require a suicide risk assessment to establish if Teen Counselling can provide sufficient support to keep them safe.

In some cases taking a detailed clinical history across the young person's lifespan may be useful, but too time consuming to be conducted in the first session. This can therefore be done in subsequent sessions.

Is there anything else we should know or that we should have asked about?

In a first session, some issues relevant to a family's main concerns may not emerge and it is important to acknowledge that this may be the case. The question *'Is there anything else we should know or that we should have asked about?'* often elicits very important information which becomes a significant focus for future work. Sometimes clients make it clear that there are other issues, which they do not wish to discuss in the present forum. In this context, normalising the fact that teenagers do not want to say certain things in front of parents is important. On other occasions, clients' reactions to the question about *'anything else we should know'* may lead counsellors to wonder if there are other important issues that clients may wish to discuss at a later stage.

When the counsellor conducting the interview and the family feel that there has been enough discussion, it is useful for the interviewer to check with their observer colleague if there is anything else that they think should be covered before taking the session break. The contribution of the team member who has adopted the observer role is critical to the process of making space for the *'not-yet-said'*. Throughout the session the observer notes half-said things that family members raised, but then moved away from, seemingly unimportant details which led to family tension or other noteworthy responses and significant non-verbal reactions. When the interviewer invites the observer to comment on anything else that they think should be covered before taking the session break, the observer may raise issues based on their observations of the session.

5.6. Session break

The session break is taken about three quarters of the way through the first session when the areas outlined above have been covered. It should be long enough for the team to develop a preliminary formulation and work plan and an agreed way of presenting this to the family. In practice the time may vary depending on the complexity of the case and the experience of the counselling team. Long session breaks may be stressful for families, so counsellors manage the tasks of the session break efficiently. Many families are not comfortable talking together and often become restless during the session break, or disappear to the bathroom or smoking area if they are left for too long.

Families are encouraged to use the session break to reflect on their experience of talking about their difficulties and to decide if it would be useful to return and talk further. Here is an example of how to introduce a session break:

"OK, if we have all the information, let's take a break now. This will give us a chance to think through what you have told us and to plan how best to help. Most importantly it will give you a chance to talk about what it was like being here and to decide whether you might come back. We'll be just a few minutes."

The main tasks to be completed by the counselling team in the session break are to:

- Decide if the service is the most suitable for the family

- Consider if additional information is required

- Decide if other family members or involved professionals need to be contacted

- Confirm the formulation explored and developed during the session

- Decide a counselling plan including which counsellor will work with the teenager and which with the parent

- Design homework assignments if appropriate

- Prepare consent forms if they are immediately necessary

- Prepare brief feedback.

Suitability of counselling for the family's problems

In the break the team consider whether counselling is the intervention required by the family. PSP is appropriate for moderate behavioural and emotional problems. It is not suitable for chronic and severe eating disorders with medical complications, psychosis, severe mood disorders with high risk of suicide, chronic drug addiction, or child protection cases in which sexual abuse has been disclosed, but has not been investigated by statutory services. Where counselling is not the most suitable intervention for families, arrangements may be made to refer them to a more suitable service.

Additional information

During the break the team consider whether additional information is required such as reports from previous assessments, telephone numbers or other contact details not available at referral. For non-resident parents in particular, their full contact details and the potential to involve them in the counselling process is often not clear from the referral.

Additional family members or professionals

During the break the team consider who else from the family or professional network needs to be involved. Despite being invited, fathers often do not attend first sessions. In such cases part of the feedback to families includes arranging for their involvement. In some instances it may be appropriate to talk with involved professionals such as a school counsellor or a social worker. In such cases, consent for such contact needs to be sought (as described below).

Preliminary formulation

In the break the team reflect on the information explored during the first part of the session and confirm the formulation (shared understanding or mini-theory) about the main problem and the key risk and protective factors associated with them. Preliminary ideas about the role of risk and protective factors in affecting the main problems are in many cases modifications of pre-session hypotheses based on specific information given during the interview and the new understandings generated during the first session.

Counselling plan

Counselling plans follow on from preliminary formulations. The main focus of counselling with teenagers and parents separately and jointly typically involves addressing factors outlined in the formulation, but may also include issues which the family did not identify, but which the team feel could warrant some attention. The counselling plan also includes decisions about whether to offer further joint sessions following the first session, or offer individual sessions for the teenager and parents.

In deciding which counsellor will work with the teenager and which one will work with the parents the following issues are taken into account:

- What connections were made between each of the counsellors and each of the family members during the first session? If the teenager formed a particularly good alliance with one counsellor, then this may be continued in subsequent individual sessions. Teenagers usually, but not always, connect with the counsellor who leads the interview.

- Do the counsellors have particular knowledge, expertise or interests relevant to meeting the needs of either the teenager or the parents?

- Would the teenager or parent benefit from working with a male or female counsellor (if the team contains counsellors of both genders)? For example, it may be particularly appropriate for female counsellors to work with teenage girls who have suffered sexual abuse; and teenage boys may find male counsellors good role models.

- What are the counsellors' *'gut'* feelings about the best match between each of them and the teenager and parents?

Client tasks

Counselling involves having conversations about challenges families face in their lives during counselling sessions, but it also involves clients making changes in their lives between sessions. To help clients make these changes they are sometimes invited to complete *'homework'* assignments between sessions. For example, keeping a record of how often a particular problem occurs, or arranging for teenagers and parents to deal with each other in a different way. Suggested tasks are designed so as to maximise the chances of success, while at the same time inviting families to take an active role in addressing their difficulties.

Consent to contact others

The first session focuses on the views of the teenager and parents. The usefulness of obtaining the views of other involved professionals, or the teenager's school, is generally introduced in subsequent sessions. However, if it is very obvious or appropriate for permission to be sought during the first session, consent forms need to be prepared during the break.

To obtain the views of other involved professionals, counsellors invite teenagers and parents to sign consent forms to give them permission to contact relevant school teachers, guidance counsellors, the family doctor, social workers, juvenile justice officers and so forth. Often it is useful to contact the teenager's school and consider if the counselling team can work co-operatively with school staff to support the family. Where other professionals have significant involvement it is useful to contact them and obtain their views and clarify the way in which they have been, and may continue to be, involved with the case. In some circumstances, it may be appropriate to convene meetings that involve other professionals and the family to clarify or propose the way professionals may best co-ordinate their input to the family.

Prepare presentation

The final task of the session break is for counsellors to agree a way to ask the family for their thoughts on the first part of the session, present them with the team's ideas, and offer them a therapeutic contract if appropriate. After a long and emotionally demanding interview families are at risk of not being able to accurately hear and remember everything, so this part of the session should be brief and in language that families are comfortable with.

In most cases the team will offer a counselling service to the family, so the first thing to check with them is if they thought the session was useful and whether they wish to return. A survey done in Teen Counselling in 2005 showed that 88% of parents and 75% of teenagers found the first session better than they expected. About 1 in 10 families attend the Teen Counselling service only once. In some cases counsellors decide that Teen Counselling is not a suitable service for them and refer them on to other more relevant services. In other cases one session is sufficient to provide reassurance about a particular concern. These families are always given the option to return in the future if the situation changes. Finally, some clients schedule a second appointment, but fail to attend. This may be because there was some level of coercion involved in the referral, the family was not ready to engage in counselling, or the family found the first session very difficult and painful, but were not able to articulate this. When families do not attend their second appointment and make no contact with the service, they receive a letter to let them know that they are welcome to re-engage at any time in the future. If the referrer was not a family member, the referrer also receives a letter to inform them of the situation.

For families who wish to attend further sessions it is appropriate to present them with the preliminary formulation in language, and at a level of complexity or simplicity that they can understand and remember. There will be opportunities in subsequent sessions to expand on this further if it is helpful to do so. The related work plan, and if appropriate, tasks to be completed before the next session are also presented, along with consent forms to contact the school and other involved professions if they are immediately necessary. These issues are reviewed at subsequent appointments.

The counsellors explain the format of counselling that they think most appropriate - continuing to work jointly, or separately initially with further joint sessions in the future. Teenagers and parents are also told that the first session is the longest and that subsequent sessions last for no more than an hour. Families are given an opportunity to consider the therapeutic contract and agree appointment times.

Therapeutic contracts are flexible. For most families an open-ended schedule is proposed – individual sessions for the teenager and their parents with their individual counsellors, with periodic joint sessions 'to see how everyone is getting on'. Counsellors and clients arrange the frequency of appointments and spacing between them so as to meet clients' needs and accommodate parents' working arrangements and teenagers' school timetables. It may be important to schedule teenagers' appointments so that they do not always miss the same class. For some families a limited number of sessions are offered with a plan to review when these have been completed, for example a set of three weekly appointments, followed by three fortnightly appointments. This can be a useful way of encouraging reluctant attenders. The critical issue is that clients and counsellors agree on a contract for counselling to address specific issues, and that the number and pacing of sessions is matched to clients' needs. Some families have misconceptions about counselling, based on television portrayals of psychotherapy as involving weekly visits for life!! It can therefore be reassuring for families to know that at Teen Counselling the average duration of counselling is 9 sessions over a period of 9 months.

Appointments with teenagers and their parents are arranged separately with their respective counsellors. Teenagers are encouraged to take responsibility for their own appointments and parents to take responsibility for theirs. This practice acknowledges the growing autonomy of the teenager and the active role they are taking in engaging in counselling.

Clients are advised on how to cancel or change appointments so that counsellors can make efficient use of their time, and schedule other clients when cancellations or changes of appointments occur. Counsellors show respect for clients by being ready to see them at agreed appointment times and encourage clients to have similar respect for them by attending scheduled sessions punctually.

5.7. Reconvening and closing the first session

When the session is reconvened, providing the counsellors consider the case suitable for counselling, they ask the family if they found the discussion useful and if they would like to return to do some more work. Here is an example of how to do this:

> *"OK so, we've had our chat and we think this would be a good place for you to look at the issues you've told us about this morning and we would like to work with you. How about yourselves? What did you think?"*

When teenagers do not want to attend further sessions

Where teenagers say that they do not want to attend further counselling and only came once because their parent told them to, the counsellor respects their decision and acknowledges that it was a great help to have their input. If parents wish to attend further, their teenager is often asked if they will return at a later date should their help be needed. This provides a face-saving option for the teenager to engage in counselling at a future date if they change their mind. This approach often works very well. If parents commit to making positive changes through counselling, the teenager may become interested and ask to be involved.

When an adolescent's problem is a calling card for parental problems

In some instances, there will be consistency between viewpoints about the reason for referral and the presenting problems. However, in other cases it will become clear that the teenager's presenting problems are relatively minor in comparison with the chief concern which is an adult-focused concern, such as marital problems, parental depression or other mental health difficulties, substance use, life-threatening illness, recent unemployment or some other crisis. In these situations, the teenager's difficulties may be a *'calling card'* to place the parents in contact with another service. In such cases it may be appropriate, without undermining the parent's position, to acknowledge this. An important decision in such cases is to decide whether to offer a service to the parents for their adult-focused difficulty, or to refer them on to an adult service. Engagement with a counselling service for teenagers may be less threatening for some parents and attendance *'to help their youngster'* can be an effective stepping stone and a gateway for them to be referred to another service which can address their adult-focused problems.

When parents do not want a service

If clients indicate that they do not wish to continue with the counselling process or that they think the service will not be helpful to them, they are thanked for attending and given the opportunity to change their minds in the future. Counsellors let them know, when appropriate, that a letter will be sent to the referrer indicating that the family had attended once, but did not wish to have further appointments.

When families want to engage in counselling

Where families indicate that the session was useful and that they want to continue, counsellors present them with the preliminary formulation, work plan, homework and consent forms if appropriate, and offer them a therapeutic contract.

5.8. Post session debriefing and recording

Conducting intake interviews is an emotionally demanding process. Therefore it is useful for counselling team members to offer each other a few minutes to process the session. That is, they may talk in an unstructured way about the session to *'decompress'* or *'ventilate'* feelings the session has evoked in them. Different counsellors have different routines for decompressing or unwinding. These include talking about the emotional impact of the family on them, talking in an unstructured way about critical moments in the interview, taking a few minutes to relax and so forth.

Ideas and hypotheses about how the family gave feedback and responded to the feedback given are shared. It may be that the preliminary hypotheses and counselling plan need to be revised in light of the family's response to feedback. The generation of hypotheses and their refining and revision is a key element in counselling team consultations as the work progresses. The key interventions planned are noted for the file and the team also complete assessment measures against which outcome can be rated (see Chapter 13). These include the Children's Global Assessment Scale[8] and the Global Assessment of Relational Functioning Scale[9].

The member of the counselling team who took the notes writes up an account of salient points from the first session. The following items (details of which are given earlier in the chapter) may be covered in this write-up:

Attendance and contact details

- Teenager, parents, counsellors who attended and the date

- Contact details not already on the referral form e.g. mobile phone numbers, non-resident parent(s) address

The presenting problem

- Outline the reason for referral and any underlying difficulties highlighted during the session

Home

- Family composition and living arrangements – a genogram may be useful

- Family routines, roles and rules

- Family relationships, significant extended family members

- Family stresses

School

- Current and previous school placements

- Family-school relationships

- Special educational needs

- Bullying

- Educational goals and expectations

Friends

- Number and quality of friendships

- After school activities

- Substance use and sexual behaviour

- Peer pressure towards antisocial peer group activity

Self

- Physical health

- Eating, sleeping and exercise routines

- Mood, self-harm and suicidality

Summary

- Formulation

- Intervention plan

- Tasks assigned

- Consent forms

- Forms (CGAS, GARF etc.).

After subsequent appointments counsellors write progress notes.

SUMMARY

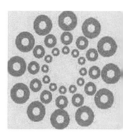

The process of conducting intake interviews with families, formulation and contracting for counselling were described in this chapter.

The aims of the first session are to lay the foundation for a good therapeutic alliance, name the issues to be addressed in counselling (while creating space for the possibility of other issues emerging) and develop a shared understanding or formulation of these difficulties.

The counselling team meet before and after the session for planning and debriefing, and about three quarters of the way through the session there is a break for formulation and planning.

A conversational style is adopted in the first and subsequent sessions in which the counselling team value all viewpoints, use a respectful, invitational approach, and show empathy, warmth and genuineness. Counsellors assume normal developmental tensions and use reframing and other interventions to promote positive and mutually respectful relationships between adolescents and parents.

In the opening of the first session counsellors explain its format to clients and let them know that both parents and teenagers must consent to attend, that the service is confidential with some limits to that confidentiality.

Starting with the teenager whenever possible, counsellors invite each person to explain their view of the reason for referral and the presenting problem. Thoughtful questioning about the presenting problem creates opportunities for reframing the problem as constituting part, but not all of the teenager's identity; as influenced by the family, school and peer group, not just the teenager's character; and as a difficulty that is transient rather than stable.

Adolescent behavioural and emotional problems are influenced by risk and protective factors within the four domains of home, school, friends and self, so detailed enquires are made in each of these four domains.

Enquires about the home cover: family composition and living arrangements; family routines, roles and rules; family relationships; and family stresses.

Enquires about the school cover: current and previous school placements; family-school relationships; special educational needs; bullying; and educational goals and expectations.

Enquires about friends cover: the number and quality of friendships; after school activities; substance use and sexual behaviour; and peer pressure towards antisocial peer group activity.

Enquires about the adolescent's self cover: physical health; eating, sleep and exercise patterns; mood, self-harm and suicidality.

A break is taken about three quarters of the way through the first session and is used by the team to develop a preliminary formulation and work plan and an agreed way of presenting this to the family. The family is encouraged to use the session break to reflect on their experience of the service and decide if they would like to return.

When the session is reconvened, counsellors check with the family if they found the session useful and would like to return. If clients indicate that they do not wish to continue with the counselling process they are thanked for attending and, when appropriate, the referrer is notified.

Where families indicate that the session was useful and that they want to continue, counsellors present them with the preliminary formulation, work plan, homework and consent forms if appropriate, and offer them a therapeutic contract.

After the intake interview the team meet briefly to process the session, note the key interventions planned and make evaluations. The note-taker then writes up an account of salient points.

CHAPTER 6

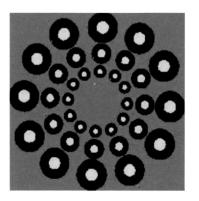

Middle and closing phases

The process of working with families through the middle phase of counselling and then concluding the counselling process is described in this chapter. The chapter covers working with adolescents, working with parents, case discussions between sessions and conducting joint sessions during the middle phase. The role of service policies is also set out. The key elements of the closing phase are also covered in this chapter.

6.1 Transition to the middle phase

Following the first session, the transition to the middle phase begins. Typically, one member of the counselling team works with the adolescent, while the other counsellor works with the parents in a series of parallel sessions with periodic joint sessions. However, in some cases joint sessions are used throughout the middle phase, where it is clear that this will be more beneficial for clients.

The dividing line between the engagement phase and the middle phase of counselling is rarely clearly drawn[1]. As the engagement phase fades out, the middle phase comes to predominate. The first session, and some aspects of the initial individual sessions with adolescents and parents constitute the engagement phase, during which the counselling team is forming therapeutic alliances with family members and developing a shared understanding of their main problems. The following processes occur during the engagement phase:

- Counsellors evaluate the context or history of the presenting problems

- Counsellors check out how the family functions and the norms that guide family members' behaviour

- Counsellors assess how open and flexible the family is to challenges which invite changes to the way family members interact with each other

- Counsellors reframe individual difficulties as family problems

- Counsellors facilitate mentalization[2] in family members, providing opportunities for them to comment on the intentions, needs, feelings, and beliefs of other family members about key family concerns

- Counsellors contain family members' anxiety

- Counsellors establish boundaries concerning attendance at counselling sessions, communication with counsellors and the limits of confidentiality within sessions

- Clients check out their counsellors and decide if there is a good match between their needs and the service the counsellors are offering

There is then a progression towards further developing a new shared understanding of the difficulties in the family. Counsellors help family members move towards this new shared understanding by showing respect for their original beliefs about the problems that brought them to counselling, but also by challenging these in ways that invite them to consider new and more useful approaches to managing their difficulties. This then creates the foundation for work on resolving the family's problems and this is what defines the middle phase of counselling.

At the beginning of the first of the individual sessions for both parents and teenagers, counsellors re-iterate the Teen Counselling policy about confidentiality and the limits of this which were explained to the family at the start of their first session as described in Chapter 5. The confidential nature of individual sessions is also repeated. Counsellors do not carry messages between parents and teenagers. That is, they do not tell teenagers what parents have said in a session, nor do they tell parents what teenagers have said in a session. When parents are separated and do not attend together, their counsellor also respects their needs for confidentiality. However, counsellors make it clear to clients that they share information to make sure that the support provided to the family is relevant and coherent.

In the first of the individual sessions, clients are asked to complete assessment forms in which they rate the severity of their concerns. There are separate forms for parents and teenagers shown in the Appendices. At Teen Counselling these are colour coded with pink forms for parents and green forms for teenagers. Similar forms are completed in the final session and comparisons made between forms completed in the first and last sessions to evaluate gains made over the course of counselling. Teenagers are also asked to complete a substance use questionnaire in their first individual session which contains questions about how much they use drugs, drink alcohol and smoke cigarettes. Responses to this questionnaire highlight the need for counsellors to work on substance use issues with teenagers. Teenagers are invited to complete the substance use questionnaire because detection of early substance misuse and preventing the development of chronic and severe drug problems is a major objective of the service and its funders. The self-report substance use questionnaire usually elicits a more accurate assessment of teenagers' use of drugs, alcohol and cigarettes than teenagers disclose in the first session in front of their parents.

Aims of middle phase

The aims of the middle phase are to maintain and deepen the therapeutic alliance, and to address the issues or themes identified in the engagement phase so as to move towards the teenagers' and parents' counselling goals. Counselling goals are usually negotiated between counsellors and clients. These goals reflect teenagers' and parents' wishes and preferences on the one hand, and counsellors' views about what is most likely to lead to a resolution of the presenting problems on the other. This middle phase of counselling is informed by the shared understanding, or formulation, of family difficulties developed in the engagement phase. In the middle phase changes in formulation may occur as a result of new information or insights so that the formulation comes to more accurately reflect the current family situation. All new information is discussed by the counselling team in regular case review meetings between the counsellor working with the teenager and the counsellor working with the parents.

During the middle phase the team and family may arrange for other members of the family or professional network to be involved in the counselling process. These may include non-resident parents, grandparents, siblings, school personnel, social workers, care workers, juvenile liaison officers, psychiatrists, or other members of specialist services. Counsellors and clients also discuss the most appropriate ways to include other members of the family or professional network. A range of options may be considered including individual meetings, joint meetings, phone calls, case conferences, letters and reports.

6.2. Working with adolescents

The counsellor working with the adolescent actively promotes their involvement in counselling sessions and helps them learn how to use sessions productively. Counsellors encourage adolescents to schedule their appointments and take personal responsibility for their attendance when possible, rather than relying on their parents. Counsellors and administrative staff make the counselling service as adolescent-friendly as possible by being positive, communicative, empathic, respectful and non-judgemental in their interactions with teenage clients. They also provide young people with a safe counselling environment, being vigilant for any threats to their well-being and development, and take steps to make sure their clients come to no harm while in counselling. They explain what they are doing and respond to the challenging questions teenagers ask. For example, *"What's it to you, why do you care?"*

A short honest answer usually suffices. For example *"It's my job, I really like working with teenagers and I hope to be able to help you and your family. This service has a lot of experience doing this and I look forward to working with you"*. Counsellors always use appropriate humour when working with adolescents.

Counsellors use their expert knowledge of adolescent development and their clinical skills for detecting issues such as learning difficulties or health problems (which may not be the primary presenting problems) to provide young people with a teenager-friendly, yet highly professional service.

Move from easy to difficult themes Where adolescents are ambivalent about attending counselling, counsellors use their creativity to make the sessions appealing. They focus the conversation initially on topics that young people feel comfortable talking about. As the alliance strengthens, they then move on to address more difficult issues. Where teenagers are reluctant to discuss difficult issues, counsellors offer a rationale for exploring these challenging concerns in a way that makes sense to teenagers and in a way that motivates them to engage in the counselling process.

Use media and materials Where teenagers have difficulty talking in response to open questions, counsellors may use structured materials to help progress the therapeutic conversation. These may include questionnaires, workbooks, experiential exercises, drawing, diaries, genograms, life story books or charts, art media, computers and so forth. Where these sorts of resources are used, their function is to support the aims of the middle phase of counselling, that is developing the relationship between counsellor and client, and deepening their alliance, and addressing the key issues or themes central to the problem formulation.

Alliance strengthening stances A range of stances, listed in chapter 3, are used to strengthen the counsellor's alliance with the adolescent. These include, for example, being genuine in relationships with adolescents, recognising the validity of the adolescent's perspective, respecting teenagers and their struggle, having a sense of humour, not over-reacting to teenagers' narratives, normalising teenagers' occasional challenging behaviours, understanding the defensive function of much problematic behaviour and accepting, and keeping present the knowledge, that parents really matter to teenagers.

Stances to promote insight and understanding As key issues and themes within the domains of home, school, friends and self are explored, teenagers may develop a new understanding of their difficulties and this may alleviate their distress. On occasion the teenager's newly developed understanding may bring parental inappropriateness, shortcomings or failures in the past into focus. Counsellors help teenagers explore these concerns, in a way that is respectful and empathic of the parents' and teenager's positions, to understand how the issues came into being. The vital communication between counsellors between sessions ensures that insights are processed and can be accepted without defensiveness. Stances that promote insight and understanding, described in chapter 3, include, for example, helping teenagers understand their parents' and other perspectives on their problems, psycho-education, exploring the pros and cons of behaviour change, and acknowledging and re-appraising negative thoughts.

Stances to promote behaviour change In some instances new understanding and insight alone are not sufficient to alleviate distress or resolve behavioural problems. Changes may be required in the young person's relationships within their family, school and peer group. Counsellors help teenagers explore options for making such changes. There may be things that the young person can do differently to effect these changes such as developing courageous or assertive behaviour or self-care routines. Stances relevant to these types of changes are detailed in chapter 3. However, it may be that what is required is a change not just in the adolescent's behaviour, but also in the behaviour of the adolescent's parents or teachers. Counsellors work with adolescents to prepare them for joint family sessions in which they can work cooperatively with their parents to address their presenting problems in more productive ways.

> *Case example: Emma, aged 17, had attended many schools. She had been diagnosed with a specific learning difficulty at primary school and despite being bright and articulate she just never found a way of coping in school and accommodating her learning problems. At 17 she was starting to worry about her future. She wanted to go to university. However, her ambitions were unrealistic. Without a secondary school Leaving Certificate, she would not be admitted to a university. Having dropped out of yet another school, she enrolled in a college of further education to do her Leaving Cert. Her attendance was appalling during the first term.*
>
> *Counselling gave her courage to persist with her studies. It also helped her to accept her learning difficulties and set realistic goals. Most importantly it helped her to elicit the support that she needed from staff in the college, rather than antagonising them as she had done in every other school she had attended.*

6.3. Working with parents

While one counsellor is working with the adolescent, the other works with the parents. In the middle phase of counselling, these sessions with the parents focus on deepening the alliance and addressing the key issues or themes central to the problem formulation.

Alliance strengthening stances A range of stances, listed in chapter 3, are used to strengthen the counsellor's alliance with parents. These include, for example, being genuine in relationships with parents, recognising the validity of each parent's perspective, accepting that conflict between teenagers and parents is inevitable, normalising teenagers' occasional challenging behaviours, understanding the defensive function of much problematic behaviour and accepting that parents really want to love and do the best for their teenagers.

Parenting issues versus personal and couple issues In working with parents of adolescents with emotional and behavioural problems, distinctions may be made between parenting issues on the one hand and personal or couples issues on the other. With regard to parenting issues, which are present in almost all cases, couples struggle to find a more useful way to meet their adolescent's needs for care, control and increasing autonomy. With regard to personal and couples issues which are present in some, but not all cases, parents may be trying to deal with their own problems such as addiction, depression, anxiety, unresolved family of origin issues, bereavement, caring for aging parents, unemployment, marital distress, separation, forming a stepfamily and so forth. Different stances are appropriate for working with parenting issues and personal or couples issues.

Stances for addressing parenting issues A range of stances, listed in chapter 3, are adopted in addressing parenting issues. These include, for example, accepting that parents are not always right, a positive influence or a resource; making it clear from the outset that violence is not tolerated; helping parents prevent destructive repetitive behaviour patterns; accepting that usually the longer young people stay in the education system the better; psycho-education; helping parents develop clarity about what they consider acceptable and unacceptable behaviour; accepting that parental over control and under control can lead to adolescent problems; respecting family and community norms; accepting that experiencing the consequences of their actions is essential for teenagers to learn to be responsible for their behaviour; accepting that mistakes are learning opportunities; helping parents to let go of directive parenting and adopt a style based on negotiation; helping parents to manage their anxiety so as to promote their teenager's independence; helping parents to provide teenagers with age-appropriate jobs to do at home; helping parents to allow their teenagers opportunities to develop strategies for protecting themselves in their social environment; helping non-authoritative parents to be parents (not friends) to their teenagers; and helping parents accept that a parent's job is to become redundant.

Case example: Fourteen year old Ciaran attended counselling with his mother, Linda. She was a single parent who had no contact with the boy's father since before Ciaran's birth. Linda complained that Ciaran's behaviour was out of control at home, school and in the community. Linda said she felt helpless and did not know how to address the situation. She recounted a catalogue of Ciaran's rule-breaking escapades with great amusement, smiling all the while at her son. From her account it became clear that Ciaran had never experienced any negative consequences for his rule-breaking behaviour. Typically his mother would sigh rather despairingly, but use no sanctions to help Ciaran understand that his behaviour was unacceptable. Before Linda came to counselling, she developed a relationship with George who had spent much of his youth in detention centres and prison. George was afraid that Ciaran's rule-breaking behaviour would lead to the boy following in his footsteps.

The couple were invited to come to counselling together and in these sessions, George offered to support Linda in establishing appropriate limits and boundaries for Ciaran and consistently implement fair consequences for rule-following and rule-breaking behaviour. For example, Ciaran was bright and liked school well enough, but he often couldn't be

Personal and couples issues For personal and couples issues, an important decision that counsellors must make is the degree to which such problems may be dealt with, within the context of an adolescent counselling service, and whether referral to another service such as addiction, relationship counselling or adult mental health service is required. Where counsellors judge that personal and couples issues may be addressed within the context of an adolescent counselling service, the aim is to do sufficient work on these issues, so that parents can be effective parents to their teenager. The counsellor clarifies that this is the purpose of personal and couple work in Teen Counselling and explicitly invites parents to engage in this work. Where parents actively seek long-term engagement for individual or couple work, it may be challenging for counsellors to maintain a focus on the needs of their teenager while also helping them to engage with an appropriate adult service.

Case example: Paul aged 12, was referred for counselling by his school. His behaviour was very oppositional. Neither his teachers nor his parents could manage his aggressive outbursts. Paul was the third child in a family of eight and his older siblings also had behaviour problems at home and school. Paul's parents, Tracy and Jeff, had a very volatile relationship. They had been together since their teens, but had never married or lived together consistently. They argued regularly. Often these arguments resulted in Tracy throwing Jeff out of the family home for unspecified periods of time until she had a crisis and needed him to come home again. The couple had never addressed the impact of their stormy relationship on their children.

It took many sessions with Tracy and Jeff, both individually and together, before they were able to agree to address couple issues and eventually accept a referral to a specialist service for couples with relationship problems. For this family, Paul had been the calling card for his parents to access the support they needed to begin to manage their relationship problems. Paul's behaviour started to improve when his parents began to work as a parenting team, providing him with the security and consistency he needed to learn how to behave in a more responsible way.

Stances for parental personal issues Stances, described in chapter 3, relevant to parental personal issues include for example, psycho-education, addressing family of origin issues, accepting that what is not said (and kept secret) is often as important as what is, helping parents accept that they cannot re-live their own adolescence through their teenagers, helping parents explore the pros and cons of changing their own behaviour, and helping parents acknowledge and re-appraise their own negative thoughts.

Case example: Ger and Mary were very worried about their 17 year old son, Thomas. He was due to sit his Leaving Certificate exam in a few months and, in their view, was not doing enough homework or study. Despite the imminence of his exams, Thomas was still expecting to be allowed to go out with his friends at the weekends, rather than stay at home and study. Thomas's expectations led to considerable conflict between himself and his father. Mary described Ger and Thomas as 'locking horns' very aggressively as Ger became more and more involved in trying to control Thomas's life, by making him stay at home and study. The conflict between father and son had a negative effect on the whole family. The younger siblings had become terrified of the arguments that occurred between Ger and Thomas. Thomas responded to Ger's attempts to control him by threatening to not sit the exams at all if Ger did not get off his back.

Ger explained to his counsellor how anxious he was for Thomas to do well in his exams and attain his evident potential. Ger had not completed his schooling. He regretted this. He also regretted that he had never had the opportunity to return to school and complete his education. He was employed doing a job that he hated. He hated his job because it was unskilled and did not challenge him enough. Like his son, Ger was very bright. He needed work that challenged him to avoid boredom. However, Ger could not obtain a job that challenged him, due to his lack of education and qualifications. He also could not leave his current unskilled boring job, because his salary was necessary to support his family. Ger wanted so badly for things to be different for Thomas, but he never discussed this with Thomas or tried to find out what Thomas wanted from his life. In counselling, Ger found it difficult to consider that he did not always know what was best for his children. He also found it very challenging to gradually let Thomas take charge of his own life.

Stances for couples work Stances, described in chapter 3, relevant for couple work include, for example, accepting that good family relationships promote well-being; helping couples communicate, negotiate and jointly problem-solve more effectively; and facilitating the processes of apology and forgiveness [3].

Throughout work with parents, the counsellor prepares them for joint family sessions, so that when these occur, parents will be in a position to relate to their teenagers more effectively and jointly address the presenting problems with their teenagers in a more productive way with support and facilitation.

6.4. Joint sessions

Counselling team members meet regularly and keep each other informed about how their work with the adolescent and parents is progressing in their parallel counselling sessions. When team members judge that the adolescent and parents have made sufficient progress, and have been sufficiently prepared to work together productively in joint sessions, these are scheduled with either the explicit rationale of 'seeing how everybody is getting along' or with the aim to focus on addressing particular issues, for example, learning to communicate needs and feelings to improve a mother-daughter relationship, addressing violence between siblings or sharing specific information. Joint sessions can be extraordinarily powerful as very sensitive issues can be addressed by clients with the support of their counsellors without 'war breaking out'. Counsellors can help family members communicate in a clear and measured way about difficult issues, without engaging in their usual destructive patterns for managing conflict.

Stances about respect for all viewpoints and family loyalty Within joint sessions counsellors are particularly mindful of a number of stances, listed in chapter 3, that promote respect for all viewpoints and highlight the loyalty parents and teenagers have for each other. They recognise the underlying validity of differing perspectives and help parents and teenagers understand each other's perspective. They accept that conflict between teenagers and parents is inevitable, but also that good family relationships promote well-being. They also accept that parents really want to love and do the best for their teenagers and that their parents really matter to teenagers.

Communication, negotiation, problem-solving Most families of adolescents with emotional and behavioural problems have difficulty with communication, negotiation and joint problem-solving. It may be the case that they have the skills to do these things in other contexts, but find it very difficult to do them effectively within the family context. Adopting the stance, detailed in chapter 3, of enhancing these processes is an important part of conducting joint sessions.

Apology and forgiveness Where parents or adolescents have behaved badly and let each other down, joint sessions may be used as a forum within which to facilitate apology and forgiveness processes. This stance has been described in chapter 3.

Case example: *Grace, aged 15, consistently worried about her father, Bernard, a heroin addict who had been in and out of prison on a regular basis throughout her life. Grace declared that she 'loved him to bits'. She wrote to him and visited him when he was 'inside', but she was also furious with him. Bernard had rarely 'been there' for her when she was growing up. He was never there for important events in her life, like birthdays, or times she played in the school concert. He was completely unreliable about arrangements to meet and spend time together with her. Sometimes he would turn up late. Other times he would not turn up at all. Most significantly for Grace, now that she was a teenager, was the shame she felt. In her community, Bernard had a reputation for being the local 'scumbag'. Grace was mortified by the crimes he had committed to feed his drug habit. She had never expressed any of these feelings to her father.*

She told her counsellor that she was certain he would not come to counselling. He surprised her by attending a joint counselling session. In this session Grace was able to let him know the impact of his lifestyle on her. With support, Bernard was able to listen to Grace and tell her that he didn't deserve such a loving and loyal daughter. This was a first small step towards rebuilding his relationship with Grace. It was also the first time he had said to her that he wanted to address his addictions, although Grace was mature enough to realise that he was unlikely to follow through on this. However, Grace did view Bernard's attendance at counselling as an act of apology or atonement. In response, over the months that followed she found her anger towards him began to be tempered with the beginnings of forgiveness.

Stances for behaviour problems When addressing behaviour problems in joint sessions, a number of stances, listed in chapter 3, are particularly relevant. These include, for example, accepting that parental over control and under control can lead to adolescent problems; helping non-authoritative parents to be parents (not friends) to their teenagers; developing clarity about acceptable and unacceptable behaviour; respecting family and community norms; and accepting that experiencing the consequences of their actions is essential for teenagers to learn to be responsible for their behaviour.

Stances to promote autonomy When using joint sessions to promote increased adolescent autonomy, a number of stances, listed in chapter 3, are particularly relevant. These include helping parents to let go of directive parenting and adopt a style based on negotiation; helping parents to manage their anxiety so as to promote their teenager's independence; helping parents to provide teenagers with age-appropriate jobs to do at home; helping parents to allow their teenagers opportunities to develop competencies, which will aid their self-esteem; to develop strategies for protecting themselves in their social environment; and helping parents accept that a parent's job is to become redundant.

Case example: Caroline, aged 14, was referred because of frequent intense arguments with her mother Natalie. Natalie had been knocked down by a hit and run driver when she, herself, was a teenager. As a result, she was very nervous of traffic and unable to let her children cross roads without her. At 14, Caroline was finding her mother's anxiety about crossing roads unaccompanied extremely difficult to cope with as she wanted to be out with friends in the neighbourhood. Prior to the referral conflict about this issue had escalated to violence. This was very distressing for both Caroline and Natalie.

The goals in this case were, through a process of desensitisation, for Natalie to 'allow' Caroline to cross a road without becoming over-anxious and for Caroline to gain an understanding of how her mother's overprotective behaviour had developed in response to her being knocked down by a hit and run driver when she was the same age as Caroline.

Stances for addressing child protection issues In cases where teenagers are at risk of neglect or abuse there are a number of stances, listed in chapter 3, that are particularly appropriate for joint sessions. These include making it clear from the outset that violence is not tolerated; helping to prevent destructive repetitive behaviour patterns; accepting that parents are not always right, a positive influence or a resource; and advocating for teenagers.

Case example: Patricia referred her 15 year old son, Mark, for counselling because of his escalating behavioural problems at home and school. Mark refused to attend counselling. However, Patricia, a single mother with several young children, attended counselling regularly with a view to developing a less problematic relationship with Mark.

Over the course of a number of counselling sessions, Patricia disclosed a history of high levels of violence between herself and Mark. Verbal conflict between mother and son had gradually escalated into loud abusive arguments, and finally into physically violent exchanges. Patricia felt overwhelmed by Mark's violence and was frightened they would eventually hurt each other seriously. The need for a referral to child protection services was evident. With the support of her counsellor, Patricia was able to report herself to the local social work team and access the support she needed at home to prevent the conflict between herself and her son escalating further. This is an example of how an intervention improves the welfare of not only the referred teenager, but all children in a family.

Stances for other issues in joint sessions Joint sessions may be used as a forum within which parents can update their teenagers on how family history has affected their current lives, as a forum for revealing family secrets or as a forum for letting go and moving on. For example an explanation of a death given to a younger child often needs to be updated during adolescence to accommodate their greater understanding and depth of insight into family dynamics. A stance concerning this issue is described in chapter 3.

Case example: Louise, aged 16, was referred because of her apparently uncontrollable aggression towards her younger brother, Sam, which was causing Sam and the parents, Peter and Paula, considerable distress.

In counselling it became clear that Louise's aggression towards Sam occurred because she was very jealous of him. She believed that her parents unfairly favoured Sam over her. She thought that they spoilt him by letting him away with behaviour for which she would be reprimanded or punished. When she complained about this, they often said to Louise that she was older and so should know better. Sam was five years younger than Louise. When the counsellor's asked about the age gap in a joint session, Louise was surprised to hear that she had had another brother who died just after his birth when she was a toddler. Peter and Paula were so distressed by this loss that they did not talk with Louise and Sam about this very significant event. During joint counselling sessions Louise's parents were gradually able to validate Louise's view that her brother was indeed 'precious' and acknowledge that his special treatment was not in the interests of either Sam or Louise.

6.5. Managing boundaries and advocating for clients

Individuation is a central feature of normal adolescence. Parents and teenagers gradually negotiate the adolescent's increasing need for privacy and independence on the journey towards adult autonomy. Counsellors facilitate the individuation process by providing parents and teenagers with separate counsellors and a confidential counselling contract. For teenagers to feel safe and secure within the counselling process, it is essential that they trust their counsellor to both advocate for them and maintain confidentiality. Throughout the middle phase of counselling, challenges to these boundaries may occur. In these circumstances, counsellors address these challenges by maintaining boundaries and advocating for their clients. For example a parent may accompany their teenager to the counselling centre and ask to have 'a quick word' with the teenager's counsellor before the teenager's session. This is a challenge to the boundaries agreed in the engagement phase, where parents are asked to share information and discuss any concerns with their own counsellor, rather than with their teenager's counsellor. If the administrative staff at counselling centres receive phone calls from parents wishing to contact their teenager's counsellor, they are reminded that the protocol is for parents to contact their own counsellors, or to request joint meetings which may be attended by the counselling team, the teenager and the parents. Where young teenagers ask an accompanying parent to bring something to the attention of their counsellor on their behalf, it is only appropriate for counsellors to agree if the information is given briefly and in the presence of the teenager. If the issue is complex, a joint appointment involving the counselling team, the teenager and the parents is the appropriate forum for these sorts of discussions.

In families where the process of individuation is progressing very slowly and is a significant focus for counselling, parents, most usually mothers, may find it very challenging to leave their teenager at the counselling centre with another adult. They may worry whether they will be OK and also what they might talk about. For these families, to facilitate the gradual process of adolescent individuation, parents who accompany their teenagers to the counselling centre are encouraged to leave and return to collect them rather than sit in the waiting room.

Case example: Anto, aged 13, arrived with his mother for his first individual appointment. His mother was encouraged to return after an hour to collect him. It took ten minutes and a great deal of reassurance from Anto that he would 'be grand' before his mother was able to briefly leave and have a 'bit of a walk'.

In some cases, without prior agreement with counsellors, parents may bring children (other than the referred adolescent) to their own individual counselling sessions or to joint sessions. This may occur for various reasons, but usually reflects parents not fully appreciating that engaging in counselling is demanding and requires their full attention without the distraction of caring for other children. Counsellors explain this to parents and arrange appointments flexibly to facilitate child care arrangements. Other than nursing infants, it is not appropriate for young children to be included in parents' sessions or joint sessions with parents and teenagers unless they are invited by the counselling team as part of the family assessment or counselling process. Younger children take the parents' focus from their teenager, which is the primary purpose of counselling.

Case example: Margaret, David's mother, arrived for an individual session with her 5 year old daughter, Julie. Julie was too young to be left to entertain herself in the waiting room and too old to be involved in an adult discussion about her older brother. Margaret thought that everything would 'go over' Julie's head until Julie asked 'Is this where David comes when he's bold?'.

6.6. Service policies

At Teen Counselling work with clients is guided by well-developed policies and procedures which are presented in a Clinical Handbook and a Child Protection Policy document to provide a definitive reference for staff. These policies have evolved from practice over many years and are reviewed every two years. They include protocols for dealing with substance use and self-harm. They specify the role of the psychiatrist attached to the service and the procedures for requesting psychiatric consultations. They also specify codes of behaviour for issues such as managing risk, critical incidents, staff changes and complaints. The Child Protection Policy covers all aspects of child welfare and safety and the relationship between Teen Counselling and the statutory child protection services. These exact policies may not be appropriate when PSP is used in other agencies. However, all agencies using PSP should develop policies to cover these sorts of issues.

Substance Use Alcohol and cannabis are the substances most often causing difficulties for teenagers referred to Teen Counselling. The use of heroin, LSD and ecstasy is not so evident amongst the teenage client group at the time of writing, but the use of cocaine and *'legal highs'* is on the increase. Solvent use is a concern for some younger teenagers and the availability of medicines at home, both over the counter and prescription, is often a problem. Trends in substance use are monitored on an annual basis.

When substance use is noted on referral an initial assessment is done in conversation with the referrer. The level of use is queried during the first session and further clarified when teenagers complete a Cigarette, Drink and Drugs form before their first individual appointment. Teen Counselling does not accept referrals for young people with well-established addictions, but may work co-operatively with a specialist service to support a teenager and their family.

In the middle phase of work with substance use, the focus is on understanding the function of the use for a particular client. The aim is to reduce risk behaviour associated with substance use and, in the case of street drugs, to work towards abstinence. In relation to alcohol, depending on the age of the client, working towards responsible drinking is appropriate.

Self-harm In 2011, 12% of new teenage clients in Teen Counselling were referred for self-harm, but subsequently 22% reported self-injurious behaviour. Many of these teenagers were referred by family doctors or Accident and Emergency Departments of general hospitals following the admission of a teenager for a drug or alcohol overdose, or other self-injury. Prior to referral some of these teenagers had a psychiatric assessment and were not considered high risk. Thus they were appropriate referrals for Teen Counselling, which does not have a crisis service. Where a preliminary risk assessment has not been conducted at a hospital Accident and Emergency Department, the appropriateness of the referral requires assessment, initially on the phone with the referrer and subsequently during the engagement phase of counselling. Protocols to use with both teenagers and parents are in place to assess the level of risk, the teenager's ability to commit to a '*contract of no harm*' and the parents' ability to maintain support during the counselling process. Internal referral to the Teen Counselling consultant psychiatrist is also considered.

The focus of work with self-harm in the middle phase is to help the family towards an understanding of the underlying issues which led to self-harming and, where possible, to resolve these issues. A key feature of this work is to reduce the shame commonly expressed by teenagers who have injured themselves or seriously considered doing so.

Psychiatric assessment Other than serious self-injury and suicide attempts the main reasons for requesting psychiatric assessments for teenagers are persistent, chronic mood and anxiety disorders. Consideration is also given to referring teenagers with medical conditions e.g. diabetes, cystic fibrosis. If after assessment medication or further treatment is recommended the psychiatrist communicates with family doctors, hospital consultants and others as necessary.

If medication is prescribed for teenagers, the prescribing psychiatrist continues to review their needs throughout the counselling process and have regular consultations with the counselling team and the parents. Generally parents are reluctant for their teenagers to take medication and the opportunity to discuss their concerns with both the doctor and their counsellor is important.

Child protection During the counselling process it is not unusual for disclosures of physical, sexual or emotional abuse to be made. Disclosures may relate to abuse of the teenager, either currently or in the past, be retrospective disclosures made by parents or relate to underage sexual activity. All concerns are notified to the Health Service Executive (the Irish Public Health Service), in line with the Irish Government's Children's First Guidelines. It is the responsibility of the Health Service Executive's Child Protection Social Work teams to assess or validate allegations.

During the middle phase of counselling where there has been abuse and/or neglect, teenagers are helped to understand the story of that abuse, and begin to develop self-protective strategies. Older teenagers are supported in developing an understanding of cycles of abuse and behaviours which protect against repetitive cycles in future relationships. Parents often need help to explore the impact of their own abusive experiences on their parenting.

Case example: *Bríd attended counselling because she was having difficulty coping with her teenage children who had multiple behaviour problems. She was a single parent separated from an alcoholic and physically abusive husband.*

In counselling it became clear that Bríd was a victim of sexual abuse. Bríd was the youngest in a large family. Her parents, both alcoholic, had failed to protect her from the sexually abusive behaviour of her older brothers. During counselling it came to light that Bríd's 13 year old daughter, Sabina, was being sexually exploited by a group of older boys in the same way that Bríd had been abused by her older brothers. This revelation was very distressing for Bríd. She had promised herself that she would never allow her children to suffer as she had. She was overwhelmed with guilt because she had failed to protect her daughter, and knew how devastating the experience was for Sabina because she had been through similar experiences herself. Counselling helped Bríd and Sabina process the trauma they had each suffered, understand the intergenerational pattern of abuse, and develop a supportive and protective mother-daughter relationship.

Legal issues A significant number of clients attending Teen Counselling are involved in legal proceedings associated with parental separations. Common legal issues include child custody, access, maintenance, barring or protection orders and child care orders. Members of the legal profession contact Teen Counselling requesting information to use in court cases. Such information is not released without written client consent. In some instances clients consent to release information that they are attending counselling. However, it is the view of the service that information disclosed during counselling is for therapeutic purposes and it is unhelpful for this information to be used for any other purpose including legal proceedings.

Sometimes teenagers with outstanding charges attend for counselling hoping that they will get a lesser sanction when they go to court. Their motivation to engage with the counselling process often does not persist beyond the date of their court hearing, but sometimes counselling gives teenagers an opportunity to reflect on their antisocial behaviour and change the direction of their lives.

Case example: Phillip, aged 17, had been involved in antisocial behaviour in the community during his early teens and two serious charges were outstanding when he was referred for counselling. He lived in a neighbourhood where the level of violence associated with the illegal drug trade had escalated. This violence involved the use of a range of weapons including fire arms. Before referring himself for counselling Philip had been the victim of a violent crime which had traumatised him and left himself and his family feeling very vulnerable.

Philip attended counselling with his parents. They used the counselling process to reflect on their lives and their hopes for the future. When Phillip's case came to court, the family asked for validation from their counsellors that Phillip had matured, that he was no longer involved in antisocial behaviour and that his parents had also changed their behaviour to provide more appropriate support for him.

6.7. The closing phase

The transition from the middle phase to the closing phase occurs when families make progress towards their counselling goals and attribute some of this progress to their own efforts. This transition may be negotiated, especially where there are no time constraints on counselling. As families express confidence that positive changes have been made, and attribute these changes to the effort of family members, then sessions may be spaced out over time. Occasionally there may be time constraints on counselling due to limited resources, counselling team members leaving or taking a break from work, or a research protocol limiting counselling to a number of sessions. In these situations the transition to the closing phase needs to be carefully managed by the counselling team.

Aims of the closing phase

The aims of the closing phase are to review progress and setbacks since the beginning of counselling, to help families develop an understanding of how they used counselling to address their difficulties and discover what they have learned, and to develop plans for anticipating and managing future lapses and relapses[4]. Stances describing ways of achieving each of these aims are given in chapter 3.

Additionally, an important element of the closing phase is to attend to any dependency issues that have developed during the course of counselling. Moving towards the end of an episode of counselling involves addressing the meaning of the ending to the particular client. Sometimes this is a very significant piece of the work. For adolescents it may mark a step towards adult autonomy. For parents, it may mark an aspect of '*letting go*' of their adolescent and allowing them to move towards greater independence. It may also mark the loss of a valued source of support for them.

During the closing phase it is also important to communicate with relevant members of the family's professional network. At the closing phase counsellors link with any other professionals who were involved in the counselling process or with whom the counsellor had significant contact during the counselling process. Usually a closing letter is written to the referrer indicating that the family is no longer attending counselling. Counsellors may also refer families or family members to other services, such as support groups, if it is considered useful.

Closing phase processes

The closing phase usually begins with a joint session attended by the parents and adolescent, and may involve a single session in which all parties consolidate their learning by sharing their experience of counselling, its advantages and its challenges. However, it does not necessarily have to involve a joint session, and may include parallel sessions with the adolescent and parents or a combination of such sessions and family sessions. The important thing is that progress and setbacks are reviewed, the lessons learned clarified, and future plans for lapse and relapse management established.

Some families do not complete the closing phase of counselling. Many of these families stop attending without any notice and do not respond to further contact from the counselling team. This may be after a few sessions, or indeed many sessions, and their reasons are generally unknown. Some families attend regularly in the engagement and middle phases and when there is improvement they become poorly motivated to attend further sessions and their attendance lapses. Other families stop attending because of changing circumstances for example the birth of other children, ill health, or moving house.

When families formally complete the counselling process, both the family and counselling team are agreed that counselling goals have been reached, or enough work has been done. As part of the closing process parents, teenagers and counsellors evaluate the family's current situation. Parents and adolescents complete end of counselling forms on which they rate improvements in their presenting problems and counsellors complete the CGAS[5] and the GARF[6]. These assessments are then compared with similar assessments conducted during the engagement phase. It is also interesting for the counselling team to hear what the family found to work well, what they considered should have been done differently and any advice they would have for other families.

Counsellors assure families that they are welcome to contact the centre again should they wish to re-engage, or to arrange a consultation. A significant number of families request further episodes of counselling for problems associated with the same teenager, or one of their siblings. At Teen Counselling, past clients are prioritised on the waiting list. In 2011, 5% of referrals to Teen Counselling were re-referrals of the same teenager and 9% of referrals were suggested by past or current clients, a number of whom were siblings.

SUMMARY

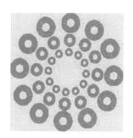

The process of working with families through the middle phase of counselling and then concluding the counselling process was described in this chapter.

The aims of the middle phase are to maintain and deepen the therapeutic alliance, and to address the issues or themes identified in the engagement phase so as to move towards the goals of teenagers and parents. Usually one member of the counselling team works with the adolescent, while the other counsellor works with the parents in a series of parallel sessions, and there are periodic joint sessions. Sometimes work is conjoint for a period or throughout the counselling process.

The counsellor working with the adolescent does so creatively to make the sessions appealing by moving from easy to difficult topics, and using media and materials with those who have difficulty talking in response to open questions.

The counsellor working with the adolescent uses alliance-strengthening stances, stances to promote insight and understanding, and stances to promote behaviour change throughout the middle phase of counselling to help them achieve their goals.

The counsellor working with the parents distinguishes between parenting issues and personal or couple issues, and in both of these domains uses alliance-strengthening stances. They use appropriate stances for addressing parenting issues, and personal and couples issues.

Counselling team members meet regularly for case discussions and keep each other informed about how their work with the adolescent and parents is progressing in parallel counselling sessions. When team members judge that the adolescent and parents have made sufficient progress, and have been sufficiently prepared to work together productively in joint sessions, a number of joint sessions may be conducted.

In joint sessions stances about respect for all viewpoints and family loyalty; communication, negotiation, problem-solving; apology and forgiveness; behaviour problems; promoting autonomy; and addressing child protection issues are adopted.

In the closing phase of counselling progress and setbacks are reviewed; lessons learned clarified; and future plans for lapse and relapse management established.

CHAPTER 7

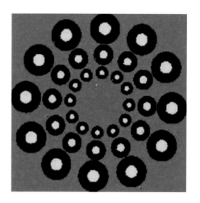

Team work, team development and supervision

In this chapter the approach to teamwork used at Teen Counselling is explained. Both practical and therapeutic elements are described. Team development and supervision of teams at different developmental stages is also addressed.

7.1. Team work

The approach to teamwork used at Teen Counselling is distinct from the style of multidisciplinary teamwork adopted in many child and adolescent mental health teams. The relationship between the two counsellors in the team is used purposefully to contain, support and challenge the perspectives of both teenagers and their parents, and provides the foundation upon which new formulations and solutions are generated and grounded. As with the fundamental stance of PSP, the particular understanding of teamwork, the support lent to it through structures and policies within the Teen Counselling organisation, and ultimately the way it is used to therapeutic advantage, lies at the heart of this model of practice.

7.2. Case discussions

Throughout the counselling process team members meet regularly to discuss the progress of their work with adolescents and parents. When these discussions are informal, they are called case meetings. When they are formal, they are called case reviews. Case meetings are brief. They are usually held prior to, and in preparation for, an individual or joint session. Case reviews, in contrast are longer and scheduled to provide a forum within which counselling teams can tease out issues in greater depth.

Case meetings and reviews are an integral part of case management and the therapeutic process. They have a number of functions. First, counsellors use them to share information about the progress parents and adolescents are making in parallel sessions. Second, they are a forum within which counsellors can evaluate and process the on-going issues within the family as they change over the course of counselling. Third, counsellors develop and devise specific family interventions which are then implemented in either individual or joint counselling sessions. As such, case discussions play a crucial role in helping families resolve their difficulties through counselling. Fourth, counsellors use case discussions to decide whether individual or joint sessions would be most productive at each stage of the counselling process. Finally, case discussions are used to consider whether contact with other family members would be useful and whether it would be helpful to have correspondence, phone calls or meetings with professionals known to the family such as school staff, social workers, child care workers, juvenile liaison officers and so forth. When reflecting on the wider professional network, counsellors may consider whether referrals to the Teen Counselling psychiatrist, or other specialist health, social or educational services are necessary.

Case discussions provide counsellors within a team with the space and opportunity to articulate their understanding of their client's position and the appropriateness, or not, of this position in their view. Such meetings therefore are always an information sharing exercise. However, process issues are also addressed in case discussions. Often subtle alignments of counsellors with their clients come to the fore and influence the relationship between counsellors within a team. This mirroring of the conflicting positions of family members within a counselling team is discussed in case discussions. Counsellors use their awareness of these processes to generate new and less blame-orientated solutions to their clients' problems. These types of conversations are central to team work and are discussed below in the section on team therapeutic processes.

7.3. Using content of parallel counselling sessions

Team members use information shared by partners to inform the way they manage their sessions with the family members with whom they are working and to pace the timing of joint sessions. Counsellors working with adolescents use information from case discussions about how the parents are progressing to inform their work with the adolescent. In a similar way, counsellors working with parents use information from case discussions about how the adolescent is progressing to inform their work with the parents. However, counsellors maintain confidentiality insofar as counsellors working with adolescents do not tell the adolescents what their parents have said or achieved in counselling, nor do counsellors working with parents tell them what their adolescents have said or achieved in counselling. This confidentiality is only breached if the teenager is found to be at risk or if it is agreed between a client and counsellor that it would be a useful thing to do.

A teenager might say how difficult or hurtful a particular parental behaviour is. A counsellor may suggest they ask their counselling team partner to raise the issue with the parents. Some teenagers are comfortable with this idea as they may feel they will never be confident enough to raise the issue directly with their parents at home, or in a joint counselling session even with the support of their counsellor.

Case example: Kenny, aged 16, had supported his mother for many years as she struggled to cope with a large family and her husband's erratic and abusive behaviour. Eventually his mother obtained a barring order against his father and seemed determined to improve the situation for her children. A short time later when Kenny returned from school to find his father in the family home eating dinner, he was furious. Kenny had never felt so angry with his mother before and could not imagine how he might express his strong feelings face-to-face. He therefore asked that the issue be raised by his mother's counsellor in her individual sessions.

Teenagers may choose to discuss the content of their counselling sessions with their parents, but parents are encouraged not to quiz their teenagers about the content of their counselling sessions and to respect their privacy. Some clients are selective in what they share at home and may use their counsellor as a '*higher authority*'. They may do this to add weight to their point of view in an argument or manipulate the other party. For example, a teenager might say: "*My counsellor thinks that I am well old enough to go to a disco on Saturday night*". A parent may say: "*My counsellor said that we shouldn't give you so much money*". As counsellors do not make such decisions for families, counsellors may share this sort of information with each other in case discussions and consider whether these sorts of exchanges might be usefully addressed in joint sessions with teenagers and parents. What a counsellor might or might not have said, or possibly said in a different context, is usually used in conflictual situations at home by either teenagers or parents. A joint session offers an appropriate way to address not only who said what, and the acceptability of such statements, but also the more revealing need for additional external authority, or support, for the position of either parents or teenagers in a disagreement.

7.4. Interventions for joint sessions

Counselling team members schedule joint sessions when they judge that parents and adolescents will derive a particular benefit from discussing issues face-to-face. This is usually when both teenagers and parents have had sufficient opportunity to explore their own perspectives in some depth, establish a more reasoned understanding of their own and the family's difficulties and, very often, have experienced the benefit of some therapeutic change, however small.

Although joint sessions are usually an opportunity for a general review of progress, counselling teams may use joint sessions for specific purposes. For example, it is not uncommon for teenagers to experience difficulty in asking questions about their parents' separation, especially if the separation was very acrimonious and occurred when the teenager was a young child. The intellectual and social maturity that occurs during adolescence increases a teenager's need for a more sophisticated explanation of the circumstances surrounding parental separation than that given to them during their childhood. Frank discussions between parents and teenagers are required if their need for more complex explanations of how parental separation occurred is to be met. Unfortunately in some cases when teenagers try to have such discussions with their parents it leads to emotional upheaval. In such cases supporting teenagers in asking questions about parental separation, preparing parents to answer these in a way that makes sense to an adolescent, and offering a rationale for why such discussions are needed, are the preparatory stages for arranging a joint session focusing on the issue of parental separation.

Joint sessions may be scheduled in various other circumstances. Sometimes joint appointments offer teams an opportunity to take a fresh look at the way a family functions, informed by the team's greater knowledge about the teenager and parents obtained from individual sessions. Joint sessions offered in this way, when parallel individual sessions for teenagers and parents have led to limited progress, can provide teams with new insights into family dynamics or help the team and family become unstuck. For more experienced teams this 'playing it by ear' or 'seeing what develops' approach to a joint session often derives significant therapeutic dividends.

Joint sessions are a useful forum within which to address problematic family power imbalances. Adolescence is a transitional developmental stage during which the task of adolescents and of parents is to shift power from the parents to the emerging young adult. In some families this shifting of power becomes stalled because parents may be reluctant to 'let go' or teenagers may be scared to 'grow up'. In these families, teenagers may develop restricted social lives, or become anxious or sad. In other families, where parents exert little control over their children, a teenager may become too powerful, too soon in their development, and use of this inappropriate power leads to problematic behaviour. Other family power imbalances include situations where grandparents or non-resident parents hold inordinate power and undermine the parents, or where one parent is overly dominant leading to an inappropriate alliance between a teenager and the non-dominant parent. The origins, facts and consequences of all of these problematic power imbalances can be explored with families at a pace they can tolerate within joint family sessions.

Case example: David, aged 16, was born when his mother was a teenager. They lived with his maternal grandparents for many years until his mother married, established her own home and had subsequent children. David did not like his stepfather as his expectations of David's behaviour, as the eldest in the family, were very different from those of his grandparents. They still treated him as 'the baby'. David often ran to his grandparents when he was in trouble at home and elicited their support against his stepfather. His mother found it extremely difficult to challenge her parents about their 'spoiling' David.

To address this power imbalance within the family, the grandparents were invited to a joint session with David, his mother and his stepfather. In the joint session, the counsellors helped the grandparents form an alliance with the mother and stepfather, so they could collectively provide a united approach to parenting David.

Joint sessions are a useful place to facilitate discussions between teenagers and parents about issues that have been raised in individual sessions, but which parents and teenagers have not previously discussed together. A parent or teenager may be prepared to raise these difficult secret issues with the support of their counsellor in a joint session. That is, parents or teenagers may use the joint session to be a 'whistle blower' about a destructive secret. In other situations, parents or adolescents may agree to talk about these issues if the counsellor asks about them in a joint session. That is, they may respond within a joint session to what may appear to other family members to be a counsellor's 'fishing expedition' questions about the secret issue. However, in some instances, family members may find that even though they see the value of discussing family secrets in joint sessions, the family tensions that this would create prevent them from doing so when the opportunity is offered to them.

Case example: *Mandy, a 17-year old, was referred for non-suicidal self-harm. She felt she had been abandoned by her mother who spent most of her time in the home of her boyfriend. Mandy's mother presented herself as the 'perfect parent' to her counsellor when she attended, although her attendance was not very consistent. She also made it very clear to her daughter that she should not disclose any family information to her counsellor.*

With Mandy's agreement a joint session was scheduled to address this issue. However, even with support from her counsellor Mandy found she was unable to challenge her mother in the joint session. Despite the opportunity provided by the joint session Mandy's mother could not engage effectively with the counselling process and hear the 'secret' her daughter needed to tell. The joint session clarified for the team that Mandy's mother would not be able to work co-operatively with them, at this stage, to provide support in addressing Mandy's self-injurious behaviour.

Case example: *Sally disclosed to her counsellor that her ex-partner, Hugh, was not the father of her eldest son, Shane age 12, and that Shane did not know. Sally's relationship with Hugh had recently broken down. She wanted to deny him access to her son because he had no legal responsibility for Shane. However, Shane told his counsellor that he did know that Hugh was not his 'real dad', but he was attached to him and wanted to maintain a relationship with him. Shane also wanted to ask his mother about his biological father. Shane discussed these issues with his counsellor in individual sessions. He talked about the distress it caused him being denied permission to discuss this matter with his mother. It was this distress that underpinned the behaviour problems which led to him being referred for counselling.*

Through teamwork, while mother and son were attending parallel individual session, counsellors working with Shane and Sally prepared them to talk about this issue in joint sessions. As a result of the joint sessions Sally consented for Hugh to continue in the role of 'Shane's dad' despite the couple's problematic relationship. To Shane's delight, Hugh remained committed to his relationship with Shane even though he was not his biological father.

For teenagers and parents who are unable to negotiate and reach suitable compromises, or resolve conflict, counselling teams may use joint sessions to model communication skills and negotiate compromises.

To model communication skills counsellors may discuss issues in joint sessions that the family want to resolve while the family observe, with the adolescent's counsellor advocating for the adolescent's position and the parents' counsellor advocating for the parents' position. In these conversations counsellors use communication skills such as listening and turn taking, being respectful and talking openly about issues without being judgemental or reactive. During these conversations, families have an opportunity to observe counsellors teasing out significant issues, suggesting possibilities, noting difficulties and using the insights gained during individual sessions to highlight the strengths of family members and acknowledge their effort, or lack of it, in trying to reach a compromise that meets the needs and preferences of the parents and adolescent.

and Vicky's need for her son's safety. In subsequent sessions, Vicky's counsellor helped her contain her anxiety as much needed freedom was negotiated for Andrew on a phased basis. Andrew gradually proved to himself and his mother that he could manage certain tasks independently, such as going to the local shops unaccompanied, and keeping himself safe while doing so.

Where parents have difficulty making the changes necessary to alleviate their adolescent's problems, counsellors may use interventions in sessions to motivate them. One such intervention is to escalate parental anxiety by highlighting the long-term negative consequences of not making the changes required. That is, information about the negative effects of not changing is dropped into the session in a dramatic way like a grenade, to shock parents into action.

Case example: Brian, a 16 year old, presented with severe chronic psychosomatic symptoms, including abdominal pains, headaches and loss of energy for which no medical explanation could be provided. Throughout adolescence, his school attendance had deteriorated. When he was referred to Teen Counselling he had not been attending school for months and had become socially isolated. His parents, Nuala and Ciaran, an unmarried, separated couple, had been involved in an adversarial relationship for all of Brian's life. Brian was caught between them. They routinely involved him in their conflicts, forcing him implicitly or explicitly to take sides. He found being drawn into their conflicts and responding to their polarised positions and inconsistent parenting very distressing. His distress and anxiety caused his stomach pains and headaches. His distress also led to nightmares, so he slept poorly and became exhausted from lack of sleep. When Brian complained to his parents of pains and exhaustion, this sometimes led to a reduction in their conflict, as they jointly focused on taking him to the GP or paediatrician, or staying quiet so as not to make his headaches worse. So Brian's symptoms had gradually become a way of preventing his parents' conflict from getting out of control.

Parallel individual sessions with Brian and his parents were slow to effect any change. A session for his parents was scheduled in which the link between Brian's symptoms and his parents' behaviour was made very clear. Their counsellor pointed out in a dramatic way that if Nuala and Ciaran did not stop drawing Brian into their on-going conflicts, his pains, exhaustion and constricted lifestyle would become a life-long problem. In view of this he would require a referral to an adult psychiatry service if the work at Teen Counselling was not successful. The idea that Nuala and Ciaran's failure to exclude Brian from their on-going conflict would lead to their son becoming a long-term psychiatric patient was introduced, like a grenade, into the conversation. This motivated Nuala and Ciaran to start making the changes necessary.

In contrast to dramatically presenting information like a grenade, to shock clients into action, in some instances it is more appropriate to introduce new information, ideas or possibilities more gently. Like a stone dropped into a still pool, this strategy can cause ripples which spread outwards and lead gradually, but inexorably to wide-ranging therapeutic changes. This strategy is particularly appropriate where a team judge that *'dropping a grenade'* might lead to clients dropping out of counselling.

Case example: *Noreen and Dermot attended counselling with their 16-year-old daughter, Catherine, after she had taken an overdose which required hospitalisation. Noreen was a very forceful woman who believed she 'did everything' in the family and in return expected unquestioning obedience from her teenage children. Dermot was a recovering alcoholic who had 'fallen off the wagon' the previous year after a long period of sobriety. This relapse reinforced Noreen's view that he was an incompetent father and that she did, indeed, need to 'do everything' with little support from Dermot to keep the family going. Catherine was close to her father, particularly as he allied himself with her against Noreen's harsh authoritarian parenting style. Catherine called her mother the 'punishment parent'. In contrast she referred to her father as 'lovely dad'. Catherine regularly elicited support from Dermot in a subversive way to undermine Noreen's harsh parenting style. This process of the father and daughter forming an alliance against the mother deprived Catherine of opportunities to negotiate with both of her parents about gaining greater autonomy, privacy and independence, appropriate for a 16 year old. It also prevented her from developing a sense of personal responsibility and accountability for her actions and finding a way to deal openly with her mother's rigid ideas.*

The counselling team did not think the therapeutic alliance with the family as a whole, and Noreen in particular, was strong enough, to directly challenge Noreen's harsh approach to parenting, and Dermot and Catherine's subversive alliance, without risking the family dropping out of counselling. They therefore did not risk confronting this process by dropping a metaphorical 'grenade' into the joint sessions. Instead they invited the family to consider what they guessed would occur if Dermot's parenting style became more like Noreen's, and Noreen's became more like Dermot's.

They also wondered aloud, in joint sessions, how it would be for Catherine if her parents took a similar view on how much freedom and responsibility was appropriate for a 16 year old girl to have. These ideas were presented subtly and gently to the family in joint sessions, like pebbles dropped into a still pool. This intervention did not lead to an immediate change in the family dynamics.

However, over a period of several months positive changes did occur. Dermot became more assertive in dealing with Catherine. Noreen became more empathic and less authoritarian in her relationship with her daughter. The couple became more united in their expectations of Catherine and the way they dealt with her limit-testing behaviour. When this change first occurred Catherine expressed confusion and resisted the joint approach taken by her parents. However, over time she adjusted well to Noreen and Dermot's better functioning parenting team. She began to explore ways to be close to both her parents, rather than being aligned with her 'lovely dad' against her strict mother.

When parents' guilt and anxiety about causing their teenager's difficulties, lead them to respond to one team member as a *'good counsellor'* who will *'fix'* their teenager and the other as a *'bad counsellor'* who is blaming them for causing their teenagers problems, counsellors respond to this defensive splitting in joint sessions in a therapeutic way. They acknowledge within their team that splitting is a common defence and arrange for the team member who is perceived as the *'good counsellor'* to address the underlying guilt and anxiety that has caused the defensive splitting, since clients usually find it easier to respond constructively to the team member they perceive as the *'good counsellor'*.

Case example: Katy, an extremely distressed 16-year old, attended an initial joint counselling session with her parents, Tara and Declan. In this session it became apparent that Tara was very angry with Katy for being distressed and causing trouble without, as far as she could see, any good reason. At the conclusion of the initial joint appointment, Katy and her parents were offered a series of parallel sessions in which Katy would work with one counsellor and the parents would work with another.

While Katy was very keen to engage in the counselling sessions she was offered, Tara and Declan were not. Tara responded to the team member who offered herself and her husband a series of counselling sessions, as if she were implicitly blaming her for failing to adequately parent Katy. In this sense, Tara responded as if she viewed this team member as a 'bad counsellor'. In contrast she responded warmly to the team member who offered to work with Katy, and seemed to view her as the 'good counsellor'.

The counselling team understood that this process of splitting the team into 'good' and 'bad' counsellors was Tara's defence against the guilt and anxiety she felt concerning her daughter's difficulties. They understood that underneath her display of splitting, Tara felt guilty that she had been a 'bad' mother, was anxious that her shortcomings had caused her daughter's distress, and did not know how to address Katy's difficulties.

Consequently she expressed anger at Katy and the 'bad counsellor' who she viewed as implicitly criticising her adequacy as a mother. On the other hand she expressed warmth towards 'the good counsellor' who she believed would 'fix' her daughter's problems, and so undo the guilt she felt for letting her daughter down. With this understanding in mind, the team avoided reacting defensively to Tara's anger at the 'bad counsellor'.

The team member who Tara responded to as the 'good counsellor' empathised with Tara's position, saying that many parents feel that when they are offered counselling, it implies that they have somehow let their teenager down by not being a good enough parent. She went on to explain that the reason parents are invited to participate in the counselling process is to help them understand their teenager's distress and provide support. Tara accepted this intervention and in subsequent sessions Tara and Declan formed a good working alliance with the 'bad counsellor'.

7.5. Team development

At Teen Counselling we have found that this approach to counselling is most successfully learnt by counsellors new to the service when they complete a comprehensive induction programme and then have the opportunity to work in a counselling team with an experienced practitioner of the model. This could be considered an apprenticeship or *'yoghurt culture'* approach to learning this model of counselling.

Induction programme

A key component of the Teen Counselling induction programme is the observation of as many different counselling teams as is practicable. New counsellors are invited to first sessions conducted by established teams with new referrals at all Teen Counselling centres. This allows them to observe the dynamics of teamwork with teams at different stages of development and with different styles, and spend time with teams after first sessions to have their questions and comments addressed. Observation of joint sessions in cases that are in the middle phase of the counselling process is also arranged, with client permission, when possible.

Team formation

For team development to occur, new counsellors work together with more experienced counsellors over a period of time. This creates a context within which the new counsellor can observe the experienced counsellor in action, and the team develop a good working relationship which is vital for effective counselling. It is essential at this initial stage for an experienced team member to be sensitive to the needs of a new member and ensure that they create space for a new perspective and support their new colleague in developing a voice in discussions and in joint sessions. This is particularly important where there is a *'power'* differential between team members due to differences in level of training, experience and age.

In newly formed counselling teams differences in professional training, counselling experiences, and clinical approaches are immediately evident. Through working together and developing familiarity with each other's styles, team members gradually develop an understanding of their partner's use of language and their clinical perspective so that they move towards a common way of discussing cases. This is a trans-disciplinary model of teamwork, in which notes are shared and disciplines plan together to achieve common goals. The style, personality, personal values and idiosyncrasies of both counsellors have also to be accommodated within the team to provide the foundations for a cohesive team relationship and team identity. This process of team development in many respects parallels the process of family counselling. Within counselling, over time, counsellors and family members accommodate to each other's differences in style and develop a shared way of addressing the problems that brought the family to counselling.

The team working relationship

Within counselling teams, the partners' experience of working co-operatively builds trust. Trust between counselling team members is essential for joint decision making and managing the inevitable disagreements which arise when counselling families with troubled adolescents. There are both advantages and disadvantages to working in counselling teams. On the positive side, teamwork is more supportive and less isolating than working as a solo counsellor. On the negative side, disagreements about how best to proceed with specific cases are inevitable when team members conduct parallel counselling sessions with adolescents and their parents involved in conflict. As part of team development counsellors must find constructive ways for managing such conflicts and disagreements.

A strong, cohesive team can manage the challenges involved in acting as advocates for parents and teenagers who are in conflict, with a view to negotiating workable solutions. That is, solutions that meet the needs of both adolescents and their parents. The challenge of teamwork is for counsellors to both advocate for their clients (parent or adolescent), and respect the advocacy position taken by their partner who is working with another family member (parent or adolescent), while working towards a shared understanding of the overall family presentation. Being able to hold the perspective of their clients, whilst remaining neutral enough to incorporate their counselling partner's position and arrive at a joint understanding of a family presentation, is the sign of a well-functioning team. Such processes provide a powerful model when working with families.

The emergence of a team identity with established team values and ways of communicating, allows counsellors to conduct very productive joint sessions. Established teams provide families with a model of how to communicate within a trusting relationship. Established teams also provide confident support for families as team members know how their partners are likely to respond to issues. On established teams counsellors are able to turn-take seamlessly and ask (often without speaking) for support when needed.

Established teams plan how to use their relationship to benefit their clients. For example, when a team is working with a conflicted family in which adolescents and parents have adopted entrenched positions, counsellors may become over-identified with the family member (parent or adolescent) with whom they are working. Within individual counselling sessions, from a client perspective, this may be very positive as clients will certainly feel understood by their counsellors. However, when counselling team members have case discussions about these sorts of families, disagreements (at worst) or emotional tensions (at best) about how to proceed are inevitable. In such cases co-operation difficulties between team members may occur unless they respect the validity of each other's positions. Where counsellors trust each other enough to respect the validity of each other's positions, they may re-evaluate their original position and develop a more complex and useful view of the case. This process requires mentalizing[1]. That is, understanding the intentions, needs and beliefs of both the adolescent and the parents, and then understanding how the positions they adopt with respect to each other and the patterns of interaction in which they currently engage prevent them from resolving their difficulties. Through the process of mentalizing counsellors develop empathy for the positions of both the adolescent and the parents and for each other's positions as counsellors working with these two factions of the family. This empathy allows counsellors to hold the difficult emotions without acting them out, something which many families with troubled adolescents find difficult to do. It may also allow counsellors to identify more creative ways of resolving families' entrenched conflicts.

Team therapeutic processes

Teamwork is central to this approach to counselling. To conduct effective teamwork a strong, trusting relationship between the two counsellors within a counselling team is essential. It is difficult to articulate in literal terms the importance of this relationship as a context within which specific pieces of teamwork are conducted. However, the team relationship may be metaphorically conceptualised as a unique territory or space within which teamwork is located. There are many advantages to the teamwork that occurs within this space.

The first of these is the alignment of one counsellor with the adolescent and the other with their parents. Within the team relationship, counsellors represent both parents' and teenager's views equally. This differs from the way these two perspectives are represented within the family, where there is often unequal articulation of the teenager's views compared to parents' views. Typically the parents' views are more competently and volubly articulated, and become the dominant perspective within the family. The teenagers' views, in contrast, are marginalised. This lack of fairness, present within families, is absent within well-functioning counselling teams.

A second advantage of teamwork is the potential of the therapeutic team to accept and hold the tensions between the two differing positions of the parents and teenager without being personally over-invested in either position, and without becoming embroiled in destructive conflict. Members of a counselling team can appreciate the merits of both parents' and teenagers' positions and understand how these positions have evolved in a more productive way than their clients, who typically become embroiled in unproductive interactions. Destructive interactions often occur because parents do not understand why their teenagers behaved in a certain way, and teenagers do not appreciate their parents' responses to their behaviour.   Counsellors working with parents can use their understanding of the adolescent's position, gained in case discussions, to help parents begin to empathise with their teenagers. Similarly, counsellors working with adolescents can use their understanding of the parents' position, also gained in case discussions, to help teenagers begin to empathise with their parents. This process of helping parents and teenagers begin to empathise with each other's positions can soften disagreements and dissolve unproductive conflicts between parents and adolescents.

A third advantage of team-work is the fact that teenagers find it easier to accept challenges to their positions from counsellors than from their parents. Similarly, parents are more accepting of having their views challenged by a counsellor than by their adolescent. This acceptability, from a client's perspective, of challenges from a counsellor occurs because clients perceive counsellors to be '*on their side*' and trying to help them find constructive solutions, rather than prove that they are wrong. This is in stark contrast to the way challenges from family members are usually experienced. When clients are challenged by family members, they typically feel that the family member is not on their side and is engaging in an '*I'm right and you're wrong*' battle.

Counsellors use a range of alliance building skills to help clients feel that they are '*on their side*'. One critical alliance building skill is mentalizing[1]. Through mentalizing counsellors develop a detailed empathic understanding of why their clients behave in a particular way and how this way of behaving has evolved. The counsellors' capacity to mentalize with their clients benefits from listening closely to their team member's perspective. Counsellors working with adolescents are better able to mentalize with them when they listen to, and understand, their parents' positions as set out by the counsellor working with the parents. Similarly, counsellors working with parents are better able to mentalize with them when they appreciate the position of their adolescents, as set out by the counsellor working with their teenagers. Thus, counselling team partners supply important information that influences their ability to mentalize with their clients. Without a trusted team member's perspective, counsellors run the risk of over-identifying with their clients and deepening rather than bridging divisions between adolescents and parents.

In difficult or complicated, intransigent cases of family disharmony, where family members have adopted defensive warring postures for many years, counsellors are at greatest risk of over-identifying with their clients and seeing them as '*right*' and the other family members as '*wrong*'. For example, parents may see their adolescents as too disobedient, depressed or difficult, and adolescents may see their parents as not understanding them and being too strict, too over-involved or too negligent. In these difficult cases, the family project their relationship difficulties onto the team and the team, through a process of over-identification, are at risk of re-enacting the family relationship problems within the team. It is in this context that good teamwork is particularly useful. In such cases counsellors who engage in skilled teamwork avoid accusing each other of being hoodwinked or manipulated by their clients, since this escalates the tension between team members. They avoid arguments about who is right and who is wrong, face-saving manoeuvres and angry stand-offs or quiet sulking, since all of these amount to acting out the family's conflicts within the team. Rather, skilled counsellors use the space within their trusting relationship to be curious about why they each entertain such contrasting or polarised perspectives. They harness the collective resources of their team to understand the processes that have led to their polarised or opposing positions. Skilled team members explore what the change in their relationship tells them about the relationship process in which the adolescent and parents are involved. They then use this information to generate possible solutions to the family's problems. Where team members have a strong trusting relationship, the team relationship is a more forgiving territory within which to conduct negotiations about the opposing positions taken by parents and teenagers, than the relationship it mirrors within the family. The strength of the team relationship and the counsellors' skill in using this relationship to negotiate about polarised family positions is often the crucial component in a case with a successful outcome.

In cases of severe and chronic family conflict, skilled counsellors always openly discuss the tension that working with these cases elicits. This necessitates a level of teamwork of a different order than is often adopted within multidisciplinary teams. Tension and the way counsellors resolve it, is used by counselling teams to inform the way teams help family members to resolve conflict in joint sessions. The functioning of counselling teams in this process is often discussed in team supervision. In this model of counselling there is a commitment to developing counselling teams that attain this level of functioning and consequently this model of counselling prioritises team support, development and supervision.

7.6. Supervision

At Teen Counselling individual supervision is provided for all clinical staff, on a monthly basis for experienced staff and more frequently for new or inexperienced staff. At present supervision is provided internally by senior staff, with external supervision arranged when requested. When resources are available Teen Counselling is committed to providing external supervision for all experienced staff.

Working in counselling teams provides clinical support and peer supervision which is particularly important for inexperienced staff and for those new to the service and this approach to counselling. Experienced counsellors, used to working on an individual basis, may find the high level of consultation and team approach particularly challenging. Each counselling team has a team supervisor who meets with established teams every two months. New teams are supervised more regularly.

Supervising new teams

The way supervision is used depends in part upon the developmental stage of the counselling team and phase of counselling at which the cases they bring for supervision are[2]. Unless a new team includes an experienced member of staff it is useful for them to review all cases with their supervisor. New teams may find that supervision focuses on the content and procedures of the counselling model. That is, counsellors may use supervision to check out that they have adequately done the main things entailed by the model and are model adherent. These sorts of questions may inform supervision with such teams:

- In the engagement phase have the team members formed a good alliance, covered all areas of the intake interview and come to a useful shared understanding?

- In the middle phase, have they strengthened the alliance, identified issues or themes to work on and goals to work towards with the parents and adolescent, a focus for joint sessions and the main stances relevant to their work?

- In the closing phase, have they reviewed progress and setbacks, clarified lessons learned, developed plans for lapse and relapse management, and arranged any further support for the family if necessary?

- In any phase, are there risks that require management?

- In any phase, are there other agencies, such as the school or referrer who should be contacted?

- In any phase, have they adhered to service policies and administrative procedures?

Supervising experienced teams

With more experienced teams who routinely adhere to the model as described in this manual, supervision may be used to address more subtle issues that focus on the counselling process and team dynamics. Here are some examples of questions that more experienced teams might explore in supervision:

- In the engagement phase, how did the family affect us emotionally, and how did we use that information to fine-tune our formulation and plan for work with the family?

- In the middle phase, how is the process in our relationship within the counselling team mirroring the dynamics between the adolescent and parents, and how can we use that to progress the counselling process?

- In the closing phase, to what extent are our own feelings about the family affecting our decisions about when to conclude counselling?

- Is there a way a joint interagency meeting could be convened so as to enhance the outcome for this family?

Matching supervision to team experience

Supervisors offer team supervision to match the developmental stage of the counselling team and the phase of counselling of the particular case brought for discussion. With newer teams they focus the discussion on the content and procedures of the model, and help the team identify steps they can take to more closely adhere to the model. With more experienced teams supervisors invite teams to acknowledge that they are adhering to the model and to consider exploring process issues that may enhance the quality of counselling they are offering to their clients.

Supervisors are mindful of the relationship in a team and aim to nurture its development and facilitate the team in addressing any issues which are impeding the process. The goal is to support the development of a cohesive team, incorporating members' strengths, which can be used creatively for the benefit of clients. It is more of a challenge to supervise experienced, established teams. Team loyalty is usually very strong and the team may appear quite self-sufficient. It is essential for team members to be aware of these team dynamics and give supervisors 'permission' to challenge them rather than present resistance to their ideas.

SUMMARY

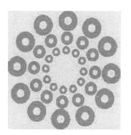

In this chapter the approach to teamwork, team development and supervision used at Teen Counselling was described.

Case meetings and reviews are used to share information about the progress parents and adolescents are making in parallel sessions; to evaluate and process the on-going issues within the family as they change over the course of counselling; to devise specific family interventions; to decide whether individual or joint sessions would be most productive at each stage of the counselling process; and to consider whether contact with other family members or members of the family's professional network are indicated.

Team development involves completion of an induction programme where counsellors observe experienced teams in action, join a team with an experienced team member and develop a trusting team working relationship.

At Teen Counselling individual supervision is provided for all clinical staff, on a monthly basis for experienced staff and more frequently for new or inexperienced staff. Each counselling team has a team supervisor who meets with established teams every two months.

The way supervision is used depends in part upon the developmental stage of the counselling team, and phase of counselling at which the cases they bring for supervision are, with new teams focusing on the content and procedures of the counselling model and more experienced teams, who have good model adherence, focusing on process issues to enhance the quality of the counselling they provide.

CHAPTER 8

Working with a family with alcohol and drug use, sexual promiscuity and adolescent depression issues

This case study illustrates the counselling process with a depressed adolescent girl who had developed a pattern of drug and alcohol misuse, and sexual promiscuity. This occurred within the context of an extended family in which a number of relatives on her father's side had alcohol problems, which heightened the parents' reactivity to the girl's substance misuse. The case shows how parallel counselling sessions with the adolescent and her parents helped the family make important changes. The girl developed control of her alcohol use, formed a more mature non-promiscuous romantic relationship and completed her Leaving Certificate. Through her family doctor she was prescribed antidepressants and this, along with the counselling, helped her to regulate her low mood. The parents were helped to work together in supporting their daughter's recovery and growth. This involved refining their joint parenting skills as well as addressing relevant issues from their own families of origin and exploring ways that they could support each other within their marriage.

8.1. Counselling team and duration

The counselling team included Emily, who worked with the parents, Mary and Paul, and Sarah who worked with Joanne, the daughter. The counselling spanned about ten months from October to August.

8.2. The engagement phase

Referral

Joanne, aged 17, was misusing alcohol and cannabis, and had dropped out of school when her father, Paul, first contacted Teen Counselling. Paul was particularly concerned because there was a history of alcoholism in his family of origin. After Paul made the referral, the counselling team, at Paul's suggestion, had phone contact with the guidance counsellor who had been working with Joanne before she dropped out of school. The school guidance counsellor was very concerned about Joanne and wanted to refer her for specialist help. The school staff had made some unsuccessful attempts to help Joanne re-enter school.

First session

Following some preliminary phone calls, Joanne and her parents came for an intake appointment with Emily and Sarah early in October. Joanne refused to engage in meaningful conversation during the session, despite gentle encouragement, but her wish to be present and observe the interview was acknowledged and understood to indicate some acceptance of the need for change. Joanne's parents said that they felt they had lost their daughter. She had been drinking heavily and using drugs. She was also being sexually promiscuous. She had dropped out of school, started a job, but then had recently lost this job because her employer was dissatisfied with her. Following an episode of significant conflict with her parents, Joanne had left home at the end of the summer and moved in with her aunt, Paul's sister, who had an alcohol problem. The parents, Mary and Paul, were very anxious, despairing, sad and distressed by Joanne's behaviour and could not make sense of how the problems had occurred. They were also at a loss to know how to resolve them. Joanne's mother was self-blaming and both parents felt rejected. They also said that they thought Joanne experienced a numbness and lack of feelings about what she was doing.

Holding, listening, and validating The main intervention in this first session was creating a safe '*holding*' context within which Mary and Paul could recount their experiences of the difficulties they had endured in the previous months, validating this, and inviting the couple to reflect on its impact on the family. During the first session, the counselling team listened carefully and unconditionally to the parents' account of the situation and its impact on them as parents and as a couple. The team offered validation for the distress and bewilderment the parents were experiencing, without offering unfounded reassurance. This was the first time the parents had spoken openly with anyone about the situation with Joanne and its impact on the family. The parents found the team's listening and validation supportive. They also found it supportive to be able to reflect on the impact of the situation on their other children, Joanne's younger siblings. This also offered Joanne the opportunity to listen quietly to her parents' concerns.

Contracting At the conclusion of the first session Emily offered a contract for on-going sessions to the parents to support them in dealing with the difficult situation. The team acknowledged Joanne's caution about becoming involved in counselling and advised the parents not to pressurise Joanne into attending, but instead, Sarah gave her a card which contained contact details for the counselling centre and let her know she could ring for an appointment if she wished.

Parents' first session

In the first session with the parents alone, the focus was helping them explore and name their worst fears about the situation, and to support them in doing this. They were frightened that Joanne was on a mission of self-destruction, that she was becoming an alcoholic and that they had lost her.

Loss, grief and depression With regard to the theme of loss, grief and depression, the mother believed she was losing the beautiful, healthy and well-adjusted daughter she once had. Joanne, who had previously been proud of her appearance, seemed to her mother to have gradually deteriorated. Joanne's health was also in decline. She wasn't eating or sleeping properly. Her relationships with her friends had become problematic. She did not have a stable group of girlfriends from whom she could get support. Rather, the group of girls with whom she socialised changed each time she changed boyfriends, which was quite frequently. For Mary, this loss of the healthy well-adjusted Joanne of former years, re-awakened her grief about the loss of her own mother about nine years previously. This bereavement had a profound effect on both Mary and Joanne. Mary became depressed following her mother's death, and spent days on end in bed. Joanne had supported her mother through this difficult time, despite the fact that she was only a child. It was also clear to Mary that now her daughter, like her, was suffering from depression.

Addiction With regard to the theme of addiction, the parents feared that Joanne was becoming an alcoholic. There was a family history of alcoholism. Paul's brother and father had been alcoholic. His father had died quite young, and his death was due to alcohol-related problems. Also Paul's sister, with whom Joanne was staying, was a heavy drinker. Paul's very distressing experience of alcoholism within his family of origin, heightened his anxiety about Joanne's drinking, drug use and promiscuity. It also heightened Paul's reactivity to Joanne when father and daughter became involved in arguments about Joanne's behaviour.

The parents found the session helpful in providing them with support. It also allowed the team to strengthen their therapeutic alliance with the couple.

Joanne's first session

Shortly after the parents' first individual session, Joanne phoned the Teen Counselling secretary and made an appointment to see Sarah.

Alliance building To begin the process of alliance building, Sarah wrote to Joanne and said she was looking forward to meeting her. Joanne attended her first appointment which was used primarily to engage with her and lay the foundations for a good therapeutic alliance. Because Joanne had not engaged in the first session, Sarah assumed that she was ambivalent about attending the service, so the focus was more on building a good relationship rather than working through an assessment agenda. Quite surprisingly, Joanne was ready to engage in the counselling process. She was *'ready to work'*.

Substance misuse and promiscuity In this session, Joanne's main referral problems (alcohol and drug use and promiscuity) were explored. There was also an exploration of her hopes for the future and career aspirations. Joanne said that she drank heavily or took hash to overcome being shy and quiet. She also mentioned that she had a reputation for sexual promiscuity, which tended to make her anxious in social situations and to lead to conflict at home with her parents. When she talked about her hopes for the future it was clear that she wanted to return to school.

Possible pregnancy However, Joanne's primary concern in the session was that she was pregnant. Joanne was apprehensive about how to deal with this and how to talk to her parents about it. Sarah offered to brief Emily, her counselling team partner, about the situation so that Emily could discuss it with Joanne's parents. Joanne accepted this way of managing the situation. Joanne was also offered practical advice on pregnancy testing. A non-judgemental supportive approach was taken to discussing Joanne's worries about possible pregnancy. This non-judgemental approach deepened Joanne's trust in Sarah and strengthened the therapeutic alliance.

Contracting Joanne made a contract to attend regular fortnightly sessions with Sarah, and gave consent for Emily to phone her mother, Mary, to inform her of the possible pregnancy.

Phone call with Mary and third session with the parents addressing Joanne's possible pregnancy

After the first session with Joanne, Sarah briefed Emily on Joanne's concerns about possible pregnancy. Emily then phoned Mary and explained the situation to her. Joanne's mother responded to the news in a very understanding way. Mary's positive response was in part due to the fact that she and Joanne had been enjoying a warm relationship in recent weeks, following Joanne's return to living in the family home after moving out of Paul's sister's, where she had stayed since the end of the summer. This type of temporary '*honeymoon*' relationship commonly occurs when teenagers return home after spending a period of time elsewhere, and in this instance provided a useful context for giving potentially distressing news to Mary.

Mary was not surprised that Joanne was worried about pregnancy. She was aware of Joanne's reputation for promiscuity and suspected that she was having unprotected sex. She was also aware that Joanne had an irregular menstrual cycle. Mary mentioned that she had asked their family doctor about prescribing contraceptives for Joanne some weeks earlier. The doctor was reluctant to do so, as he thought the priority was to start Joanne on a course of antidepressants, in view of her low mood, low self-esteem, loss of appetite, sleep disturbance and family history of maternal depression. He was of the view that she was suffering from clinical depression. Joanne had been on antidepressants for a few weeks prior to attending counselling and continued on them for the duration of the counselling process.

In the next session with the mother, concern about the possible pregnancy was resolved. Joanne found out she was not pregnant. The process of the family using the services of the counselling team to deal with a possible unplanned pregnancy had positive effects. Within the family, it strengthened the relationship between Joanne and her parents, particularly her mother. Joanne learned that her mother would support her even if she did something that was taboo, such as having an unplanned pregnancy. Within the therapeutic system, the effective management of this crisis strengthened the alliances between Joanne and Sarah, and between the parents and Emily. It showed the family that the counselling team could be trusted to help them manage difficult situations effectively.

8.3. The middle phase

Further sessions with Joanne

Joanne attended fortnightly and participated in about 18 individual sessions. Over the course of counselling her main presenting problems improved dramatically. She eventually stopped binge drinking and regular drug taking. She stopped having frequent promiscuous sex with multiple partners. She formed a long-term relationship with a boyfriend. Her depressive symptoms (low mood, low self-esteem, low appetite, sleep difficulties) abated. She completed her Leaving Certificate and got a job. She deepened her relationship with her best girlfriend and developed stable friendships with a group of girls from school. However, her recovery process was marked by periodic setbacks and relapses.

Therapeutic alliance There was a good fit between Sarah and Joanne, and this facilitated the development of a strong working alliance. Within the context of this trusting relationship Joanne felt safe about discussing very private issues. Sarah also skilfully used a variety of therapeutic techniques to address the presenting problems and deepen the therapeutic alliance. Some of these are described below.

Sensitivity to the alliance and session outcome For many of the sessions Sarah used ten point outcome and alliance rating scales[1]. Before most sessions Joanne was invited to rate on ten point scales how she felt individually, socially and overall. After most sessions she was invited to rate on ten point scales how useful she found the session and what it was within the session that she found helpful or unhelpful. This allowed Sarah to fine-tune her therapeutic style to Joanne's preferences. For example, Joanne rated one session as seven on a ten point scale. When Sarah asked about this, Joanne said it was because she had not been ready to cover the sexual material raised in the session. Sarah apologised for this intrusion and said she would be clearer about giving Joanne control over the sort of material covered in sessions in future. That process of acknowledging mistakes and mismatches in timing helped to build trust and strengthen the therapeutic alliance.

Family relationships Throughout the counselling process there was an emphasis on strengthening the relationships between Joanne and both her mother and father. The fact that all three were attending concurrent sessions with a view to helping Joanne work through her problems was the main technique used to strengthen family relationships. However, Joanne was also invited to explore ways of managing potentially conflictual situations with her mother and father. This exploration created opportunities to help her plan to use more effective communication skills in talking with her parents about contentious issues.

Psycho-education Psycho-education about the dangers of concurrently taking alcohol and antidepressants was an important early intervention. In an early session Sarah told Joanne about the dangers of drinking alcohol while taking antidepressants. It can cloud judgment and lead to erratic or risk-taking behaviour. The possibility of a referral to the Teen Counselling consultant psychiatrist for assessment and advice on antidepressant medication was discussed with Joanne. However, Joanne was nearly 18 and her family doctor had referred her to a community adult psychiatrist, so this did not become necessary.

Educational and occupational support Joanne wanted to complete her Leaving Certificate and get a job. A number of sessions focused on helping her to explore this goal and work strategically towards achieving it. She eventually returned to school and started working productively. She also controlled her drinking so she would be able to engage and work at school.

Re-appraisal of negative beliefs Joanne confided that she believed she was not an attractive looking person and so used sex as a way of keeping boyfriends interested in her. Sarah used cognitive behavioural procedures to help Joanne understand and change repetitive patterns of thinking, feeling and behaving based on her negative self-concept. For example she invited Joanne to explore how her negative beliefs about herself, such as '*I am not worth much*', made her feel depressed; and how low mood made her act in ways that reinforced her negative self-concept and depressive feelings by for example, having promiscuous sex to retain boyfriends; and how this in turn reinforced her negative reputation in her district as promiscuous; and how she then used alcohol to cope with the social anxiety she experienced when she felt negatively judged by others. Sarah also invited Joanne to look for evidence for her negative beliefs about low self-worth and also to look for evidence to support alternative more positive beliefs. Joanne was also invited to explore and experiment with alternative ways of behaving based on positive views of the self.

Relationship skills   Before coming to counselling, Joanne spent more time with peers, particularly male peers that jeered her and had little respect for her, than with peers who respected her. Sarah invited Joanne to recognize that she spent very little time with the one good female peer who really respected her, Lucy, while spending much time with disrespectful male peers. She then invited her to begin making more conscious choices about who she spent time with. There were a couple of key incidents to do with relationships that served as a focus for the middle sessions of therapy. One of these concerned managing the process of apology and forgiveness in her relationship with Lucy. The other, involved dealing with the urge to be responsible for solving her boyfriend's problems in a long-term romantic relationship.

Apology and forgiveness   In a critical incident in mid-counselling, Joanne had the opportunity to address the issues of apology and forgiveness in close relationships. She went on a school trip with her best friend, Lucy. The two girls had a falling-out while on tour that could have marked the end of their relationship. In the sessions that followed this incident, Sarah invited Joanne to identify and own her own part in the conflict and to consider the consequences of never apologising for this. This could potentially end their relationship forever. After a lapse of some time, this intervention led to Joanne spontaneously going to Lucy's house and apologising to her. Joanne's relationship with Lucy was strengthened by this apology, and the forgiveness it elicited. In counselling, the impact of the process of apologising and being forgiven was explored, and Joanne found that apologising led to positive feelings and also to a renewal of her friendship. This marked the breaking of a habitual pattern of ending peer relationships through engaging in conflict and not making attempts to repair these fractured attachments.

Relinquishing responsibility for solving boyfriend's problems   The second incident occurred when Joanne developed an intense relationship with a new boyfriend, David, who had an alcohol problem. This was after she had stopped drinking heavily and had begun to work productively at school. Joanne found that her mood dropped when her boyfriend drank heavily. She believed she was responsible for helping him to control his

169

drinking, but she also believed she was powerless to help him resolve the difficulties that led him to drink so heavily. The urge to help him, and the experience of powerlessness led to feelings of frustration, sadness and distress. Sarah encouraged Joanne to focus in these situations not on resolving her boyfriend's problems, but on self-care. She invited Joanne to consciously not take responsibility for her boyfriend's problems which required professional help, because this would only '*drag her down into the pit of depression*'. This was very challenging for Joanne, but over time she gradually relinquished responsibility for solving her boyfriend's problems and he eventually sought professional help for his difficulties. Concurrently Emily supported Joanne's mother who found Joanne's involvement in this relationship very difficult (as described below).

Further sessions with parents

During the course of counselling Emily held three-weekly sessions with the parents. Mary and Paul attended all sessions, of which there were about 12 in total. These sessions focused on parenting issues, and also on Mary and Paul's personal and marital issues. Over the course of about nine months, during which Joanne's main presenting problems abated, improvements occurred in the relationship between the parents and Joanne. In particular, Joanne and Paul became embroiled in fewer escalating conflicts. There was also an improvement in the extent to which Mary and Paul supported each other, and a reduction in the amount of conflict they experienced about managing Joanne. However, Paul found the recovery process which was marked by periodic setbacks and relapses, very challenging.

Parenting work

Those aspects of sessions that focused on parenting addressed such issues as the parents' perception of Joanne and their relationships with her, ways they could support her, and ways they could reduce conflict between themselves and Joanne. In this work, Paul was vocal about the emotional quality of his relationship with his daughter. In contrast, Mary, who was less articulate, said she showed her care for Joanne by providing practical support, by for example giving her lifts to school, or commenting on her appearance when she asked for reassurance before going to work.

Observing positive alliances The parents frequently commented on Joanne's investment in the counselling process. They said that Joanne looked forward to counselling sessions with Sarah, and would go to considerable effort to be punctual. This observation of the good alliance between Joanne and Sarah gave Mary, Paul (and Emily) hope that Joanne would recover and make a good life for herself.

Reframing Reframing was frequently used to help Paul develop a more useful way of interpreting Joanne's problematic behaviour, that would lead to more positive and fewer negative interactions. When Joanne moved back into the family home having stayed with her aunt for several months, there was an initial honeymoon period. However, old destructive patterns of father-daughter conflict began to re-emerge. These involved Joanne behaving in ways that irritated Paul, and Paul interpreting his daughter's behaviour as intentionally hurtful. To address this, Emily helped Paul reframe Joanne's behaviour in other ways, notably in terms of Joanne's low self-esteem. So for example, instead of seeing drunkenness, promiscuity or misbehaviour as a personal attack, Paul was invited to see it as a reflection of Joanne doing things to cope with a low sense of self-worth. Gradually over time, Paul developed a facility for understanding his daughter's behaviour in this way, and empathising with her, rather than viewing it as a personal attack on him. This led Joanne to gradually engage in less conflict with her father.

De-escalating negative father-daughter behaviour patterns Direct interventions were used to de-escalate negative father-daughter behaviour patterns. Emily helped Paul to explore ways of being less immediately reactive to Joanne and slightly more emotionally independent of her. This was to help father and daughter avoid becoming involved in spiralling conflictual behaviour patterns. For example, to avoid escalating shouting matches about misbehaviour, Paul was helped to develop strategies such as temporarily withdrawing and taking a walk to the park and then coming home and addressing the issue with Joanne in a calm, respectful, problem-solving manner.

Managing relapses During recovery Joanne periodically relapsed and drank heavily, for example while on holidays or at Saint Patrick's weekend. During these times, Paul's mood would drop and he would become distressed. He viewed these relapses as total and complete, wiping out all hope of recovery. At these times he viewed Joanne as '*throwing it all to the wind*' again. On these occasions, Paul used the sessions to express this distress in an extreme way, and Emily gave Paul time and space to do so. However, Emily would respond not by affirming or validating Paul's negative mood state as she had done in the first session. Rather, she would reframe Joanne's relapses as part of a progressive recovery process. In this sense Emily would '*hold the hope*' for Paul. Emily found that regular team discussions with Sarah, in which she got feedback on Joanne's progress and potential, empowered her to remain optimistic about Joanne's recovery.

Managing the transition to adulthood When Joanne became intensely involved with a new boyfriend, David, who had a drink problem, Emily supported Mary who found Joanne's involvement in this relationship very difficult. Joanne was spending every minute she was not in school with him. Mary saw this as part of Joanne's addictive process, transferred from an addiction to alcohol to an addiction to being with her new boyfriend. This was anxiety-provoking for Mary because of her experience of the addictive processes within Paul's family. She had witnessed the lives of Paul's family become devastated by addiction. She also felt a rivalry towards David because she saw him as taking Joanne away from her. Mother and daughter had undergone reconciliation when Joanne returned home after her period living with Paul's sister. Now Mary felt that David was luring Joanne away from her again. This all occurred at about the time of Joanne's 18th birthday. Mary's anxiety may have been fuelled by Joanne's imminent transition to adulthood. With this in mind, Emily invited Mary to reflect on Joanne's transition from being a teenager to being an adult. This was challenging for Mary because she tended to view Joanne as less mature than an 18 year old and was apprehensive about according her increasing autonomy.

Couples work

Alongside the parenting work, some of the work that Emily did with Mary and Paul focused on them as a couple, and as individual adults.

Recognising and disrupting destructive patterns In the sessions with Mary and Paul, the impact of Joanne's behaviour on them as a couple was explored. Joanne's behaviour caused considerable tensions between them. Paul became angry at Mary because of her ability to avoid becoming embroiled in escalating battles with Joanne. Mary, in turn, would become exasperated with her husband for repeatedly falling into these conflicts with their daughter. They discussed this process openly in the couple's sessions and developed ways of interrupting these destructive behaviour patterns.

Facilitating mutual support They also worked out ways of supporting each other. For example, they scheduled some evenings or weekends away from the family for themselves as a couple.

Facilitating joint problem-solving Many of the ways Mary and Paul found to interrupt destructive patterns of interaction and to support each other, they worked out in the sessions without direction or suggestion. In these sessions with Mary and Paul, Emily invited the couple to talk to each other about significant issues; listened carefully to what they said to each other; and then reflected her understanding of what they had said back to them. That is, Emily created a facilitative context within which the couple could engage in productive joint problem-solving. Mary and Paul were a strong couple who had endured significant life stress, such as caring for their aging dependent parents. They were strongly attached to each other and had good communication and problem-solving skills, so formal skills training was not necessary. However, creating a context for joint problem-solving was very useful for them in dealing with the issues that brought the family to counselling.

Self-care In working with Mary and Paul as individual adults, there was a focus on facilitating the development of self-care routines. Mary had become exhausted and stressed by the situation with Joanne and also by the demands of caring for her aging father. Following exploration of self-care options, Mary enrolled in an art class. Mary also used the sessions to revisit her feelings of grief about her mother's death. This work with Mary paralleled similar self-care work that Sarah was doing with Joanne, particularly when Joanne felt stressed by David's heavy drinking. Mary's capacity to remain emotionally detached from the stresses of Joanne's problematic behaviour was affirmed by Emily as a useful coping strategy that permitted her to remain productive within her occupation.

8.4. The closing phase

The disengagement phase involved a joint session in which the counselling team, Sarah and Emily, met with Joanne and her parents. Then this was followed by a session involving Joanne and Sarah, and a session involving both the parents and Emily. In these sessions progress made over the course of the counselling process was reviewed. The ways the family had used the counselling process to resolve their difficulties were discussed.

The counselling team noted that for the family as a whole, attendance over the 10 months of counselling had been excellent. Mary, Paul and Joanne had not missed any sessions. Clearly they were a highly motivated family that had used counselling productively to resolve their difficulties.

There were many positive changes highlighted in these final sessions. Joanne had turned 18 and begun to make the transition to adulthood. Her Leaving Certificate had gone well and she was invited to stay working in the restaurant where she had got a summer job. Her mood, appetite and sleep pattern had all returned to normal. She was no longer binge drinking. She had developed a healthier balance in the amount of time she spent with her boyfriend, her girlfriends and her family. She no longer went straight to her boyfriend's house every day and was no longer trapped in feeling responsible for rescuing him from his problem drinking. She went out with girls from school at weekends. Her boyfriend had started counselling to deal with his drink problems.

There was also a focus on the way Joanne and the parents were adjusting to Joanne's relationship with her new boyfriend, David. One of the parents' concerns was that Joanne's boyfriend's drinking would have a negative impact on her, by making her depressed and possibly causing her to relapse and start drinking heavily again. In the closing joint session there was an opportunity for Joanne to say that she was aware of this danger and that she was consciously deciding not to be '*dragged into the pit*' by her boyfriend's drink problems. This reduced parental anxiety and potential conflict between Joanne and her parents about her spending time with David. It also was a demonstration to Mary and Paul of Joanne's increasing maturity.

In the final session with the parents, they reported seeing Joanne managing the relationship with David as she had described in the joint session. They saw her avoiding getting '*dragged into the pit*' with him. They also discussed their concerns about the future and possible situations in which Joanne might relapse, because they considered that she had an addictive disposition.

Paul used the final session to reflect not only on Joanne's recovery, but also on his own therapeutic journey. He reflected on how he had learned to have a better quality of relationship with his daughter and to manage, not just the stresses associated with parenting Joanne, but also other stresses in his life, such as dealing with difficult work colleagues.

Mary and Paul reviewed how the counselling process had helped them as a couple. For example, Paul clearly recognised that when he was very worried about Joanne and compelled to be emotionally over-involved with her, his wife's apparent emotional detachment was a trigger that made him experience rage at her for not feeling the concern and distress that he did. In the final session he was able to acknowledge that her calm detachment was her way of coping, and that it allowed her to continue to function well in her job and to manage practical aspects of family life in an efficient way. He also saw that his emotional reactivity to Joanne was problematic and that if both he and his wife were that emotionally reactive to Joanne it would make things worse, not better.

The pacing of the final weeks of counselling was in part influenced by the fact that the counsellor, Sarah, was taking a career break. She discussed this with Joanne, so that Joanne would be prepared to either conclude counselling or transfer to another counsellor. However, as it transpired, Joanne and her parents were ready to disengage from counselling before Sarah's leave began.

Reflecting on the outcome of this case, Sarah noted that a critical aspect of her positioning was her sensitivity to Joanne as a highly sensitive girl and a willingness to be non-judgemental despite the description of Joanne, given by her parents in the first session, as an antisocial teenager who misused drugs and alcohol and was promiscuous.

CHAPTER 9

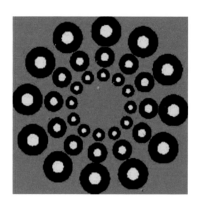

Working with a family with a violent father-son relationship

This case study illustrates the counselling process in a case where father-son conflict had escalated into physical violence. The conflict was, in part, rooted in the difficulties the father had in disengaging from his family of origin. This in turn, compromised his capacity to work co-operatively with his wife in jointly parenting his son and supporting his son's increasing independence as he moved towards adulthood. The case shows how parallel counselling with the adolescent and the parents, and joint sessions with the parents and teenager helped reduce intense conflict between the father and son. The teenager was helped to develop negotiation skills and to control his anger. The father was helped, within the context of couples' sessions, to differentiate from his family of origin and form a more viable parenting team with his wife. During the parallel adolescent-focused and couples-focused sessions, the two counsellors through regular consultation fine-tuned the work they did with the teenager and his parents to help resolve the father-son conflict.

9.1. Counselling team and duration

In this case Helen and Celine were the counselling team. Celine worked with Luke, the adolescent, and Helen worked with the parents, Fintan and Brigid. The counselling spanned 9 months from September to June.

9.2. The engagement phase

Referral

Luke, aged fifteen, was referred by his mother because he had difficulty controlling his temper and often became very angry. There was frequent conflict between Luke and his father. Luke's mother, Brigid, said she was often the peacemaker between the father and son. Luke had also been apprehended by the Gardaí for stealing from a shopping centre. Luke was the eldest of four children. He had a twelve year old brother, and six and eight year old sisters. The referral was precipitated by an incident in which Luke and his father, Fintan, had become involved in an altercation. Luke's younger brother called the Gardaí because he was frightened his father and brother would hurt each other or other family members.

First session

Luke and his parents, Fintan and Brigid, attended the first session. In response to questions about the difficulties that brought them to counselling, it became clear that violent conflict between Luke and his father was the family's primary concern. Against a history of frequent conflict between Luke and Fintan, there had recently been a traumatic incident in which Luke had become very angry at his father and Fintan had responded by pinning Luke to the floor and punching him. This incident represented an extreme escalation of a longstanding pattern of father-son conflict. Luke became very distressed in the session when he recounted this episode. He was tearful and distressed by recalling the details of the incident. He was also distressed by the fact that he had been unable to talk about the incident to his father and had only been able to discuss it with a friend. He felt angry at his father and let down by him for resorting to violence in this way. Fintan, who worked in a bank, was ashamed at his loss of control and the violent way he had treated his son.

Confronting family violence Celine made it clear to Fintan that violence was not acceptable for any family member. He agreed that there would be no more violence and that he would not hit his son again. A verbal contract of no violence was agreed with the family, with the understanding that if violence recurred, a referral would be made to the statutory services. Celine was strong in her challenge to Fintan about his violent behaviour. Helen wondered if the challenge was too strong and whether it would lead to the family dropping out of therapy after the first session. It is often difficult to judge if confrontative interventions like this offered early in the counselling process will cause parents to drop out of treatment or fail to engage. However, in this case Celine accurately judged that the family's readiness to engage in counselling was strong enough to risk this type of early confrontation. Celine based this judgement on the fact that the father indicated that he really wanted to support his son, but was at a loss to know how to do this and was aware that if he didn't find a way to do this, his son would develop serious long-term difficulties. The confrontative stance that Celine took with Fintan, led to herself and Helen deciding that it would be best if Celine worked with Luke, rather than with the parents because Fintan might find her too threatening.

This confrontation of family violence had a significant impact for both Luke and Fintan. Luke said that he had been to a number of other services and no-one had ever told his father that it was not acceptable to use physical force or to hit his son. He had not got the impression from these services that they viewed his father's violence towards him as completely unacceptable. Nor had these services directly confronted his father and told him that hitting his son was not acceptable and if it continued they would need to take further steps to ensure Luke's safety. So for Luke, hearing Celine confront his father helped him engage in the counselling process. He knew that the counselling team did not accept violence and was prepared to confront his parents about this.

In the first individual session with the parents, Fintan told Helen that he had found being confronted by Celine, about his violence towards his son, very difficult. However, it also had had the effect of making him stop using physical force in conflicts with Luke and become committed to avoiding family violence.

The discussion of this violent incident between father and son in the first family session was used as a starting point for exploring who else in the family became involved in hitting or physically hurting others. Brigid acknowledged that she had hit Luke and his younger brother on a few occasions. Thus, Fintan's violence was not an isolated incident. There was a culture within the family that condoned violence.

Apology and forgiveness The discussion of the violent incident between Fintan and Luke led on to inquiries about the sort of things that the family needed to do to move forward from this difficult predicament. The theme of apology and forgiveness was explored. It became clear that the family had never talked about this theme and no one in the family had ever said sorry for hitting or hurting another. There was also no experience within the family of the process of forgiveness. In light of this, Helen and Celine indicated that a contract for further counselling would involve working on creating a context within which apologies could be made so that there might be a possibility of forgiveness in the future. Addressing the issues of apology and forgiveness was viewed as essential for strengthening Luke's relationship with his parents, which in turn was viewed as an important process in helping him control his temper, his anger and his antisocial behaviour.

It is noteworthy that the contract for counselling was not premised on identifying who was right and who was wrong; punishing the perpetrator or removing the perpetrator from the family; or putting the victim in a place of safety. A child-protection perpetrator-victim frame of reference was not adopted. However, child protection issues were addressed in the context of a systemic-relational frame of reference which was the guiding model for the subsequent counselling process. The counselling would focus not on the father as 'the bad guy' and the son as 'the good guy' or vice versa. But on enhancing the quality of the relationships between Luke and his parents through processes such as apology, forgiveness and understanding.

Reframing   Towards this end, in the first session Luke's anger, aggression, theft and apparent disrespect for his parents were reframed as upset, hurt, a cry for help and a need to be understood and cared for by Fintan and Brigid. Luke and his parents had not previously considered this sort of reframing and it had the effect of reducing the polarised conflict between the parents and adolescent. However, it did not excuse Luke's antisocial behaviour, but rather created a context within which he could learn to identify more appropriate ways to get his needs for parental care and support met, and control his anger, aggression, violence and theft and learn how to deal with authority figures.

Communication training   In order for Luke to have his need to be understood by his parents, particularly by his father, met it was essential that the father and son communicated effectively with each other. In the first session their style of communication was explored. It became clear from enquires about this, that their routines for communicating with each other were problematic. When Luke spoke with Fintan with a view to being listened to and understood, his father typically gave him well-intentioned advice and directives on how he should behave and manage his life. There was a consistency and 'sameness' to the advice Fintan gave. In these situations Luke felt that Fintan was lecturing him, from a monotonous repetitive script, and not hearing that he needed to be understood. In response, Luke would speak in a disrespectful way to his father, who in turn would increase the intensity of his ineffective way of advising his son on how to behave. This confirmed for Luke that his father had little interest in understanding him, and increased the anger and disrespect he showed towards his father. This type of cycle repeated and escalated into angry conflictual battles that left both Luke and Fintan feeling misunderstood and unsupported. In the first session this

{ 179 }

pattern was noted and it was proposed that counselling focus on helping father and son find more effective ways of communicating with each other. In particular it was noted that there was a need for Luke to find a way to speak respectfully and calmly to his father and for his father to find a way to listen attentively and hear what his son was saying, rather than *'lecture'* him.   Subsequently, Luke attended sessions with Celine and the parents attended parallel sessions with Helen. However, there were periodic joint family sessions and in all of these Luke and Fintan were coached in effective father-son communication.

Mismatch between adolescent's and parents' vision of Luke's life goals Luke was not achieving his potential at school. When this was explored, it became clear that Luke had a certain idea of what he wanted to do with his life and his parents had a very different view of what he should do. Luke felt that his parents did not understand or condone his life plans. This sense of being misunderstood and unsupported underpinned his poor achievement in school and exacerbated the adolescent-parent conflict. This mismatch was flagged as a focus for counselling.

Father's family of origin issues In the first session Brigid spontaneously mentioned that the father-son conflict in which Fintan and Luke were engaged mirrored similar problems in Fintan's family of origin. This was noted as a potential issue to be addressed in the parents' sessions with Helen, but was not explored in detail in the first session. Helen and Celine judged that Fintan was not ready to explore these sorts of personal issues in the presence of his son. There was a triangulation process within the family within which the mother and son were closely aligned and the father was more peripheral to this dyad. Helen and Celine judged, that in light of this process it would be counterproductive to explore Fintan's family of origin issues within the family session. They thought there was a risk that it would make Fintan feel that he was being labelled as the cause of all the family's problems, which in turn might lead to him dropping out of counselling or failing to engage.

9.3. The middle phase

Sessions with the parents

There were four interrelated recurring themes within the couple's sessions. The first was that Brigid viewed Fintan as *'the problem'*. The second was Fintan's continued enmeshment in his family of origin. The third was helping the couple deepen their own relationship. And the fourth was helping the couple develop a shared approach to parenting to help Luke move towards becoming a responsible independent adult.

Reframing '*Fintan is the problem*' as a couples issue and retaining neutrality From the outset Brigid made it clear that she saw Fintan as the problem. For example, in an early session she pointed out to Helen, in a self-righteous way, that she had completed the homework assignment of reading some material on parenting and that Fintan had not bothered to do so. As this process repeated, Helen developed a hypothesis that Brigid saw counselling as a context within which she could get Fintan '*fixed*' or '*put right*'. There was a covert invitation for Helen to take sides with Brigid against Fintan. Helen had to consciously manage the sessions in a way that allowed her to maintain a neutral position with respect to Fintan and Brigid, since to take sides would jeopardise the possibility of helping the family. Reframing was the main strategy used to retain neutrality. That is, when it was stated or implied that the family's problems were all due to Fintan, the alternative perspective that the family problems were due to the couple not having found a way to work together as a team was proposed or implied as an alternative. For example, when parenting issues were being discussed, and Brigid implied that the problems with Luke would be resolved if they did things her way (which was right) and not Fintan's (which was wrong), the issue was reframed as the need for the couple to find a shared approach to joint parenting. When family of origin issues were being explored, Helen was careful to reframe Brigit's view that her family was right and Fintan's was wrong, by observing that Brigid and Fintan came from families with different styles and family cultures, and the challenge was for Fintan and Brigid to develop their own shared family culture and style.

Fintan's enmeshment in his family of origin A major challenge for the couple was finding a way to help Fintan disengage from his family of origin so the couple could deepen their relationship, and develop a joint shared parenting style through which to address Luke's behaviour problems. Even though the couple had been married for 20 years, Fintan still had not disengaged from this family of origin. When Fintan and Brigid were with Fintan's parents, Fintan became strongly aligned with them against Brigid and undermined or negated her views on important family issues including parenting. This had a detrimental impact on the couple's relationship and their capacity to jointly parent their first adolescent, Luke, and help him move towards increased responsibility and autonomy.

Couples work Fintan's difficulty in disengaging from his family of origin was preventing him from deepening his relationship with Brigid. The couples work focused on helping Fintan and Brigid become more separate from Fintan's parents, and psychologically more intimate and closer to each other.

Parenting work The parenting work with Brigid and Fintan focused on helping the couple understand how Fintan's problematic relationship with his parents mirrored Luke's problematic relationship with Fintan and Brigid. It also focused on helping the couple become more of a team in parenting Luke. That is, helping Brigid and Fintan work together and also helping Fintan develop a less authoritarian stance as a parent in which he listened to and respected Luke's views.

Sessions with Luke

Luke felt undermined and negated by his parents and in particular by his father's attitude towards him in many areas of life. He felt that his parents would not take account of his wishes and preferences. For example, in the area of sport, they insisted he play rugby whereas his preference was to play Gaelic football. In the area of clothing, his parents would not give him money to buy his own clothes in case he bought drugs.

He identified the relationship with his father as more problematic than that with his mother. Because he experienced his father as not listening to his wishes and preferences and not trying to understand him, he felt disrespected. In return he disrespected his father's authority. He then generalised this to other authority figures in his social network.

Much of the work with Luke involved helping him appreciate that if he continued to aggressively demand things from his parents, and from his father in particular, it was unlikely that they would listen to him and accord him the privileges, autonomy, respect and trust he desired.

Reframing Celine framed the issue of learning to get on with his father and respect his authority, as an impersonal thing, that is, learning to respect authority in general. Celine took the position that it wasn't a question of who was right and who was wrong. It was a question of how he and his parents (and other authority figures) could develop a way of co-operating so that he could get some of what he wanted. This included, for example, respect and trust at a general level, and the right to buy his own clothes and play the sport he preferred.

Communication and negotiation skills training This framing of the problem as finding ways of co-operating with his parents so he could get more of what he wanted, paved the way for helping him to develop a way to negotiate more patiently with his parents. He explored how to demonstrate respect for his parent's authority in the way he spoke to them, even if he didn't feel emotionally as if he respected them. He practiced planning carefully what he wanted to say in negotiations with his parents, rather than giving vent to his feelings of frustration and anger. He also made efforts to listen to his parents' responses to what he had said without interrupting and to reflect on what they had said before responding. As Luke developed skills for containing his anger and negotiating more respectfully with his parents, and with his father in particular, he began to develop a less conflictual relationship with his father.

Arising from these negotiations, the parents did allow him to play Gaelic football and gave him some discretion to buy his own clothes. This was within the context of a very significant reduction in his antisocial behaviour both outside the family and at home. During the counselling process he stopped stealing outside the home and had no further involvement with the Gardaí. Also, at home, his episodes of aggression diminished in frequency and intensity.

Homework experiments In setting up homework assignments, Celine invited Luke to try out his communication and negotiation skills at home, not as definitive ways of making everything better, but rather as experiments, that would allow him to find out how his parents would respond if he communicated with them in a different way. He was invited to try to find times when it was possible to talk to his parents in a low key way about issues of concern to him. During these times, he was to carefully say things that he had planned before hand and then listen to and record his parents' replies. He was very responsive to this idea of carrying out experiments for homework.

Team work

Throughout the counselling process Helen and Celine met regularly to discuss the progress of the parents and the adolescent. Initially, Helen took the view that Celine would have to work with Luke to help him to be more respectful and less aggressive towards his father, or progress would not be possible. Concurrently Celine took the view that Helen would have to work with Fintan to help him listen to his son, and to be more respectful and less controlling of him, or little progress would be made. As the case progressed Helen and Celine noticed a tension about their polarised positions and after carefully listening to each other's perspectives reached a consensus that father and son each had responsibilities for engaging with each other in more tolerant and respectful ways. This joint position of the counselling team guided the work that Helen did with the parents and that Celine did with the adolescent. Helen found that the empathy she developed for Luke's position, by talking with Celine about the work she was doing with him, made it possible for her to push for Fintan to be more accommodating to his son. Similarly Celine developed empathy for Fintan's position, through discussing the work he was doing in counselling with Helen and this provided a context within which she could invite Luke to be more respectful of his father.

Family sessions

This case began with a family session which was followed by a series of parallel sessions in which Celine worked with Luke, and Helen worked with Fintan and Brigid. Towards the end of the counselling process there were further family sessions. Within these sessions there was an opportunity for Luke, Fintan and Brigid to talk with each other, listen to each other and appreciate each other's different perspectives. There was also an opportunity for them to negotiate about issues concerning Luke's freedom, privacy, privileges and responsibilities. In one of these sessions Luke said he wanted a tattoo and his parents strongly objected to this. To test out his parents' reactions, Luke spontaneously got a fake tattoo. His father, Fintan, predictably responded very intensely and negatively to the tattoo, while his mother took a very low-key permissive approach, accepting that what was done could not be undone so there was little to be gained by fighting about it. When Luke revealed that the tattoo was fake, and he had worn it as a joke to test his parent's reactions, Fintan saw the humour in this and responded to Luke positively. This incident illustrates how the counselling process strengthened the relationship between Luke and his parents. If this incident had happened before counselling had begun, it could have led to a violent exchange between father and son.

9.4. Closing phase

Final session

The team agreed to finish the counselling process after two family sessions. It was clear that Luke and Fintan were ready to conclude counselling. However, Brigid asked Celine if a third family session could be scheduled. The team guessed that Brigid was anxious that the gains that had been made would become undone once the family disengaged from counselling. This anxiety was similar to her rigorous compliance with homework assignments at the start of counselling.

In the two family sessions progress made over the course of the counselling process was reviewed. The ways the family had used the counselling process to resolve their difficulties were discussed. The mood in the final session was light-hearted. There was much laughter and a strong sense of achievement. The family had moved a long way. There had been no further violence and respect among family members had increased. Fintan and Brigid were working well as a parenting team. Luke was more respectful of them and negotiated with them about his increasing need for autonomy as he moved towards adulthood.

In the final session there was also a discussion of future situations in which the family might view themselves as being at risk of becoming involved in their destructive patterns again. Luke was asked what advice he would give to his parents to avoid the family difficulties recurring in the future. He said that they should become a *'wall of steel'*. This referred to them consolidating their relationship as a couple and taking a united front when dealing with him, but may also have referred to their need to be united when dealing with Fintan's family of origin.

CHAPTER 10

Working with a family with mother-daughter conflict

This case study illustrates the counselling process with a family where the main focus was on resolving mother-daughter conflict which followed in the wake of the father leaving the family home. The mother-daughter conflict, which contributed to low mood in the 17 year old daughter, revolved around a range of issues including the daughter's reluctance to follow rules her mother set, her erratic school attendance and academic performance, and her involvement with boyfriends and peers who did not meet with her mother's approval. The conflict occurred within the context of the mother's directive and inconsistent parenting style. This in turn was related to the mother's own experience of being parented by her mother in a dominant manner. The case shows how parallel counselling with the daughter and mother, and conjoint sessions with them improved the quality of communication between the mother and daughter. It also helped the mother to move to a style of parenting based on negotiation rather than direction that is more appropriate for helping an adolescent make the transition to adulthood.

10.1. Counselling team and duration

The counselling team included Gerry and Kate. Gerry worked with the parents, Molly and Brian, although most of the sessions were with Molly. Kate worked with the adolescent, Sue, who was 17 years of age. The counselling spanned ten months from February to November. There were ten sessions with the parents and eight sessions with the adolescent.

Referral

Molly referred her daughter Sue, aged seventeen, to counselling because she was arguing with her and her younger brother Ray a great deal. This followed in the wake of Brian, the father, leaving the family home some weeks earlier without explanation and without leaving any information about where he was going.

First session

Gerry and Kate conducted a conjoint initial session with the mother, Molly, and her daughter, Sue.

The mother's concerns In the first interview, Molly said she was distressed because she had previously had a good relationship with her daughter, Sue, and this had deteriorated drastically since her husband, Brian, had left the family home some weeks previously. In the weeks prior to Brian's departure there had been a gradual deterioration in Sue's behaviour, but Molly viewed this as manageable. However, once Brian left Sue's behavioural problems escalated significantly. Brian was still supporting the family financially, but was uncertain about his future with the family and gave no clear explanation for leaving. Molly was also worried about the deteriorating relationship between Sue and herself. Molly liked to have clear rules and routines, whereas Sue was a free spirit and liked to take a less rule-bound approach to life. Molly had been arguing regularly with Sue about her coming in later than agreed at night and about Sue not following through on chores she had agreed to do. Molly disapproved of Sue's boyfriend and of the peer group of girls with which she associated.

The daughter's concerns In contrast to her mother who was concerned with external issues such as arguing about curfew times, chores and school attendance, Sue's concerns were largely internal. Sue was concerned that in recent weeks her mood had been very low and she couldn't understand why this was happening or how to change it. She had also lost motivation to achieve in school over the preceding months and this sense of just not caring about how she did in school was distressing. She was not attending school regularly and her grades were deteriorating. This was less of a concern for Sue than for her mother. Sue had previously been an excellent student, achieving honours in her Junior Certificate and being at the top of her class. In the preceding couple of years her social adjustment in school had been good and she had gone to Morocco on holidays with school friends, although she had been bullied in her first year of secondary school. (In later sessions it became clear that Sue was unhappy with her school placement and wanted to change to another school). Sue had a wide circle of friends and a boyfriend. She was involved in amateur drama with her friends and boyfriend. Her involvement in acting and her relationships with her friends and boyfriend were all very important to her. Sue's mother, Molly, was funding the drama courses and Sue appreciated this. However, she was distressed that her mother disapproved of her boyfriend, her friends and the amount of time she spent at the theatre.

Preliminary hypothesis Towards the end of the first session the team took a break and developed a preliminary hypothesis. The team's preliminary hypothesis was that the mother-daughter relationship problems, Sue's low mood and school problems were due to a number of factors including the father leaving the home, the differing ways the mother and daughter were dealing with that, and the normal adolescent process of individuation. The team saw the daughter's distress at the father leaving, just as she was making the transition to adulthood, as increasing her need for support and her need to make sense of the complex family situation. However, the team saw the mother as not recognising this need and focusing her concern and anxiety instead on limit-setting and school performance. This, unfortunately, led to the daughter feeling greater distress and so being more apt to spend much of her time away from home and arguing with her mother about limits, friends and school issues when she was at home. This, in turn, reinforced the mother's conviction that she must focus on these issues, rather than on supporting her daughter and helping her make sense of the complex family situation. The mother was also inconsistent in her limit setting, which was confusing for the daughter and led her to argue with her mother more, since often her mother would '*cave in*' on limits she had previously set. The team understood that the mother was coping with her husband's absence, running the household singlehanded, doing all the chores, paying the bills and setting limits for the two children in the best way that she knew. However, they thought she needed to be given sufficient therapeutic support and opportunity for reflection to see that she would meet Sue's needs for individuation better if she relaxed the tight restrictions she was placing on her, set a few consistent limits about safety issues, and focused her energy on building a supportive relationship within which Sue could makes sense of her situation. The team thought the daughter, Sue, needed an opportunity to explore and make sense of her complex life situation, including mood management, school issues, her relationships with her parents, boyfriend and peers and her transition to adulthood.

Contracting After the break towards the end of the first session, the mother and daughter were offered a contract for further counselling. It was suggested that this would focus on helping them improve their relationship and address the tension between them about various issues, including Sue's boyfriend, her friends and the amount of time she spent at the theatre. It was also proposed to explore ways of helping Sue manage her low mood and recent lack of motivation in school. It addition it was suggested that they explore the impact of Brian's absence from the family home on both of them with a view to understanding how this might be associated with their other difficulties. The mother and daughter were offered concurrent individual sessions and some periodic conjoint sessions. Both Molly and Sue agreed to this contract, with neither showing any ambivalence. It was agreed that Kate would work with Sue, and Gerry would work with Molly and also Brian if he wished to be involved in counselling.

10.3. The middle phase

Individual sessions with the daughter

In a series of individual sessions Sue, the daughter, discussed a number of themes, all of which were related to her low mood.

Assertiveness with boyfriends The first theme was her relationships with boys. She found it difficult to be confidently assertive with boyfriends. For example, she lent one of her boyfriends her new racing bike. He didn't give it back and ended the relationship. She didn't feel confident about taking a stand on this issue and let it go without confronting him. With another boyfriend, if he called to cancel a date he had made with her, she would say it was fine with her even though she was very disappointed. Kate helped Sue to explore the thoughts and feelings she had in response to these sorts of interactions with boyfriends, by asking her to describe her inner experiences in considerable detail. Through probing for details and responding non-judgementally, Kate gradually helped Sue to move from a position where she made excuses for her boyfriends' behaviours, to a position where she expressed dissatisfaction with them. Kate then invited her to explore assertive ways of expressing her dissatisfaction to her boyfriends when these types of situations arose.

Conflict with her mother about friends A second theme was Sue's disappointment, hurt and anger towards her mother, because her mother would not accept her peers or boyfriends and was quite hostile towards them. Sue said she felt like her mother did not listen to her, understand her point of view, or appreciate how important her friends were to her. This made Sue argue forcefully with her mother, spend as much time away from home as possible, and not want to respond to her mother's text messages and phone calls. Kate helped Sue to see that this type of reaction confirmed for Molly that Sue's friends were a bad influence on her and was driving a wedge between them, which in turn led her to disapprove of them more strongly. She invited Sue to consider alternative ways of responding to her mother that might not have this undesired effect.

Conflict with her mother about school A third theme was the distress Sue experienced because her mother could not appreciate her very strong wish to change schools. Sue felt that her current school was putting too much pressure on her to achieve well academically and she found this too stressful. She had gradually lost motivation to go to school and to do well academically. She felt her mother could not hear and understand her position on this. Kate helped Sue explore many options including dropping out of school and not finishing her Leaving Certificate, moving to another school and doing her Leaving Certificate over two years, and taking a break from school and finishing her Leaving Certificate at another time. Kate also invited Sue to consider how she might talk to her mother about her preferred options.

Relationship with her father A fourth theme was Sue's relationship with her father. While Sue appreciated intellectually that her father's absence could potentially affect her mood, she experienced her low mood to be more closely linked to her conflict with her mother about rules, friends, boyfriends and school. She saw herself as a 'daddy's girl' and used counselling to explore ways to continue to stay connected to him by having occasional visits and meetings, and texting him on her mobile phone. She thought she had a more privileged relationship with her father than her younger brother did. She felt a bit guilty about this. She did see that her father's absence affected the way her mother managed the home and family, and this in turn affected Sue. So in this sense she did gradually acknowledge the indirect effect of Brian's absence on her.

Individual sessions with parents

Gerry conducted a series of individual sessions with Molly in which she addressed parenting issues and also Molly's relationship with Brian, although little time was spent on this theme. Gerry also had a couple of sessions with Brian.

Parenting and limit setting In the individual sessions with Molly, the most appropriate way to parent Sue and to set limits was a central theme.

The adolescent behaviours that led to greatest maternal anxiety Molly was very anxious about Sue being more disobedient and argumentative than she had been as a child, staying out late, associating with friends who she did not approve of and bringing home friends who Molly had not met to stay at the house without permission. She worried about all of these issues a great deal and found parenting Sue, without the support of her husband Brian, very challenging. Molly also worried for her own safety now that Brian was not in the house. She worried that if she left the door open late at night for Sue, the house would be burgled. She worried that if Sue brought home some friend Molly didn't know to stay in the house, the stranger might harm her or her children as Brian was no longer there to protect them.

Identifying inconsistent parenting as a core problem Molly coped with her anxiety about failing as a parent and her worries for her own safety by setting very strict limits for many of Sue's behaviours. However, she typically 'caved in' and set more permissive limits or did not follow through on threatened consequences. This was because Sue became very angry with her and argued very forcefully with her. She stayed away from the house for long periods and would not communicate with her by phone while she was away. All of these reactions to strict limit setting distressed Molly a great deal. Through working with Gerry, Molly came to see how confusing it must have been for Sue to have strict limits set and then relaxed. She came to see how this parenting style may have reinforced Sue's argumentative and oppositional behaviour and her staying out late, since often these behaviours led to her mother relaxing strict limits.

Setting a few consistent limits Gerry invited Molly to identify a few areas which she thought were a priority for limit setting, and then in each of these to consistently set clear limits for Sue that could not be altered by argument or oppositional behaviour. Molly settled on two areas that would, in her view, create a degree of safety particularly for herself, but also for Sue and so reduce her anxiety.

She set limits for how late Sue could stay out at night and locked the door at this time each evening. This was partly because she wanted Sue to come home at a reasonable hour, but also because she was quite frightened about leaving the door unlocked. She also banned Sue from having friends stay over in the house if she did not know them. This was mainly because she was frightened of having strangers in the house while she was asleep. She explained the limits calmly to Sue and her reasons for setting them. She also set very clear consequences for violations and followed through on these.

Over time Molly found that consistently setting these limits worked and this gave her courage to continue to be consistent. Sue conformed to these limits that were set and argued much less with Molly and so their relationship improved. Alongside this consistent limit setting, Gerry encouraged Molly to let go of the restrictive rules she had inconsistently enforced about other issues. In response, she found that Sue argued with her less and the quality of their relationship improved.

Marital issues and sessions with Brian

In the individual sessions, Molly conveyed that she had hoped the counselling process would have a positive impact on her relationship with Brian. That is, at some level Molly's referral of Sue for counselling was a 'calling card' for her to get marital counselling for Brian and herself. However, Brian did not accept an offer for a joint session with Molly, so no marital sessions were held.

However, Gerry met with Brian for a couple of individual sessions. Brian explained that he was considering developing a relationship with a new partner, but was uncertain about the permanence of this new relationship and did not wish his family to have knowledge of it. He felt he needed time to think about what to do for the best. He was feeling troubled about the dilemmas he was facing. Should he return and live with Molly and the children, or should he move towards making his new relationship permanent? In the sessions with Gerry, Brian explored ways he could remain connected to Sue and his son. Various options for visitation were considered, ranging from helping out with transporting them to sports activities, to brief meetings, to more extended visits. He did not follow through on many of these and had limited contact with Sue and her brother.

Work was a priority for Brian. Even during his brief meetings with his daughter he took work phone calls.

Molly took the view that Brian needed a lot of time and space to think about what to do. However, through work with Gerry, her permissive approach to Brian was gradually replaced by a more assertive one. She took the position that if after six months he could not make a decision, then they should discuss him removing his belongings from the house. She also insisted that he make an effort to maintain his relationships with the two children. She extended invitations for him to visit for family occasions. He accepted some of these invitations. However, his contact with Molly, Sue and his son was sporadic and he declined an invitation to attend sessions with Molly or joint sessions with Molly and Sue.

Conjoint work with mother and daughter

The conjoint work with Molly and Sue focused on helping the mother actively listen to Sue, understand her point of view and help her arrive at solutions to her problems or negotiate solutions that were acceptable to both of them. It also involved exploring the historical factors that made it challenging for Molly and Sue to communicate in this way. This communications training was essential, because Molly's very directive parenting style was appropriate for a pre-adolescent child, but inappropriate for an older teenager about to leave school. It was also creating conflict between mother and daughter and leading Sue to distance herself from Molly.

Problematic mother-daughter communication   For Sue's difficulties with romantic relationships, school achievement and low mood, Molly would work out solutions and then try to '*fix*' Sue by directing her to follow these solutions. This was all motivated by her desire to be a good mother and bring up her daughter well. For example, she would tell Sue to keep away from certain boyfriends, to work harder at school and to spend more time at home where she would be cared for. This parenting style led Sue to experience her mother as not taking her views and capacity for independent problem-solving into account.   Consequently Molly's parenting style made Sue feel hurt and angry. Not surprisingly, Sue responded to Molly's advice by arguing with her mother, staying away from home, not answering her mother's phone calls and rebelling against the advice her mother gave her. Some of her mother's advice may have been useful, but the directive way Molly offered it to Sue was not. Molly would respond to Sue's oppositional position by becoming more critical and more directive, which in turn would alienate Sue further and elicit more oppositional behaviour from her. Molly's directive and dominant parenting style, and the negative mother and daughter interaction pattern associated with it, was a very significant factor contributing to Sue's low mood.

Mother-daughter communication training The joint work which Kate and Gerry did with Molly and Sue aimed to help Molly listen to Sue's difficulties non-judgmentally, understand her perspective and invite her to explore possible solutions to her difficulties. Only after that had been achieved was Molly invited to comment on Sue's views and to offer these comments in a supportive way, rather than being critical of them and directing Sue to follow Molly's agenda.

Advocating for Sue In doing this communications training, the team acted as an advocate for Sue, helping her to present her position clearly. Presenting her position clearly was challenging for Sue because from all of her previous conflicts with her mother she had come to expect that Molly would not listen to her and would always be critical of her ideas.

The impact of Molly's family of origin experiences on her parenting style The team also supported Molly in doing her best to hear her daughter out and in checking that she had fully understood her daughter's position before commenting supportively on it. This was very challenging for Molly to do, because her own mother had been very critical of her and this was the role model she had for communicating with Sue. In fact her mother's critical style still had an impact on Molly's relationship with her. Molly felt her efforts to become independent were hampered by her mother's dominance. Molly said that she did not want to dominate Sue as her mother had dominated her, because she wanted Sue to mature and become independent. However, it gradually became clear to Molly that her parenting style was inadvertently compromising Sue's capacity to develop autonomy. Molly felt compelled to make Sue obey all of her rules (just as she had followed all of her own mother's rules when she was a teenager), otherwise she would be failing in her duty as a mother, according to the standards of her own mother.

Negotiating age-appropriate responsibilities Sue had developed a lifestyle where she stayed out very late at night and spent much of the day asleep in bed, particularly at the weekends, but also during the week when she wasn't attending school. Molly responded by being critical of this lifestyle. Sue's lifestyle not only exacerbated mother-daughter conflict, but may also have had a negative effect on her low mood. The team invited mother and daughter to explore age-appropriate responsibilities that Sue could take on so that there would be a genuine reason for her to get out of bed and be active. Through negotiation it was arranged that Sue would work on a regular basis at the theatre, helping with coaching classes for the younger kids. This would reduce the drama tuition fees that her mother had to pay the drama teacher. This was an important intervention because it provided mother and daughter with an opportunity to negotiate about an issue that was of concern to both of them and to reach a satisfactory conclusion. For Sue, she got to spend more time at the theatre (which she liked) and she also got to take on responsibilities that contributed to family finances. In addition, Sue began to consider that her career might in the long-term involve working as an actress. In this sense, the negotiation increased her sense of autonomy. For Molly, the arrangement made her feel like she was being a more effective parent, since it prevented Sue from spending days in bed and offered her a chance to begin to earn her keep.

Negotiating about pocket money The negotiation about Sue working at the theatre led on to an exploration of how she received pocket money and how she had contributed to the household finances in the past. The issue of managing household finances more prudently was becoming a priority since Brian had moved out, because Brian and Molly had to support two houses. The team thought that it would also be important for the mother and daughter to find a better way to manage pocket money, because Molly had become very angry about the current situation which she felt was unsatisfactory. She saw herself as paying large sums for Sue's school and drama classes. In response Sue wasn't attending school and had developed friendships which Molly did not approve of at the theatre. Within this overall financial context, Molly became increasingly angry when Sue was aggressive in how she asked for pocket money and ungrateful when she received it.

Mother and daughter described how when Sue needed money she asked her mother for it as there was no set limit on pocket money. Usually, if her mother offered some money, for example €20, Sue would argue that she needed €40, and in response to forceful arguing Molly would eventually give Sue the amount she requested. Molly complained about Sue bullying her into giving her more pocket money than she wished to provide and how angry and upset this made her. The team pointed out how Molly's approach was training Sue to argue with her, since arguing forcefully usually led to her to getting more funds. Agreement was reached that a more organised approach to pocket money would be developed and this was negotiated within a joint meeting involving Sue and Molly.

Teamwork issues

This case required careful teamwork between Gerry and Kate. Both counsellors developed strong alliances with their respective clients. There was some tension between the counsellors feeling unheard by the other. It was challenging for them to balance the differing needs of the clients – the need for Sue to do her internal work and deal with the stresses of her complex family situation and her drive for individuation, as against the difficulty of Molly managing in a practical way her daughter's very difficult behaviour, while also dealing with her family of origin issues. Kate and Gerry discussed this issue together. They agreed that in a joint meeting, Kate, who had developed a strong alliance with Sue, would challenge Sue about the appropriateness of her problematic behaviour (staying out late etc.). This showed Molly, that it was possible for an adult to be both understanding and supportive of her daughter, while also challenging her behaviour. This created a context within which Gerry, who had developed a strong alliance with Molly, could explore the family of origin issues that were preventing Molly from adopting this caring, but challenging position with Sue. Gerry helped Molly acknowledge that her conscious message to her daughter was that she loved her and would do anything for her. However, at an unconscious level, the message was that unless Sue followed all of Molly's rules, she was making Molly a failure as a mother according to the standards of Molly's own mother. These two conflicting messages "*I love and accept you and will do anything for you*" and "*I'm angry at you and reject you because you make me a failure as a mother*" underpinned many of Molly's interactions with Sue, and led Sue to become frustrated and confused. These complex issues were discussed by Gerry and Kate in case review meetings and informed the way they worked with the mother and daughter.

10.4.   Closing phase

This work spanned eighteen sessions over ten months. In the disengagement phase, progress made over the course of the counselling process was reviewed and the way the family had used the counselling process to address their difficulties was discussed.

The quality of the mother-daughter relationship improved significantly and Sue's low mood improved over the course of this time. There were a number of factors that contributed to this. Molly made a major shift from using a very directive and critical parenting style to developing a style based on open communication and negotiation. Mother and daughter developed a clearer understanding of each other's positions and viewpoints. Molly and Sue adjusted to Brian living outside of the family home, but Sue continued to hold a position of anger and rebellion toward her mother.

The challenging aspects of the joint work, particularly coaching the mother and daughter to communicate more clearly with each other and to negotiate, was made possible by the strong alliances Molly developed with Gerry, and Sue developed with Kate in individual sessions, and the empathy they had for the mother and daughter's positions as they struggled to develop a more effective way of communicating together.

The adoption by Gerry and Kate of a non-judgemental approach in their individual work with Molly and Sue was a central factor in building their therapeutic alliances. It was in stark contrast to the highly judgmental positions that the mother and daughter took towards each other at the outset of the counselling process. In the disengagement phase, the risks of Molly and Sue falling back into their old patterns were discussed, and ways of recognising this and talking about it in a calm way were considered.

In the disengagement phase, there was also a focus on the future challenges. Sue and Molly reached a position where they could negotiate about Sue's future educational and occupational development. Sue was beginning to think that she would like to work as an actress. Molly had become more flexible about considering Sue's wishes in planning her schooling and occupational training. Joint mother-daughter sessions focused on this issue.

Molly reached a position where she wanted greater clarity on Brian's future role in the family and was being more assertive with Brian about this.

CHAPTER 11

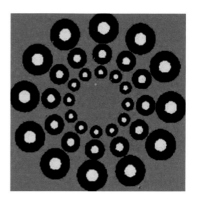

Working with a family with bullying, sexual abuse and family violence issues

This case study illustrates the counselling process in a complex case where a highly conflicted family was attempting to cope with the fallout from intrafamilial child sexual abuse, and family violence. Stacey, the 13 year old teenager in this case, had been multiply traumatised (beaten by her parents, bullied at school, sexually abused by a cousin and betrayed by her boyfriend) and responded by engaging in escalating aggressive conflict with her mother in particular, but also with others. The case shows how counselling was effective in supporting this traumatised girl and in preventing an extreme escalation of family violence, while being relatively ineffective in transforming the family's habitual conflictual style. The case also illustrates how the statutory reporting of child abuse was managed during the counselling process.

11.1.   Counselling team and duration

In this case Ciara and Ruth were the counselling team. Ciara worked with Stacey, the adolescent, and Ruth worked with the parents, Patrick and Margaret. The counselling spanned about eighteen months.

11.2.   The engagement phase

Referral

Stacey was a thirteen year old girl referred by her mother, Margaret, at the suggestion of the school. The main concerns mentioned by the mother in the referral phone call were that Stacey was being bullied at school, was feeling ill in the mornings and refusing to go to school, and was harming herself. It was also mentioned that there had been deaths within the family, although this issue was not subsequently highlighted by the parents as a key concern in the first session.

First session

Stacey attended the first session with her parents, Patrick and Margaret. They presented as a highly conflictual family. There was frequent fighting, shouting, verbal abuse and violence within the home involving the parents, Stacey and her older brother and sister. Patrick and Margaret had many complaints about Stacey's aggressive behaviour and Stacey complained that her parents had punished her difficult behaviour by hitting her.

For this family, the process of attending the first and subsequent sessions was marked by significant conflict. For example, Stacey and her parents typically disagreed about the timing of sessions and transportation arrangements. These disagreements often escalated into angry rows. Stacey's difficulty resolving conflict within relationships was not confined to the family. She also had difficulty maintaining peer relationships. Stacy had been bullied in school and had been in conflict with many of her close friends.

11.3.   The middle phase

Sessions with Stacey

Ciara conducted a series of sessions with Stacey. During the first couple of sessions Stacey was ambivalent about being in counselling. She never settled comfortably into her chair and her concentration was poor. She flitted from one topic to another and often lost her train of thought.

Alliance building   Because of Stacey's ambivalence, Ciara took advantage of various opportunities to build a good working alliance with Stacey. For example, in one of the early sessions Stacey and her mother had been fighting before the appointment and Stacey refused to come in with her mother. Ciara went down and sat with Stacey in the car. After a few minutes Stacey agreed to walk around the block and the session was held in that way. Stacey appreciated the tolerance Ciara showed in that and other similar situations.

Conflict with parents   In the first two sessions Ciara explored the source of Stacey's immense anger. There was a longstanding history of conflict within the family. Some of

Stacey's anger stemmed from the verbal abuse and physical chastisement to which she had been subjected by her parents, particularly her mother.

Sex-education In the first couple of sessions, Stacey also wanted to talk about sex a good deal. Ciara responded to this curiosity by engaging Stacey in some sex education, using an appropriate sex education book. Stacey had not been able to talk with her mother about sex and had only a sketchy knowledge about sexual functioning, so she appreciated Ciara's willingness to talk openly about sex.

Disclosure of sexual abuse In the third session Ciara continued to explore Stacey's views of her relationships with her parents. Stacey complained about their emotional unavailability to herself and her two siblings. Then she moved on to talk about her past boyfriends. At this point she asked if she could tell Ciara something distressing about sex, but with a note of caution. She said to Ciara "*Can I tell you something gross, but I don't want to gross you out*". Ciara invited her to talk about whatever was on her mind at the time. Stacey then gave a detailed account of a series of incidents of sexual abuse. In all incidents her cousin was the perpetrator. Ciara had to inform Stacey that this '*gross*' secret was in fact one she could not keep and reminded Ciara of what had been said at the first session. Ciara assured Stacey that nothing would happen too quickly and certainly not before their next session.

In retrospect, Ciara suspected that Stacey had used the first couple of sessions, and the talk about sex and sex education, to see if Ciara was the sort of person to whom she could disclose sexual abuse, and the sort of person who could tolerate high intensity negative emotions and conflict. Ciara saw the early sessions as Stacey's way of testing her, to see if they could tolerate and contain the intense emotions, conflict and sexual information that she needed to talk about.

Consolidation of the therapeutic alliance, trauma work and managing conflict From the third session (in which Stacey disclosed sexual abuse) onwards, Stacey engaged well in counselling and formed a strong alliance with Ciara. The ambivalence about counselling she had displayed in the early sessions was no longer evident. She used the sessions to process the intense emotions she felt about the abuse and also to address her on-going conflicts with her mother and friends. Ciara invited her to ventilate her feelings about these conflicts, to develop an understanding of the repeating patterns of interaction that typified these conflicts, and to explore alternative and more productive ways of resolving conflict.

Stacey's betrayal Stacey used the counselling sessions to express the extreme distress she felt, in response to her experience of betrayal. When Stacey was self-harming her boyfriend asked her about it and she told him about her experiences with her cousin when she was younger. This boy challenged the cousin who lived locally. When Stacey found out about this, she was very upset that her boyfriend had betrayed her trust and told others her secret. She was also aware that news of her abuse had got back to Patrick and Margaret through conversations they had had with various people in the close knit community in which they lived. This caused terrible upheaval within the wider family.

Sessions with the parents

Ruth conducted a series of sessions with Patrick and Margaret. In the early sessions there was a focus on understanding conflict and violence within the family. During their sessions the parents, especially Patrick, expressed shame and distress about their involvement in this conflict, and particularly about the violence. It also became clear that the family was divided. Patrick got on better with Stacey than her older sister. In contrast, Margaret got on well with the older boy, but her relationships with Stacey and her sister were more problematic, and characterised by frequent intense conflicts that occasionally escalated into violence.

Breaching the split in the family Patrick and Margaret were invited to complete various homework tasks to explore the degree to which this split in the family could be breached. For example, Ruth invited Patrick to make an effort to watch sport with his son when the opportunity arose (something that was very challenging for him to do); concurrently, Margaret was invited to be less reactive to Stacey and her sister's negative behaviour. Margaret was invited to look to Patrick for support in this, to help her to walk away from escalating conflict. Margaret found this very challenging as she was quite depressed at the time and had taken two weeks off work so she could get her mood under control.

Parents' disclosure of sexual abuse At the same time that Stacey had told Ciara about her sexual abuse, Patrick and Margaret had told Ruth about the same incidents.

They had heard about the incidents from neighbours and from members of the extended family.

Other family stresses Patrick and Margaret also told Ruth about other stresses within the family. The older sister, Lydia was going out with a lad who had been in prison for burglary and was facing other charges. She had recently told them that she was pregnant.

Joint family session and the family's reaction to the team reporting the sexual abuse to the Health Service Executive (HSE)

After the disclosure of sexual abuse, Ciara told Stacey, and Ruth told the parents, that they had to inform the statutory authorities (HSE Community Care) about Stacey's allegations of sexual abuse, in keeping with the Irish national child protection guidelines. Stacey, Patrick and Margaret seemed to understand and accept this.

However, in the subsequent joint session they were very angry. They said they would never have disclosed the abuse if they had known that the team would tell social workers at Community Care about their difficulties. (The family, like all clients attending Teen Counselling, had been told about the limits of confidentiality and the requirement to report child abuse at the time of referral, in the first session and at the beginning of their individual sessions). Patrick and Margaret spoke on behalf of Stacey in the joint session and said she was very angry and felt betrayed. The fact that it was intrafamilial abuse, and that Patrick's brother's son was the perpetrator, and that he might be subject to investigation and prosecution, were very distressing for the parents and Stacey.

Ciara and Ruth listened to Margaret's and Patrick's anger and distress about reporting the abuse to the social workers. They adopted an understanding and non-reactive stance. They explained that they were bound by the national guidelines to report allegations of abuse, but that Stacey had a choice about whether or not she made a statement to the social workers. This information had a calming effect on the family. By the end of the session the rupture in the therapeutic alliance was repaired and the counselling process continued.

Margaret recalled some uncomfortable and potentially abusive experiences which she had experienced as a child, and also the fact that a friend who had visited herself and Patrick had been mildly sexually inappropriate with the children some years previously. She reflected on this to try to understand her daughter's experience and to consider possible causes for the abuse Stacey had suffered.

Managing risk to others

A second incident occurred in which confidentiality had to be broken because Stacey gave Ciara information about another person being at risk of significant harm. Stacey told Ciara that her boyfriend intended to assault the cousin who had abused her. The team had to contact Stacey's mother and let her know of this impending danger. Despite breaching confidentially in this way, the family retained a good alliance with the team and remained in counselling. They could understand the importance of this risk management procedure. This was an indicator of the strength of the therapeutic alliance that had been established between the counselling team and the family.

Mother-daughter sessions focusing on conflict management

Three sessions involving the mother and daughter were held in the weeks following the disclosure of sexual abuse. The mother and daughter sessions were held because concurrent parallel sessions were not helping Stacey and Margaret find a way to resolve their repeated episodes of conflict. In the parallel sessions there was a recurring pattern in which Stacey and Margaret would each describe conflictual events and understand them, but find themselves unable to change the way they handled these conflicts when they recurred between sessions.

One episode of conflict had escalated to physical violence. Stacey threw a computer printer at her mother and Margaret pushed Stacey, which caused Stacey to fall and hit her head. Stacey was bruised and brought to hospital. At this point Stacey said to her mother *"There is something else I'm not saying"*. Margaret asked if it was something to do with the family or something that had happened at school. Stacey said that it was neither of these, but was clearly letting her mother know that she had experienced further trauma that had not been disclosed. Later she let her mother know that she had been abused by another perpetrator as well as her cousin and had felt too ashamed to let anyone know. The family had no difficulty with the service adding this piece of information to the referral to the statutory authorities.

The sessions with mother and daughter were very difficult because Stacey and Margaret would come to them in such a state of anger that they were barely able to look at each other. In these mother-daughter sessions, Stacey was invited to explain how her experience of sexual abuse made her highly sensitive to Margaret's use of words like '*bitch*' and '*knacker*' to describe Stacey, when mother and daughter were involved in heated conflicts. The words that Margaret and Patrick used also made Stacey feel as if they were referring to the fact that she had participated in abusive sex. Stacey also explained to her mother that when others called her a '*slut*' or a '*tramp*', she felt as if they had x-ray eyes and could see into her past and know that she had been sexually abused. When Stacey explained her sensitivity to Margaret's language in this way, Margaret was able to empathise with the distress her language caused Stacey and she became committed to refraining from calling her daughter derogatory names.

In the mother-daughter sessions Stacey and Margaret were also invited to do simple joint tasks that would allow them to have the experience of co-operating with each other. The mother-daughter sessions were effective in preventing family conflict from escalating, particularly over the Christmas period, often a stressful time for families challenged by conflict.

11.4. Closing phase

During the disengagement phase, therapeutic progress was reviewed. The family and counselling team acknowledged that this family was highly committed to the counselling process. In the eighteen months of counselling there was only one cancelled appointment. The family had flagged bullying, school refusal and self-harm as reasons for referral and tested out the team's capacity to deal with complex family issues in the first few sessions, before letting the team know the core issue was helping them cope with the impact of child sexual abuse on the family. The child sexual abuse heighted the level of conflict within the family, which already had a very conflictual style. The family thought that the counselling process had prevented the escalation of episodes of family conflict into violence, and that episodes of conflict probably would have been more frequent and intense if the family had not engaged in counselling. Thus, the counselling process prevented the family's difficulties from getting worse.

In the joint family session which occurred after the mother-daughter sessions, the mother and daughter acknowledged that their relationship was still a stormy one, and would continue to be so into the future. In this joint session the old habitual patterns of family conflict re-emerged. However, there was also some evidence of Margaret and Patrick taking a more protective and supportive stance towards their daughter. In fact they facilitated Stacey in changing schools, which helped her put her 'bad reputation' behind her.

CHAPTER 12

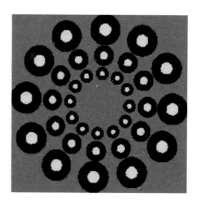

Working with school expulsion, cannabis use, ADHD and family conflict issues

This case illustrates the counselling process with a seventeen year old adolescent girl with attention deficit hyperactivity disorder (ADHD) who was using cannabis to control her symptoms of inattention and over activity. She had been expelled from school for cannabis use and stealing. She also had a long history of school problems associated with ADHD. In addition there was significant conflict between the girl and both her father and mother and her older siblings. At the time of referral the girl had dropped out of treatment with the child and adolescent mental health service (CAMHS), and had stopped taking stimulant therapy which had been prescribed for her ADHD. Her parents however, continued to link in with the CAMHS psychiatrist.

The referral to Teen Counselling came from CAMHS. The parents had complained about their daughter's anger and the psychiatrist hoped that the Teen Counselling model of support for the family would be helpful. The team negotiated with the CAMHS psychiatrist to ensure clarity around working co-operatively with them and to establish appropriate boundaries and limits of confidentiality. It was noted that a review of Teen Counselling's commitment in cases, such as those referred from CAMHS, is indicated at any stage after counselling has commenced if the change in presentation is such that the case would probably not have been accepted by the service.

The case shows how parallel counselling sessions for the girl and her parents were used to help the girl disclose her worsening depression and risk of self-harm. The case also shows how work with the parents, softened their harsh critical attitude towards the girl and helped them to understand her need for their support as she made the transition from adolescence to adulthood. The case indicates that counselling was successful in reducing the risk of self-harm and improving family relationships. However, counselling did not help the adolescent achieve regular school attendance or reduce her cannabis use.

12.1. Counselling team and duration

Margaret and Noreen were the counselling team in this case. Margaret worked with the daughter, Gina, and Noreen worked with the parents, Sally and Shay. The counselling spanned about 11 months. There were 10 sessions with the adolescent, 6 sessions with the mother, 3 sessions with both parents, an initial joint session with mother and daughter and three later joint sessions with both parents and their daughter.

12.2. The engagement phase

Referral

Gina, aged seventeen years, was referred for support with anger management. She was suspended from school for using cannabis. At school Gina had learning difficulties, was overactive, aggressive and had been caught stealing from classmates. She had attended her local CAMHS and received a diagnosis of Attention Deficit Hyperactivity Disorder (ADHD). In addition there was significant conflict between Gina and both her father, Shay, and her mother, Sally. Gina was working for a neighbour while out of school. Conflict between Gina and her parents arose because the neighbour was giving the money she earned at work to Gina's mother, who retained it for her, but would not let her have access to it. She did this to prevent Gina from buying cannabis. In the first session Gina said she wanted her father to stop fighting with her, and her mother said she wanted Gina to stop using cannabis and to return to school.

First session

The first appointment was attended by Gina and her mother, Sally. The father, Shay, was invited, but he didn't attend.

Orientation to the counselling process

The counselling team began by introducing themselves, explaining the duration and format of the interview, and the limits of confidentiality. Margaret said that the interview would be about an hour and a half in duration, that she would conduct the interview and that Noreen would take notes. She mentioned that there would be a break of a few minutes towards the end so that the team could reflect on the information they received from the family, and Gina and Sally could reflect on whether they wanted to attend further appointments. (Teen Counselling is a voluntary service, so different from the statutory service that Gina was referred from). The team also explained that if the family wanted to have further counselling sessions, one counsellor would work with Gina and the other would work with Sally and Shay. They were told that the contents of individual sessions would be confidential, so things that Gina said would not be discussed with her parents, and things Sally and Shay talked about would not be mentioned to their daughter. However the team, Margaret and Noreen, noted that they would talk together about progress both parents and daughter were making and jointly explore ways that information from the parallel sessions with parents and daughter could be used to help the family work out their problems. It was also explained that no other agency would be informed about the details of the counselling, unless there was a risk of someone hurting themselves or others, or information that someone had been abused in the past.

This introduction was done in a friendly, informal caring way to put Gina and Sally at their ease and to give them time to settle in. Finally, Margaret mentioned that first Gina, and then Sally, would be given an opportunity to present their separate accounts of their main concerns in this, the first session. The aim of this approach, it was explained, was to get a clear understanding of their different viewpoints: not to find out who was right and who was wrong.

Engaging the adolescent

Margaret began by asking Gina about her main concerns and the difficulties that had led her to come to counselling. (Whilst this is the Teen Counselling protocol, Margaret was also aware that it was a '*leap of faith*' for Gina to present herself at '*yet another service*'). Margaret addressed her initial questions to Gina to show her mother that the counsellors considered that young people should be listened to and respected so that their point of view could be understood. Margaret also wanted to let Sally know that the counsellor's job was not to side with the parent against the young person. Rather it is to be impartial and listen to each person's perspective with curiosity, empathy and respect.

Pacing the interview to suit ADHD limitations Gina did her best to co-operate with the interview. She mentioned her school-based difficulties, her suspension from school, her regular use of cannabis to try to relax and control her hyperactivity, and her conflict with her parents. Gina responded to Margaret's questions hesitantly. She gave short answers and had difficulty answering long questions. It became clear that by the time the end of a multiclausal question was reached, she had forgotten the beginning. Margaret took account of this significant attention problem by using very short questions. She also limited the amount of time she spent talking with Gina in the first session to the first 15 or 20 minutes. After this period of time Gina had significant problems maintaining attention and controlling her agitation and activity level.

Attunement to non-verbal signals Margaret attuned her responses to Gina, both by listening carefully to what she said, and by taking account of her non-verbal behaviour. For example, she monitored the direction of her gaze, and her level of activity and agitation to let her know if Gina's attention was wandering or if she was becoming distressed.

Alliance building with the adolescent through empathy Margaret acknowledged the difficulties that Gina was having with attention, impulsivity and over activity. She empathised with the fact that she found it distressing when her impulsive behaviour got her into trouble with school teachers, and when her attention problems prevented her from doing well at school work.

Acknowledging different perspectives on cannabis use Gina and her mother held very different views about her cannabis use. Sally thought that Gina was a relatively infrequent cannabis user. In contrast, Gina admitted that she used cannabis very frequently. Gina saw many benefits to cannabis use, particularly helping her to stay calm and control her hyperactivity. In contrast, Sally saw no benefits to Gina using cannabis. Gina saw reducing her cannabis use as very challenging. Sally, on the other hand, believed that if she controlled how Gina spent her time by making her work with her neighbour, and controlled the amount of money she had, then she could control her use of cannabis. Sally believed that Gina could stop using cannabis abruptly without difficulty. Gina, in contrast believed that she had become dependent on cannabis and could not stop using it. When Gina talked about her regular use of cannabis, Margaret empathised with Gina's perception of the benefits of cannabis use, in terms of controlling her hyperactivity and calming her down, but balanced this with a consideration of the downside of cannabis use. Sally was helped to listen actively and attentively to this part of the interview. She had not previously considered the self-medicating function of Gina's drug use. While Margaret empathised with Gina's position on the benefits of using cannabis, she also empathised with Sally's position in worrying about Gina's well-being and the negative effect of cannabis use. She empathised with Sally's expression of this worry and concern by trying to control how Gina spent her time and how much money she had. Thus there was an attempt to allow both mother and daughter's positions to be heard and understood.

Addressing family conflict On the issue of family conflict, Gina was adamant that she did not want her father involved in the counselling process. Margaret said that the policy of the service was for both parents to be involved, so that each person's viewpoint could be heard. She added that the involvement of both parents created an open-ness among family members. However, she made it clear that she respected the fact that Gina was uncomfortable about her father's attendance, and did not expect Gina to fit in with her father's position, only to listen to it. This may have given Gina a sense that the team would help her to reduce conflict between herself and Shay.

Reflections on alliance building with the adolescent Gina engaged well with Margaret. In the first part of the intake interview, Gina said that she had been to a number of different services in the past for her attention and over activity problems and for her drug use. However, she had dropped out of all of these services after a brief period, because they did not help her or because she did not like the staff at the services. She had attended her family doctor, a school counsellor and a child and adolescent mental health team. She had been prescribed methylphenidate (Ritalin) by the psychiatrist at the community mental health team, but now refused to see her or to take her medication. Margaret guessed that Gina engaged well with her because she gave her the opportunity to speak first in the interview, facilitated communication between herself and her mother, listened respectfully to her, empathised with her attention, impulsivity, drug use and family problems, and did not side with her parents against her.

Engaging the mother in the first session

When Gina's turn at outlining her concerns and difficulties was concluded, Margaret invited Sally to take a turn and give her account of the situation. In contrast to Gina who spoke hesitantly, Sally spoke fluently and forcefully. She spoke with anger and frustration in her voice, and conveyed by both what she said, and the way she that she said it, that she had been finding parenting Gina very challenging.

Alliance building with the parent through empathy Margaret allowed Sally to speak without interruption, giving her space to set out her main concerns about Gina, and the difficulties as she saw them. When she concluded her first fluent account of the situation, Margaret summarised Sally's concerns about Gina's ADHD, her school problems, cannabis use, stealing and involvement in conflicts with herself and Shay. She empathised with the challenges Sally had experienced in parenting an adolescent with ADHD and all of the problems that had arisen from that. She also invited Sally to explore the main things she wanted to get from the counselling process. Sally vacillated between saying that she wanted Gina to return to school and then recognising that Gina's ADHD and the limited resources of the school would make it difficult for Gina to benefit from school attendance. Margaret empathised with this dilemma. This process of giving Sally a '*long turn*' to put forward her viewpoint, just as Gina had been given a similar turn first, allowed Sally to feel understood, and to know that Margaret was not '*taking sides*' with Gina against her.

Creating parental hope by engaging the adolescent Sally said that she had become gradually more despondent when Gina had failed to co-operate with the school's attempts to help her, and then failed to engage with the CAMHS team. Sally seemed pleasantly surprised that Gina had engaged so well with Margaret during the first part of the interview. This seemed to give her hope and help her to engage with the team also.

Exploring parental attitudes about control, responsibility and adolescent autonomy Sally's frustration about being unable to control Gina's cannabis use led her to control Gina's access to money. Although Gina was working for her neighbour five days a week, Sally was keeping the money she earned from her, so that she would not use it to buy cannabis. Margaret engaged Sally in a discussion about how much control is appropriate in adolescence. That is, there was a consideration of what constitutes parental over-control and under-control in rearing a teenager. Margaret explored Sally's view on what she believed was an appropriate level of parental control for a pre-adolescent and an adolescent. Margaret proposed that one of the tasks of adolescence is learning money management and learning to make wise choices about how to spend money. She suggested that Sally's well-intentioned attempt to have total control over the amount of money that Gina had, and how she used it, was inadvertently preventing her from learning this important developmental task. There was also an exploration of the household jobs or chores and responsibilities that Sally and Shay expected Gina to do. Gina had almost no domestic responsibilities, because her parents did not see her as capable or reliable. The negotiation of age appropriate domestic responsibilities for Gina was identified as a possible counselling goal.

Facilitating adolescent-parent communication   Margaret facilitated communication between Sally and her daughter. She helped Sally carefully listen to, and hear, Gina's point of view on living with ADHD, self-medicating with cannabis, school attendance and other issues. This was challenging for Sally, who was so frustrated with Gina's ADHD, school difficulties, and drug use that she had given up listening to her. She had developed a style of talking '*at*' her daughter rather than trying to understand her. Margaret empathised with both the mother's frustration with her daughter, and with Gina's distress about not being heard or understood by her mother. This approach helped both Sally and Gina develop trust in Margaret and Noreen. Enhancing communication between mother and daughter was identified as a focus for future counselling.

Conclusion of the first session

After about an hour Margaret suggested that they take a break, so that the team and the family could reflect on the interview and how to proceed after the first session. When the meeting was reconvened, Margaret said that she appreciated the severity of the problems that had brought them to counselling. She said she understood that Gina was distressed by coping with her attention and impulsivity problems, her school difficulties, the conflict she was having with her father and the difficulties she had communicating with her mother. Margaret also said she understood that Sally was frustrated by the difficulties she and Shay were having in helping Gina control or stop her cannabis use, and in helping her to fit in at school. Helping Gina, Sally and Shay find a way to work out these problems, so that Gina could make the transition to adulthood was proposed as the overall goal of counselling, if this was what Gina and Sally wanted. Both mother and daughter said that they wanted to come back for further sessions. Margaret said that in future sessions, she would work with Gina, and concurrently Noreen would work with Sally and Shay, and that when some progress had been made in these meetings, there would be some joint family sessions to check how everybody was progressing. Sally and Gina agreed to this arrangement and the session concluded with the dates of the next appointments being offered.

12.3. The middle phase

Further sessions with the adolescent

Gina attended ten individual sessions. She took responsibility for getting to and from these appointments. She made it clear, early on, that conflict with her father was too intense for her to be comfortable in joint family sessions, so these were postponed until the team judged that sufficient progress had been made for her to be comfortable with them.

Separating the problem (ADHD) from the person (Gina) There were a number of issues covered in the individual sessions. One of the most pressing issues was coping with having a very limited attention span, and severe difficulty regulating impulsivity and over activity. Gina found living with these aspects of ADHD very challenging, especially when she was in school. She found sitting still in class, paying attention to her teachers and learning what was being taught very difficult. She found being criticised by teachers and mocked by peers for her failure to learn at the same rate as others extremely distressing. Margaret empathised with these difficulties, emphasising that Gina was a well-intentioned and well-motivated student, who was doing her very best to keep up with school work despite having a limited attention span and a constant uncomfortable feeling of being '*revved up*' that made it hard for her to sit still and do school work. Having Margaret empathise with her in this way about the challenges in her life was a new and positive experience for Gina. From her perspective, she thought her parents, teachers and peers viewed her as stupid, lazy, bad, or '*a messer*'. Over her years in school she had come to accept these self-descriptions and had very low self-esteem and self-confidence. She found it supportive to be seen by Margaret as a good person, trying her best to cope with difficult limitations imposed on her by ADHD. This process of separating the problem from the person, separating the ADHD from Gina's self or identity, was a consistent theme that Margaret introduced throughout the individual sessions, to help raise Gina's self-esteem. She helped her to move from seeing herself as a '*bad person*' to seeing herself a '*good person coping with ADHD*'. During this work, Margaret complimented Gina when she coped well or reported that she had coped well in particular situations. Gina responded to these compliments with suspicion. She said she thought Margaret did not mean the compliments, because at home and school no one ever complimented her. It was challenging for Margaret to offer compliments to Gina in emotionally congruent ways so that Gina could accept them as genuine, rather than discount them as being insincere.

Facilitating decision making about pros and cons of drug use Cannabis use was a second recurring theme in the individual sessions with Gina. Gina was distressed that she had become dependent on cannabis. She explained that this had occurred gradually and without her awareness. Initially she found that when she smoked cannabis it made her feel relaxed and mellow. She found she felt less *'revved up'*, uncomfortable and angry when she was stoned. Consequently, she behaved less aggressively, got into fewer fights, and got on better with peers when she had smoked cannabis and was a bit *'stoned'*. However, she had progressed from smoking grass or weed to smoking hash, and from smoking at the weekends to smoking almost every day. She believed her parents didn't appreciate how dependent she had become on cannabis, and how distressing this was for her. She was scared that her dependency on cannabis was making her more, rather than less aggressive. When she had no access to cannabis, she felt intolerably uncomfortable, angry and *'revved up'*. She wanted to return to occasional use and to use weed instead of hash. Margaret empathised with Gina's need to use cannabis to self-medicate and her distress at her drug dependency. She also supported her plan to reduce and control her drug use. She pointed out the various health risks that go with chronic frequent cannabis use. However, this was an area where considerable sensitivity was required. On the one hand, if Margaret confronted Gina too intensely about the negative effects of cannabis and the necessity of abstinence, there was a risk that this would undermine the therapeutic alliance and Gina would disengage from therapy. On the other hand, there was the risk that if Margaret empathised with the benefits to Gina of cannabis use without pointing out the associated health risks, that she would be supporting her continued drug use. Margaret addressed this dilemma by helping Gina consider the risks and benefits of continued drug use and reducing or stopping drug use, and then supporting her in engaging with the decision making process.

Risk management and suicidality A further theme which emerged in the third individual session was low mood and suicidality. Gina told Margaret that her distress concerning her attention problems and impulsivity, her sense of failure at school, her guilt for stealing from others in school to get money to buy cannabis, and her low self-confidence and self-worth had gradually led to her having very low mood, and to feeling hopeless. She had been through an episode where she planned to hang herself, although she had not made an actual attempt. She had gone so far as to get a rope and learn to make a noose. She also told Margaret that this was the first time she had ever talked about her suicidality to anyone. The alliance she formed with Margaret was strong and secure enough for her to feel safe to talk about these very painful issues. She valued Margaret's willingness to talk about what she called the '*dark stuff*': her plan to hang herself, her feelings of hopelessness and helplessness, and her low mood. Margaret explained to Gina that it was important for her parents to know that she felt so low and that she had previously planned to harm herself, so that they would understand the severity of her current difficulties and so that they could help to protect her until she had worked out her problems and felt more in control of her life. After some discussion about Gina's preferred way of doing this, it was agreed that Margaret would brief Noreen and she would then explain the situation to Sally and Shay. Margaret also talked to Gina about the need to speak to the psychiatrist who had referred Gina to Teen Counselling, Dr. Maloney, to discuss an assessment of her low mood and to ensure optimum support for Gina regarding her risk of self-harm.

Interagency working: **contacting the psychiatrist** After Gina told Margaret about her low mood and her episode of suicidal intent Margaret and Noreen had a meeting with Dr. Maloney, the child and adolescent psychiatrist. It is the policy at Teen Counselling for adolescents at high risk of self-harm to be regularly monitored by a psychiatrist. This would usually be managed internally with the support of the consultant psychiatrist who attends the Teen Counselling centres as needed. However, as Gina was already a patient of Dr. Maloney, Margaret and Noreen discussed with her the most useful way to collaborate in working with Gina's family to manage Gina's risk of self-harm and address the other problems they had. Dr. Maloney said that she viewed Gina's core problem as ADHD, and her other behavioural and emotional problems as secondary reactions to this main difficulty. She had tried to treat Gina's ADHD with methylphenidate (Ritalin). However, treating her had been very challenging. She often missed appointments, rarely took her medication, and found it difficult to engage with the child and adolescent mental health team. Dr. Maloney said that she would continue to try to engage with Gina and her parents, explore ways of helping Gina take her medication, and monitor her low mood and risk of self-harm. Margaret and Noreen said that if the family agreed to the arrangement they would concurrently engage in counselling with Gina and her parents. Gina refused to attend appointments at CAMHS and co-operate with this arrangement. A compromise was reached in which Sally and Shay attended appointments with Dr. Maloney and kept her informed of Gina's mood and behaviour. Along with regular telephone contact with Margaret, Dr. Maloney used this information to monitor Gina's risk of self-harm. This level of monitoring was considered sufficient for Margaret and Noreen to continue counselling with Gina and her parents.

Further sessions with the adolescent, Gina

Two key themes emerged in further work with Gina. First, re-establishing the therapeutic alliance after the three-week gap between sessions which occurred while the team arranged psychiatric support; and second, identifying dealing with Gina's low motivation and the prevention of deterioration as a focus for work with her.

Dealing with low motivation and preventing deterioration   There was a period of about three weeks when Gina did not attend regular weekly appointments with Margaret. This was because Gina refused to see Dr. Maloney, the child and adolescent psychiatrist, and the policy at Teen Counselling requires an adolescent at high risk of self-harm to be medically assessed by a psychiatrist. When an arrangement was reached that Gina's risk level could be monitored through her parents' attendance with the psychiatrist, and Margaret's telephone contact, Margaret resumed regular sessions with Gina. In the first session after the three week gap, Margaret explained the importance of the service policy with regard to keeping young people safe even though she knew that Gina was not impressed by it.

Gina was invited to identify what she had been finding useful about the sessions before the break occurred. She vacillated between acknowledging that they offered her a chance to talk about life difficulties in a way that she had not done before, and saying she didn't care because they were of no value to her. In a subsequent session she was invited to explore therapeutic goals, such as taking responsibility for managing her ADHD symptoms by visiting Dr. Maloney, considering taking Ritalin, and reducing her use of cannabis. Gina expressed little motivation to commit to these types of goals. Margaret asked her to consider how counselling could be of value to her, if at the moment, she had little motivation to make positive changes in her life. She found this line of enquiry, very challenging and confronting. However, she did not say so in the session with Margaret. Rather, her mother, Sally, said to Noreen in her next session that Gina had come home from this session in a very angry mood. In view of Gina's low readiness for change in the areas of ADHD management and substance misuse, the main goal in this case was preventing self-harm and deterioration until Gina's readiness to change increased.

Repairing a rupture in the therapeutic alliance after a long gap between sessions
Gina was ambivalent about attending sessions with Margaret after she had let her know about the service's policy on medical monitoring of low mood and suicidal risk. Also the

lapse of three weeks since her previous appointment had reduced the strength of the therapeutic alliance. However, she eventually re-engaged with Margaret. Reflecting on the fact that Gina did re-engage with her, Margaret believed the key aspects of Gina's work with her that supported this repair of the rupture in the therapeutic alliance were the fact that she expressed genuine care for her, acknowledged the challenges she faced in her life, acknowledged the severity of her dependence on cannabis and her distress about this, and the fact that she did not push her too rapidly towards having a joint family session with her father and mother.

Work with the parents

In Noreen's work with the parents, there were five main themes. These were (1) risk monitoring, (2) managing ADHD, (3) school issues, (4) control and autonomy and (5) focusing on positive potential.

Risk monitoring Sally and Shay provided Noreen with regular information on Gina's mood and behaviour, so she could have their perspective on Gina's risk of self-harm. Their reports indicated that she did not show signs of self-harm, although her mood fluctuated a great deal. Sally and Shay also met regularly with Dr. Maloney the psychiatrist and kept her briefed on Gina's mood and behaviour, so she could monitor her risk of self-harm.

Managing ADHD Sally and Shay also kept Noreen informed about Gina's willingness to manage her ADHD in the way Dr. Maloney recommended. Over the course of 11 months there was little change in this. She adamantly refused to attend the psychiatrist or to consider taking Ritalin (or other medications such as amoxetine or clonadine).

School issues Noreen invited Shay and Sally to consider the pros and cons of Gina returning to her old school or finding some alternative educational placement. Arising from these discussions and the school staff's willingness to give Gina another chance, she returned to school. However, there was conflict between Gina and her teachers. Eventually she stopped attending school and refused to return. Shay was somewhat open to the idea of exploring other educational placements, but Sally was ambivalent about this because such placements would reduce the amount of supervision and control they had over Gina. Sally preferred Gina to remain working with the neighbour. This was because she knew where she was and she could control the amount of money she received, because the neighbour would pass Gina's earnings to her. Sally worried that Gina would use her money to buy cannabis or to save for a car. Sally was concerned at the risk posed by Gina's continued drug use or her driving a car.

Control and autonomy Noreen invited Sally and Shay to consider giving Gina some degree of control over the amount of money she received. They responded by giving her all of her wages from work. She spent all of the money on cannabis. Sally and Shay, pointed out to Noreen that this was evidence that they could not trust Gina to manage her money. Noreen invited Sally and Shay to move away from this '*all or nothing*' approach to helping Gina learn how to manage her money, and to negotiate with Gina about having control over a portion of her money each week. This issue was taken up again in the joint family session.

Focusing on positive potential Sally and Shay took a strongly negative view of Gina. They focused predominantly on her limitations, her school problems, drug use, impulsivity and so forth. In a series of sessions, Noreen helped Sally and Shay shift their focus to their daughter's positive attributes and potential. Noreen proposed that for Gina to be able to believe that she could overcome her limitations, she would first need to see that her parents believed she could do so. To help the parents make this switch from focusing on Gina's limitations to focusing on her strengths, it was important that Noreen believed that Gina had the potential to make positive changes in her life. In this sense she was '*holding the hope*' for both the parents and the daughter in this case. For those periods when the parents were able to maintain a more positive view of Gina, their behaviour towards her was more supportive. In response she was less oppositional and more co-operative at home. However, these periods were relatively brief, as the parents easily fell back into focusing on Gina's negative characteristics.

Noreen used a variety of techniques to help the parents articulate their daughter's strengths and positive potential. For example, she invited Sally and Shay to say what they thought Gina would need to help her to be able to pay attention more, to return to school, to be better at money management, to be less impulsive, to use less cannabis or to have a car in the future. The parents said that she would need to accept help. In response Noreen said that by attending counselling Gina was acknowledging that she did have problems such as cannabis dependency, and was trying to find a way to address this through counselling. This acknowledgment of her limitations and her attempt to address her problems in counselling were framed as strengths.

The parents, particularly Sally, found it very difficult to maintain a focus on Gina's positive potential. She repeatedly slipped back into focusing on her negative behaviour and attributes. Sally's anxiety underpinned this process of returning to a focus on Gina's negative characteristics. She was genuinely worried that her drug use, low mood and suicidality, educational underachievement and conflict with her and Shay would persist indefinitely. She worried that Gina would have a difficult and problematic life. She anticipated that she would be at continual risk of harm. She may also have felt guilty that she was responsible for this and yet powerless to do anything to change it. Noreen contained Sally's anxiety by empathising with her worries and helping her to return her focus to Gina's strengths. When Sally could hold an appreciation of her daughter's strengths in mind, this reduced her anxiety about her limitations somewhat.

Joint family session

A joint family session was convened to discuss cannabis use within the family in an open and constructive way. The session was scheduled because it came to light that Shay was using cannabis regularly. Gina had stolen cannabis from her father's stash. On one occasion Gina stole all of Shay's cannabis to deal to others to make some money. However, Shay had not challenged Gina about this. The joint family session was scheduled because of this revelation that Shay was using cannabis and also because of Gina's willingness to take part, and the parents increasing acknowledgement of Gina's positive attributes as well as her problems. All of these factors led Noreen and Margaret to judge that time was right to conduct a joint family session, and that such a session would be helpful rather than counterproductive. Gina, who had previously been reluctant to attend a joint session with Shay agreed to come to the session when she understood that her father would be open about his cannabis use also. In prior conversation with Noreen, Shay agreed that he would talk about his cannabis use with Gina. Three main issues were addressed in the session (1) cannabis use within the family, (2) Gina's positive potential and (3) negotiation of greater autonomy.

Cannabis use within the family Noreen and Margaret invited Shay to talk about his cannabis use within the session. Sally knew that Shay had smoked cannabis in the past, but was surprised to hear that he still did so. She confronted Shay and questioned the validity of bringing Gina for counselling for cannabis use, when Shay was now admitting to on-going use of cannabis himself. Shay said that he was using the drug in a controlled way and that it did not affect his work performance or relationships. However, he did not approve of Gina using cannabis because it was having a negative impact on the development of her adolescent brain, and negatively affecting her relationships at home and school. The open discussion about Shay's cannabis use had the effect of reducing conflict between father and daughter, but increasing conflict within the couple. However, Shay and Sally did not acknowledge the degree of dependence on cannabis that Gina was experiencing, and her wish to have support in overcoming it. They took the view that if she took Ritalin prescribed by the psychiatrist to deal with her attention and over activity problems she would not need cannabis.

It seemed to Margaret that Gina's initial reluctance to attend conjoint sessions with her father arose from her frustration with her father's hypocrisy about cannabis use. She may also have feared that it would create a forum where Shay could respond to Gina's theft of his stash of cannabis.

Gina's positive potential Gina's positive potential was a second important theme within the joint family session. Noreen and Margaret invited the parents to comment on their daughter's positive characteristics. They said that the neighbour was very impressed with Gina's performance at work. The neighbour also mentioned that Gina seemed to be able to control her attention and impulsivity problems at work and had been doing a very good job.

Negotiation of greater autonomy In the joint session Noreen and Margaret facilitated a negotiation between Gina and her parents about two key issues: money and holidays. Arising from this, Gina was given control of some of the money she earned working with the neighbour. She was also given permission to go on holidays to Austria with her friends. In a subsequent session Shay and Sally reported that Gina managed the holiday in a responsible way and they were pleased with that.

Teamwork

Throughout the middle phase of this case, Noreen and Margaret met regularly to discuss progress being made by Gina and her parents in their parallel counselling sessions. Key themes in these team discussions were parental monitoring of Gina's low mood and risk of self-harm, arranging for a reduction in the level of control Sally was exerting over Gina, Shay's use of cannabis and how best to arrange and manage the joint family session focusing on substance misuse within the family.

12.4. Closing phase

It became necessary to conclude the counselling process because the company Shay worked for relocated him to another town over 100 miles from the counselling centre. Disengagement spanned two family sessions during which progress made over the course of the counselling process was reviewed, and the ways the family had used counselling to address their difficulties were discussed. There was also some discussion of future plans.

Problems that did not improve In reviewing progress the family made over the course of the 11 months of counselling, there was agreement that the process had no significant impact on Gina's school attendance or cannabis use.

Benefits of counselling However, Shay, Sally and Gina agreed that the counselling process had some demonstrable benefits for the family. There was an improvement in family relationships. The overall level of conflict within the family decreased. The degree of parental criticism of Gina decreased and the parents focused more on their daughter's positive potential. The parents, particularly Sally, became less anxious about her daughter, relaxed the very tight level of control she had been exercising over how Gina spent her time and her access to money. This involved the parents using negotiation skills. Gina became more aware of her need to take responsibility for her ADHD into the future and to be proactive in finding a job. The counselling process prevented an escalation of the daughter's risk of self-harm, and may have prevented Gina's suicide. All of these benefits helped Gina with the developmental task of making the transition to adulthood.

The future Gina was pleased to be moving and looked on it as a fresh start. She had written to some of the supermarkets near where she would be living to see if she could get work as a cashier, similar to the work she had done for her neighbour, and had been invited to two interviews. She was sorry to be leaving her old job, but welcomed the adventure of starting somewhere new. Shay and Sally had mixed feelings about moving to a new town. Shay was pleased that the new job he was due to start would involve a significant promotion and salary increase. However, Shay and Sally were sorry to be leaving the area where they had lived for the previous twenty years. They would be leaving close friends and family behind. Shay and Sally recognised that moving homes would be stressful, but hoped that they would all use the calmer way of communicating they had developed during counselling to talk to each other about managing the many challenges that they would face in setting up their new home. Noreen and Margaret offered to refer Gina to a mental health service in her new town, with whom she could link up when she arrived there. Gina was now 18 and so eligible for referral to an adult service. The primary concern was that Gina would have mental health professionals she could link up with, who would support her in managing her mood problems and risk of self-harm, as well as her cannabis dependency. There was a discussion with Gina, Shay and Sally about how to recognise if Gina's mood was dropping, her risk of self-harm was increasing and so the need for contact with mental health services was increasing.

A challenging but likeable family Noreen and Margaret found this a challenging family to work with. It was difficult to establish a regular schedule of appointments with both the daughter and the parents. The daughter's schedule of appointments was disrupted by her refusal to attend for medical monitoring of her mood and suicidality. The parents' schedule of appointments was sometimes interrupted by the father's work commitments or the mother's level of anxiety. Sally on occasion phoned to cancel an appointment at very short notice, and then a day later phoned in crisis. Having discussed the crisis with Noreen her anxiety would drop, and she would be reluctant to accept an immediate appointment, but would prefer to postpone it for a few days or a week. Sally felt she could not trouble Shay for support when crises occurred with Gina because he and Gina would become involved in escalating conflict and this would upset Gina more. Margaret and Noreen found that they were also a very likeable family to work with. They were very engaging, particularly Gina. Margaret saw her as a caring young woman, concerned about the future, yet very sad. Despite her lack of motivation to change her drug use and ADHD management, Margaret really liked working with her. Shay and Sally were also likeable. Shay was affable. Sally was very anxious initially, but over time relaxed and was more caring towards her daughter.

CHAPTER 13

Evaluation of Positive Systemic Practice

Evaluation is central to PSP. At Crosscare Teen Counselling, PSP is routinely evaluated by counsellors in the normal course of their clinical work. Each year Crosscare Teen Counselling publishes an annual report which includes a detailed service evaluation. As we are writing, the first controlled trial of PSP is nearing completion. In this chapter, procedures used for routine case evaluation will be described; key findings from a three-year service audit will be presented; and preliminary results from the controlled trial will be given.

13.1. Case Evaluation

Data are routinely collected using four sets of measures to evaluate the effectiveness of the therapeutic service offered in each case. These include:

- Intervention aims
- Client problem ratings
- Counsellor problem ratings
- Adolescent and family adjustment ratings.

Intervention Aims

During the first session with a family a mutual understanding of the presenting problems is reached and mutually agreed goals set. These are noted from the client's point of view. After the session the counselling team devise a set of intervention aims to help clients to achieve their goals. For example:

Johnny lives with his mother. His biological father ceased contact with him 5 years ago and his step-father has recently left the home. There is a great deal of conflict between Johnny and his mother. It has recently escalated to involve physical contact. Johnny is 15 years old and regularly will not get up to go to school. The family's goals identified in the first session were for mother and son to fight less and for Johnny to attend school more frequently. The counsellors decided on 3 intervention aims for Johnny to work towards in counselling and 3 for his mother to work towards to help achieve the family's goals.

The intervention aims for the mother were:

- To help the mother understand Johnny's anger and acknowledge that he needs nurturing despite his adult size and rejecting stance towards her
- To help the mother understand how Johnny's life experiences have contributed to his anti-authority stance and to work out strategies she can use to help him develop a more constructive stance towards authority
- To help the mother set limits in an assertive, non-provocative, consistent way.

The intervention aims for Johnny were:

- To help Johnny acknowledge and process the anger and sadness arising from the lack of contact he has had with his biological father
- To help Johnny acknowledge and process the anger and sadness arising from his step-father recently leaving the home, and the way this has compounded the impact of the absence of his biological father from his life for the past 5 years
- To help Johnny learn anger management techniques.

These intervention aims were reviewed when the case was closed.

Client Problem Ratings

Adolescent and parent problem ratings are made before and after counselling. Adolescents are invited to rate the extent of their difficulties at home, in school, with their friends and for them as individuals. Parents are invited to rate the severity of their teenager's difficulties and their own ability to manage these. Ratings are made on 5 point scales where low scores indicate better adjustment.

Counsellor Problem Ratings

After the first appointment with parents and adolescents, counsellors record the main presenting problems (for example, school non-attendance and family conflict) and underlying problems (for example, adjustment to father absence and limit setting problems). When closing cases, counsellors assess change in these presenting and underlying problems.

Adolescent and Family Adjustment Ratings

Counselling teams use the Children's Global Assessment Scale (CGAS[1]) and the Global Assessment of Relational Functioning scale (GARF[2]) to make ratings of adolescent and family adjustment after the first session and when closing each case. These ratings are made on 100-point scales where high scores indicate better adjustment.

Summary of routine clinical evaluation procedures

In summary there are four ways in which the effectiveness of PSP with teenagers and their parents is routinely evaluated in Teen Counselling:

- Intervention aims are noted by the counselling team at the start of counselling and reviewed on closing cases

- Teen and parent ratings of problems are made by clients before counselling and change assessed after counselling

- Presenting and underlying problems are noted by counsellors at the beginning and end of counselling and changes evaluated

- Assessments of adolescent and family functioning are made by counsellors before and after counselling using the CGAS and GARF.

In addition clients are invited to complete an anonymous service satisfaction questionnaire and leave this in the comment box in the waiting room.

13.2.   An Archival Study of PSP

Each Teen Counselling centre is audited three times a year and the results of these audits are summarised in a Centre Review Report. Combined data from all six centres are presented in Crosscare Teen Counselling Annual Reports. An archival study of PSP was conducted using annual report records for the three year period 2007-2009. The aim of the study was to describe the referral sources, demographic characteristics, clinical problems, patterns of counselling service usage and clinical outcomes for families who attended during this period.

Participants

For all new families that engaged in counselling between 2007 and 2009, data were extracted from the Crosscare Teen Counselling database. Seven hundred and fifty four cases were included in the study. Of these 317 (42%) continued in PSP from the year in which they started into the next year; 190 (25.20%) began and concluded PSP in the same year, 170 (22.55%) dropped out before completing 6 sessions, and 77 (10.21%) dropped out after 6 or more sessions.

Referral sources

When possible Crosscare Teen Counselling asks agencies that wish to refer families to encourage them to make self-referrals. This policy led to 486 (64.45%) referrals being made by mothers, 64 (8.48%) by fathers and 20 (2.65%) by teenagers themselves. The remaining 184 (24.40%) were referred directly by health, educational and other agencies. Of 570 self-referred families, 184 (32.23%) reported that the referral was suggested by health professionals such as the family doctor, 159 (27.89%) said that the referral was suggested by the adolescent's school, and 227 (39.82%) reported that other community services or former clients suggested the referral.

Demographic characteristics

The teenagers' ages ranged from 11-19 (M = 15.0, SD = 4.77) and there were almost equal numbers of boys (378) and girls (376). Families were predominantly white and of Irish nationality; only 19 (2.50%) families were non-Caucasian or non-nationals. With regard to family composition, 297 (39.38%) adolescents were living with both biological parents; 198 (26.25%) were living in single parent families; and 85 (11.27%) were living with a biological parent and a step-parent. The remainder were living with extended family (42, 5.57%); foster care (25, 3.31%); in residential care (26, 3.44%); or had other living arrangements (81, 10.74%). With regard to education and employment, 648 (85.94%) teenagers were attending secondary school; 77 (10.21%) were attending some other educational establishment or were employed; and 29 (3.84%) were not attending school or were unemployed.

Clinical problems

At intake 309 (40.98%) adolescents were assessed as having primarily emotional problems such as depression, anxiety or suicidality; for 240 (31.83%) teenagers behavioural problems such as disruptive behaviour, rule-breaking, aggression or drug use were the principal concern; and for 205 (27.18%) cases, family conflict or other difficulties were the main problems.

In all cases risky behaviours, including self-harm and drug use were assessed during the first session. With regard to self-harm, 138 (18.30%) adolescents reported suicidal ideation; 60 (7.95%) reported suicidal intent; and 116 (15.38%) had engaged in non-suicidal self-harm. With regard to substance use, 302 (40.05%) reported regular alcohol use; 151 (20.02%) smoked cigarettes; and 122 (16.18%) used street drugs, of which cannabis was the most common. Excessive alcohol use was reported for 118 (15.64%) fathers and 74 (9.81%) mothers.

Service usage

The time families spent on the waiting list ranged from 1 to 516 days with an average of 93 days *(SD = 55.21)* or about 3 months. The length of time they attended counselling ranged from 1 to 42 weeks with an average of 16.5 weeks (*SD* = 2.57) or about 4 months. The number of treatment hours per case, including family sessions and individual sessions with adolescents and parents, ranged from 2 to 63 hours. The average number of sessions attended by families was 15 (*SD* = 13.07). The number of conjoint family sessions ranged from 1 to 13, and the average number was 2 (*SD* = 1.18). The number of sessions held with adolescents ranged from 1 to 24 and on average adolescents attended 5 sessions (*SD* = 3.66). The number of sessions held with mothers ranged from 1 to 37 and on average mothers attended 4 sessions (*SD* = 2.53).

The number of sessions held with fathers ranged from 1 to 28 and on average fathers attended 3 sessions (*SD* = 2.07).

Table 13.1. Comparison of ratings of indices of problem severity made at intake and closure by parents, adolescents and counsellors

		Intake	Closure	t
Parents rating of problem severity	N	89	89	
	M	2.93	1.29	14.48**
	SD	0.88	0.85	
Parents rating of competency to deal with the problem	N	89	89	
	M	3.06	1.28	11.49**
	SD	1.30	1.08	
Adolescents' rating of problem severity in school	N	91	91	
	M	1.68	0.47	7.67**
	SD	1.43	0.79	
Adolescents' rating of problem severity at home	N	91	91	
	M	2.03	0.61	9.77**
	SD	1.32	0.72	
Adolescents' rating of problem severity with friends	N	91	91	
	M	1.07	0.25	5.95**
	SD	1.39	0.46	
Adolescents' rating of problem severity with self	N	91	91	
	M	1.97	0.51	8.94**
	SD	1.53	0.69	
Counsellors' Child Global Assessment Scale rating	N	191	191	
	M	57.97	69.521	13.59**
	SD	11.08	12.74	
Counsellors' Global Assessment of Relational Functioning rating	N	188	188	
	M	58.64	70.63	11.95**
	SD	15.03	14.43	

Note: N = Number of cases for which intake and closure data were available. M = mean. SD = Standard deviation. t = t test result. **p<.01.

Treatment outcomes

At Crosscare Teen Counselling, when families formally complete PSP, adolescents and parents use questionnaires to evaluate any improvement or deterioration in their problems since the beginning of treatment. Parents rate problem severity and their own coping ability, and adolescents rate improvements in school, home, relationships with friends and personal adjustment. All ratings are made on 5-point scales where low scores indicate improvement.

Of the 754 cases in the study, it was noted earlier that 190 families started and completed PSP in the same year. Of these 190 cases, 89 teenagers (47%) and 91 parents (48%) filled in questionnaires before and after counselling (see Appendix 3). From Table 13.1 it may be seen that in all areas rated by adolescents and parents before

{ 229 }

and after PSP, statistically significant ($p < .01$) improvements occurred. Clinical improvement rates were as follows. After PSP, out of 89 parents, ratings of greatly improved or improved were given by 81 (91.01%) for problem severity and 74 (83.14%) for coping ability. After PSP, out of 91 adolescents, ratings of greatly improved or improved were given by 70 (76.92%) for adjustment in school, 77 (84.61%) for adjustment at home, 44 (48.35%) for relationships with friends and 76 (83.52%) for personal adjustment.

For 191 teenagers at intake and closure, counsellors rated adolescent adjustment on the CGAS[1] and in 188 cases rated family adjustment on the GARF[2]. Both the CGAS and GARF are psychometrically robust 100-point rating scales on which high scores indicate better adjustment. From Table 13.1 it may be seen that CGAS and GARF ratings improved significantly ($p < .01$) from intake to closure, moving up on average by 12 points. CGAS ratings at intake and closure in round numbers were 58 and 70 respectively. GARF ratings at intake and closure were 59 and 71 respectively.

Figure 13.1 illustrates the significant (p<.01) reduction in adolescent and parent rated problem severity from intake to closing. Figure 13.2 shows the significant (p<.01) improvement in counsellor-rated adolescent and family adjustment on the CGAS and GARF from intake to closing. These figures are based on data in Table 13.1.

Figure 13.1. Reduction in adolescent and parent rated problem severity from intake to closing

Figure 13.2 Improvement in counsellor-rated adolescent and family adjustment on the CGAS and GARF from intake to closing

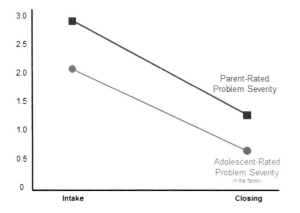

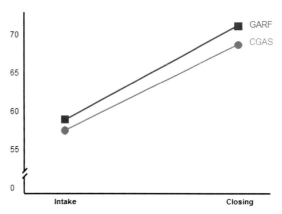

Conclusions from the archival study

This archival study showed that families of adolescents with significant behavioural and emotional problems, most of whom were self-referred, engaged with PSP for an average of 15 sessions over 4 months. For a subsample of cases where pre- and post-treatment data were available, there was evidence for statistically and clinically significant improvement on parent and adolescent self-rating scales, and on psychometrically robust therapist rating scales. The main limitations of this study were the amount of missing outcome data; the lack of psychometric data on adolescent and parent questionnaires used to rate improvement; and the lack of inter-rater reliability data for the CGAS and the GARF. With regard to missing data, there may have been a serious selection bias due to sample attrition as families *'dropped out'* of counselling, and it may be that only families who improved provided data at both intake and closure. Because of these limitations the outcome results required cautious interpretation. However, despite the limited validity of the results of this archival study, they did suggest that PSP was a promising approach to family therapy for adolescent emotional and behavioural problems and they provided the impetus for conducting a prospective controlled trial.

13.3.   Preliminary Results from a Controlled Trial of PSP

A controlled trial to evaluate the effectiveness of PSP was started in 2010 and at the time of writing is almost complete. Families of adolescents aged between 12 and 18, with clinically significant emotional and behavioural problems were invited into the trial if they scored above the clinical cut-off range of 16/17 on the total difficulties scale of the parent version of the Strengths and Difficulties Questionnaire (SDQ[3]). The SDQ is a reliable and valid index of adolescent emotional and behavioural problems. 122 families were recruited into the trial and 66 of these (54%) had completed all the assessment questionnaires required before a preliminary analysis of the results was conducted. There were 33 families in the PSP treatment group and 33 families in the waiting-list control group. Families in the treatment group were assessed before they started counselling (Time 1) and again 16 weeks later (Time 2) after they had received at least 9 sessions of counselling. Treatment group families were also followed up 6 months later (Time 3). Families in the Control group were assessed when they went onto the waiting list (Time 1) and before their first appointment (Time 2). One parent (usually the mother) completed the SDQ to assess their teenager's problems and the 28-item version of the

Systemic Clinical Outcome and Routine Evaluation (SCORE-28[4]) to assess family adjustment.

Figure 13.3. Clinical improvement rate for adolescents from families treated who engaged in PSP and those in a waiting list control group.

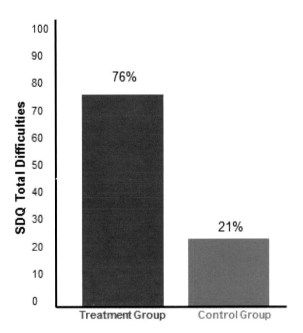

Clinical improvement rates

Figure 13.3 shows that clinical improvement occurred in 76% of families where adolescents and their parents engaged in PSP, compared with an improvement rate of 21% in the waiting-list control group. This difference was statistically significant (Chi Square = 19.65, p<.01). Families were classified as clinically improved if their scores on the total difficulties scale of the SDQ had fallen from above the clinical cut-off score of 17 at Time 1, to below 17 at Time 2. That is, in clinically improved cases parents rated their adolescents as no longer having clinically significant problems on the SDQ, 16 weeks after the start of the trial.

Improvement in average scores

Figures 13.4 and 13.5 show that average scores on the SDQ total difficulties scale and the SCORE-28 total family adjustment scale decreased significantly from Time 1 to 2 in the treatment group that received PSP, but not the waiting-list control group. Further analyses of the treatment group data found that the improvements shown in adolescent problems and family adjustment after 9 counselling sessions over 16 weeks were still evident 6 months later.

Figure 13.4. Mean scores of the PSP treatment group and the waiting-list control group on the SDQ Total Difficulties Scale at Times 1, 2 and 3.

Figure 13. 5. Mean scores of the PSP treatment group and the waiting-list control group on the SCORE-28 Total Family Adjustment Scale at Times 1, 2 and 3.

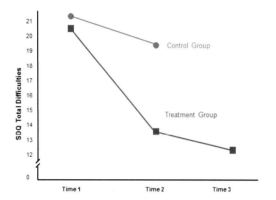

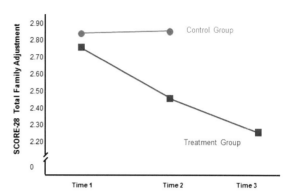

Preliminary conclusions from the controlled trial

The preliminary results from this trial, based on data from 66 cases, support the effectiveness of PSP. In 3 out of 4 cases that completed at least 9 sessions of PSP over 16 weeks, adolescents showed clinical improvement on the SDQ (compared with 1 in 5 in the control group). Improvement in family functioning occurred in parallel to improvement in adolescent emotional and behavioural problems. Improvement in emotional and behavioural problems and family adjustment continued during the 6 month follow-up period.

The full results, analyses and conclusions of this trial will be available in summer 2013.

SUMMARY

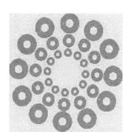

Evaluation is central to PSP. Data are routinely collected using four sets of measures to evaluate the effectiveness of the therapeutic service received by each family. These include:

- Intervention aims
- Client problem ratings
- Counsellor problem ratings
- Adolescent and family adjustment ratings.

Each year Crosscare Teen Counselling publishes an annual report which includes a detailed service evaluation. An archival study of annual report data for the period 2007-2009 showed that families of adolescents with significant behavioural and emotional problems, most of whom were self-referred, engaged with PSP for an average of 15 sessions over 4 months. For a subsample of families where pre- and post-treatment data were available, there was evidence for statistically and clinically significant improvement on parent and adolescent self-rating scales and on psychometrically robust therapist rating scales.

Preliminary results from a controlled trial indicate that in 3 out of 4 cases where at least 9 sessions of PSP over 16 weeks were completed, adolescents showed clinical improvement (compared with 1 in 5 controls). Improvement in family functioning occurred in parallel to improvement in adolescent emotional and behavioural problems and this improvement was maintained at 6 months follow-up.

Taken together, evidence from the archival study and controlled trial support the effectiveness of PSP as a clinically useful intervention for treating adolescent emotional and behavioural problems.

REFERENCES

Chapter 1

1. Shaffer, D., Gould, M., Brasic, J., Ambrosini, P., Fisher, P., Bird, H. & Aluwahlia, S. (1983). A children's global assessment scale (CGAS). *Archives of General Psychiatry*, 40 (1), 1228-1231.

2. Yingling, L. C., Miller, W. E., McDonald, A. L., & Galewaler, S. T. (1998). *GARF assessment sourcebook: Using the DSM-IV global assessment of relational functioning.* New York: Brunner/Mazel.

Chapter 2

1. These principles hold much in common with principles on which other evidence-based approaches to systemic practice are based such as: Henggeler, S., Schoenwald, S., Bordin, C., Rowland, M. & Cunningham, P. (2009). *Multisystemic therapy for Antisocial Behaviour in Children and Adolescents* (Second Edition). New York: Guilford; Liddle, H. (2010). *Multidimensional family therapy for adolescent drug abuse and delinquency.* New York: Guilford; Lock, J., LeGrange, D., Agras, W., & Dare, C. (2001). *Treatment manual for anorexia nervosa. A family based approach.* New York: Guilford; Sexton, T. (2010). *Functional family therapy in clinical practice: An evidence-based treatment model for working with troubled adolescents.* New York: Routledge; Szapocznik, J., Hervis, O. & Schwartz, S. (2002). *Brief strategic family therapy for adolescent drug abuse.* Rockville, MD: National Institute for Drug Abuse.

2. Carr, A. (2004). *Positive psychology.* London: Routledge; Lopez, S. & Snyder, C. (2009). *Handbook of positive psychology* (Second Edition). New York: Oxford University Press.

3. Carr, A. (2006). *Family therapy: Concepts process and practice (Second Edition).* Chichester, UK: Wiley; Sexton, T., Weeks, G. & Robbins, M. (2003). *Handbook of family therapy.* New York: Brunner-Routledge.

4. Lerner, R. & Steinberg, L. (2009). *Handbook of adolescent development. Volume 1, Individual basis of adolescent development. Volume 2, Contextual Influences on adolescent development* (Third Edition). Chichester: Wiley.

5. The concept of phases is shared by other evidence-based approaches to systemic practice such as Liddle, H. (2010). *Multidimensional family therapy for adolescent drug abuse and delinquency.* New York: Guilford; Lock, J., LeGrange, D., Agras, W. & Dare, C. (2001). *Treatment manual for anorexia nervosa. A family based approach.* New York: Guilford; Sexton, T. (2010). *Functional family therapy in clinical practice: An evidence-based treatment model for working with troubled adolescents.* New York: Routledge.

6. Carr, A. (2009). *What works with children, adolescents and adults? A review of research on the effectiveness of psychotherapy.* London: Routledge.

7. Carr, A. (2009). *What works with children, adolescents and adults? A review of research on the effectiveness of psychotherapy.* London: Routledge; Weiss, J. & Kazdin, A. (2010). Evidence-based psychotherapies for children and Adolescents (Second Edition). New York: Guilford.

8. Anderson, C. & Stewart, S. (1983) *Mastering resistance.* New York: Guilford.

9. Todd, T. & Storm, C. (2002). *The complete systemic supervisor: Context, philosophy, and pragmatics.* Lincon, NE: Universe

Chapter 3

1. Rogers, C. (1961/1995). *On becoming a person. A therapist's view of psychotherapy.* New York: Mariner books.

2. Lanyado, M. & Horne, A. (2009).*The handbook of child and adolescent psychotherapy: Psychoanalytic approaches* (Second Edition). London: Routledge.

3. Carr, A. (2006). *Family therapy: Concepts process and practice (Second Edition).* Chichester, UK: Wiley; Sexton, T., Weeks, G. & Robbins, M. (2003). *Handbook of family therapy.* New York: Brunner-Routledge.

4. American Psychiatric Association (2000a). *Diagnostic and Statistical Manual of the Mental Disorders (Fourth Edition-Text Revision, DSM –IV-TR).* Washington, DC: American Psychiatric Association.

5. World Health Organization (1992.) *The ICD-10 Classification of Mental and Behavioural Disorders.* Geneva: WHO.

6. Carr, A. (2006). *Handbook of child and adolescent clinical psychology* (Second Edition). London: Routledge.

7. Lerner, R. & Steinberg, L. (2009). *Handbook of adolescent development. Volume 1, Individual basis of adolescent development. Volume 2, Contextual Influences on adolescent development* (Third Edition). Chichester: Wiley.

8. Cassidy, J. & Shaver, P. (2008). *Handbook of Attachment (Second Edition).* New York: Guilford.

9. Imber-Black, E. (1993) *Secrets in families and family therapy.* New York: Norton.

10. Miller, W. & Rollnick, S. (2002). *Motivation interviewing* (Second Edition). New York: Guilford.

11. Beck, A. (1976). *Cognitive Therapy and the Emotional Disorders.* New York: International Universities Press; Friedberg, R. & McClure, J. (2002). *Clinical Practice of Cognitive Therapy with Children and Adolescents.* New York: Guilford; Graham, P. (2005), *Cognitive Behaviour Therapy for Children and Families* (Second Edition) Cambridge: Cambridge University Press.

12. Worthington, E. (2005). *Handbook of forgiveness.* New York: Routledge; McCullough, M., Pargament, K. & Thorsen, C. (2000). *Forgiveness. Theory, research and practice.* New York: Guilford.

13. O'Donohue, W. & Ferguson, K. (2001). *The psychology of B. F. Skinner.* Thousand Oaks: Sage.

14. Ollendick, T. & March, J. (2004). *Phobic and anxiety disorders in children and adolescents: a clinician's guide to effective psychosocial and pharmacological interventions. A clinician's guide to effective psychosocial and pharmacological interventions.* New York: Oxford University Press; Morris, T. & March, J. (2004). *Anxiety disorders in children and adolescents* (Second Edition). New York: Guilford.

15. Alberti, R. & Emmons, M. (2008). *Your perfect right: Assertiveness and equality in your life and relationships* (Ninth Edition). Atascadero, CA: Impact.

16. Shaffer, D., Gould, M., Brasic, J., Ambrosini, P., Fisher, P., Bird, H. & Aluwahlia, S. (1983). A children's global assessment scale (CGAS). *Archives of General Psychiatry*, 40 (1), 1228-1231.

17. Yingling, L. C., Miller, W. E., McDonald, A. L., & Galewaler, S. T. (1998). *GARF assessment sourcebook: Using the DSM-IV global assessment of relational functioning.* New York: Brunner/Mazel.

Chapter 4

1. Carr, A. (2006). *Family therapy: Concepts, process and practice (Second Edition).* Chichester, UK: Wiley; Sexton, T., Weeks, G. & Robbins, M. (2003). *Handbook of family therapy.* New York: Brunner-Routledge.

Chapter 5

1. Carr, A. (2009). *What works with children, adolescents and adults? A review of research on the effectiveness of psychotherapy.* London: Routledge.

2. Carr, A. (2006). *Handbook of child and adolescent clinical psychology* (Second Edition). London: Routledge.

3. Carr, A. (2006). *Family therapy: Concepts process and practice (Second Edition).* Chichester, UK: Wiley.

4. Cecchin, G. (1987). Hypothesizing, circularity and neutrality revisited: An invitation to curiosity. *Family Process,* 26, 405-413.

5. Rogers, C. (1961/1995). *On becoming a person. A therapist's view of psychotherapy.* New York: Mariner books.

6. Kelly, G. (1955). *The Psychology of Personal Constructs* (Volumes 1 and 2.) New York: Norton.

7. Lerner, R. & Steinberg, L. (2009). *Handbook of adolescent development. Volume 1, Individual basis of adolescent development. Volume 2, Contextual Influences on adolescent development* (Third Edition). Chichester: Wiley.

8. Shaffer, D., Gould, M., Brasic, J., Ambrosini, P., Fisher, P., Bird, H. & Aluwahlia, S. (1983). A children's global assessment scale (CGAS). *Archives of General Psychiatry*, 40 (1), 1228-1231.

9. Yingling, L. C., Miller, W. E., McDonald, A. L., & Galewaler, S. T. (1998). *GARF assessment sourcebook: Using the DSM-IV global assessment of relational functioning*. New York: Brunner/Mazel.

Chapter 6

1. The concept of phases is shared by other evidence-based approaches to systemic practice such as Liddle, H. (2010). *Multidimensional family therapy for adolescent drug abuse and delinquency.* New York: Guilford; Lock, J., LeGrange, D., Agras, W. & Dare, C. (2001). *Treatment manual for anorexia nervosa. A family based approach.* New York: Guilford; Sexton, T. (2010). *Functional family therapy in clinical practice: An evidence-based treatment model for working with troubled adolescents.* New York: Routledge.

2. Allen, J. & Fonagy, P. (2006). *Handbook of mentalization-based treatment.* Chichester: Wiley. Allen, J., Fonagy, P. & Bateman, A. (2008). *Mentalizing in Clinical Practice.* Washington, DC: American Psychiatric Publishing.

3. Gurman, A. & Jacobson, N. (2002). *Clinical Handbook of Couples Therapy* (Third Edition). New York: Guilford.

4. Carr, A. (2006). *Family therapy: Concepts process and practice (Second Edition).* Chichester, UK: Wiley.

5. Shaffer, D., Gould, M., Brasic, J., Ambrosini, P., Fisher, P., Bird, H. & Aluwahlia, S. (1983). A children's global assessment scale (CGAS). *Archives of General Psychiatry*, 40 (1), 1228-1231.

6. Yingling, L. C., Miller, W. E., McDonald, A. L. & Galewaler, S. T. (1998). *GARF assessment sourcebook: Using the DSM-IV global assessment of relational functioning*. New York: Brunner/Mazel.

Chapter 7

1. Allen, J. & Fonagy, P. (2006). *Handbook of mentalization-based treatment.* Chichester: Wiley. Allen, J., Fonagy, P. & Bateman, A. (2008). *Mentalizing in Clinical Practice.* Washington, DC: American Psychiatric Publishing.

2. Todd, T. & Storm, C. (2002). *The complete systemic supervisor: Context, philosophy, and pragmatics.* Lincon, NE: IUniverse.

Chapter 8

1. Duncan, B. L., Miller, S. D., Reynolds, L., Sparks, J., Claud, D., Brown, J. & Johnson, L. D. (2003). The session rating scale: Psychometric properties of a "working" alliance scale. *Journal of Brief Therapy, 3*(1), 3–12; Miller, S. D., Duncan, B. L., Brown, J., Sparks, J. & Claud, D. (2003). The outcome rating scale: A preliminary study of the reliability, validity, and feasibility of a brief visual analogue measure. *Journal of Brief Therapy, 2*(2), 91–100. http://124.254.10.21/scott/node/6

Chapter 13

1. Shaffer, D., Gould, M., Brasic, J., Ambrosini, P., Fisher, P., Bird, H. & Aluwahlia, S. (1983). A children's global assessment scale (CGAS). *Archives of General Psychiatry,* 40 (1), 1228-1231.

2. Yingling, L. C., Miller, W. E., McDonald, A. L., & Galewaler, S. T. (1998). *GARF assessment sourcebook: Using the DSM-IV global assessment of relational functioning.* New York: Brunner/Mazel.

3. Goodman, R. (2001). Psychometric properties of the Strengths and Difficulties Questionnaire. *American Journal of Child and Adolescent Psychiatry*, 40, 1337-1345.

4. Cahill, P., O'Reilly, K., Carr, A., Dooley, B., & Stratton, P. (2010). Validation of a 28-item version of the Systemic Clinical Outcome and Routine Evaluation in an Irish context: The SCORE-28. *Journal of Family Therapy*, 32, 210-231.

SUMMARY OF PSP

PSP is based on ten principles

1. Counsellors adopt a **positive perspective** in which they are hopeful that counselling can make a difference; where they are sensitive to family strengths; and where families may become more optimistic.

2. Counsellors adopt a **systemic perspective** where adolescents are viewed as embedded in multiple social systems. The domains of family, school, friends and self provide a framework for assessment in the intake session.

3. Counsellors adopt a normal **developmental perspective**, seeing individuals and families as progressing through a series of normal developmental stages over the course of the life cycle, and viewing adolescence as a transitional period.

4. Counsellors adopt a preventative and **therapeutic perspective** by encouraging early engagement in counselling, and where following an initial conjoint family session, adolescents and parents most usually engage in parallel confidential sessions, and periodic conjoint family sessions.

5. Counselling evolves through **phases** of engagement, a middle phase and a closing phase, with different tasks at different phases: assessment and alliance building in the engagement phase; working out problems in the middle phase; and reflecting on gains made and how to manage future challenges in the closing phase.

6. Counsellors prioritise building a **strong working alliance** with clients and promote positive and mutually respectful relationships between adolescents and parents; between families and schools; and between adolescents and pro-social peers.

7. Counsellors **draw on the available evidence-base** about *'what works?'* but customise these interventions to clients' unique individual needs; they conduct counselling in a conversational style.

8. Counsellors accept that setbacks in counselling are common and these *'resistance issues'* are openly and respectfully discussed as they arise.

9. Counsellors **work in teams of two** and engage in regular team consultation and supervision to develop their teams.

10. Counselling **outcome is evaluated** and counsellors take responsibility for helping families achieve positive outcomes.

Counsellors adopt specific stances to translate the principles of PSP into therapeutic interventions

The **four elements** of the **fundamental stance** are:

- Be genuine in your relationship with adolescents and parents

- Understand the defensive function of much problematic behaviour

- Recognise the underlying validity of differing perspectives of adolescents, parents and others in their social networks

- Only adopt an *'expert clinical position'* where there are clear benefits for clients.

1. The **10** stances which **enhance engagement** are:

- Accept that a teenager's perspective is valid

- Respect teenagers and their struggle and have a sense of humour

- Accept that teenagers are not a homogeneous group

- Do not over-react to teenagers' narratives (as this inhibits further communication)

- Accept that conflict between teenagers and parents is inevitable

- Normalise teenagers' occasional challenging behaviours

- Accept that good family relationships promote well-being

- Accept that parents really want to love and do the best for their teenagers

- Accept that parents really matter to teenagers

- Accept that counsellors working with teenagers and their parents have multiple roles.

2.   The **5** stances which **facilitate child protection** are:

- Make it clear from the outset that violence is not tolerated

- Make it clear that usually the longer young people stay in the education system the better

- Help families prevent destructive repetitive behaviour patterns

- Accept that parents are not always right, a positive influence or a resource

- Advocate for teenagers.

3.   The **8** stances which **promote insight and understanding** are:

- Help parents and teenagers understand each other's perspective (even if they do not agree with it)

- Provide psycho-education to give parents and teenagers information relevant to their problems

- Help parents update their teenagers on how family history has affected their current lives

- Help parents address family of origin issues

- Accept that what is not said (and kept secret) is often as important as what is

- Help parents accept that they cannot re-live their own adolescence through their teenagers

- Help teenagers and parents explore the pros and cons of changing their behaviour

- Help parents and teenagers acknowledge and re-appraise negative thoughts.

4.   The **10** stances that **foster behaviour change** are:

- Help family members communicate, negotiate and jointly problem-solve

- Facilitate the processes of apology and forgiveness

- Help parents and teenagers develop clarity about acceptable and unacceptable behaviour (because *'everybody does not do stuff'*)

- Accept that parental over control and under control can lead to adolescent problems

- Respect family and community norms (unless they are too permissive or oppressive)

- Accept that experiencing the consequences of their actions is essential for teenagers to learn to be responsible for their behaviour

- Accept that mistakes are learning opportunities

- Help anxious adolescents develop courageous behaviour

- Help adolescents develop assertive behaviour

- Help family members develop self-care routines.

5.   The **7** stances that **facilitate the transition to adulthood** are:

- Help parents let go of directive parenting and adopt a style based on negotiation – because when primary school is over parenting must change

- Help parents to manage their anxiety, so as to promote their teenager's independence

- Help parents provide teenagers with age-appropriate jobs to do at home

- Help parents allow their teenagers opportunities to develop strategies for protecting themselves in their social environment

- Help non-authoritative parents to be parents (not friends) to their teenagers

- Ask teenagers to take responsibility for their attendance at counselling

- Help parents and teenagers accept that a parent's job is to become redundant.

6. The **3** stances that **facilitate closing the counselling process** are:

- Review progress and setbacks

- Help families discover what they have learned

- Help families plan for lapses and relapses.

APPENDIX 1: Summary of PSP

FREQUENTLY ASKED QUESTIONS

Is it just for teenagers?

Teen Counselling is for teenagers and their parents. We find that working with both is usually the best way of making a difference. Most difficulties for teenagers affect parents and vice versa.

How does it work?

If parents live together we invite them both to come with their teenager to the first appointment. We call this a joint appointment. If parents are separated we decide whether to invite both parents, or just the parent that the teenager lives with. If you decide to return for counselling we involve the other parent whenever possible. Sometimes separated parents need separate appointments.

Who will be at the first appointment?

Usually you will be met by our secretary who will show you to the waiting room. You will be introduced to the counselling team - two, sometimes three, counsellors – and have your first counselling session together. This usually lasts about one and a half hours. We know you will be nervous, but most teenagers (and parents) say that the first session was better than they had expected.

What will happen?

The first appointment is an opportunity for teenagers and parents to say what is not working for them. It is for gathering information and deciding whether Teen Counselling is the right place for you to sort out the difficulties you are experiencing. The counsellors will ask a lot of questions and one counsellor will take some notes so that we remember what you tell us.

Is it private and confidential?

What you tell us about your family is confidential and information is only shared with other people in exceptional circumstances e.g. if we are given information about anyone being hurt, we cannot keep this private. If this happens we talk to you about what we need to do to keep people safe as this is our number one priority.

Can I talk to a counsellor on my own?

After the first appointment, one counsellor will be assigned to the teenager and one to parent(s). In most cases teenagers and parents attend their second appointments separately. We call these individual appointments and they usually last about an hour. Further appointments, individual or joint, are arranged depending on what seems the best way to help.

What happens to the information you have about my family?

Everything to do with your case is kept in a confidential file. The counsellors share information, but sometimes teenagers and/or parents want to keep some information private. As above, this is not possible when it involves anyone being hurt or hurting themselves and your counsellor would talk to you about this.

Do you keep records?

We have forms which we fill out anonymously for each family. We use this information for our Annual Report, for research, for fund raising and also to note trends so that we can provide the sort of service teenagers and families need. We use Data Protection and Freedom of Information guidelines.

How much does it cost?

Teen Counselling does not charge for counselling. We receive funding from several different sources and we are part of the charity, Crosscare. However, donations are always welcome. Should you wish to make a donation, envelopes are available in the waiting room and should be given to the secretary.

Can parents attend without their teenager?

Sometimes teenagers decide that they do not want to attend counselling. In such cases a counsellor will meet with a parent, or both parents, to discuss their concerns. This usually works much better than 'forcing' a teenager to attend. If the teenager changes his/her mind, another appointment can be made.

How long does counselling take?

Every family is different. Some families only attend once or twice and some find it useful to keep in touch for a long time. The average time is about 9 sessions over 9 months. Teenagers and parents often have a few sessions quite close together when they first start, say every two weeks, and then if things are going well, appointments are less often.

Do I have to attend?

Some teenagers ask for counselling themselves, but most teenagers attend Teen Counselling because an adult (most often a parent) thinks it is a good idea. Parents are often (not always) right, so it is usually worth giving it a try. You may be surprised at how well it works.

Why does anyone go to counselling?

Families come to Teen Counselling because they have problems that they feel stuck with. Teen Counselling gives teenagers and parents a 'space apart' from their everyday lives and with the support of the counselling team they can often find new ways of doing things so that life gets back on track.

Teen Counselling Referral Form

Counsellors_____

1. Age (12-18) **( )**   **2.** Catchment area/Substance use **( )**   **3.** Child Protection Responsibility **( )**   **4.** GP suggested **( )**

Caller's first name: **Teen's first name:**

Referral Date: _____   **Date 1st Appt:**_____   **Time:**_____

Still Interested: _____   **Date 1ˢᵗ Appt Confirmed**: _____**By**:_____

CAN 1ˢᵗ appt no further service:_____ DNA 1ˢᵗ appt no further service:_____NFU:_____

To take a referral, I have to ask you some details about the problem. The information you give me is confidential, except if there is concern that any young person may be at risk. We have policies to deal with this which I can explain later if I need to. OK?

REASON FOR REFERRAL:_____

_____
_____
_____
_____
_____
_____
_____
_____
_____
_____
_____

HOW LONG HAS PROBLEM EXISTED? _____
HAS PERSON EVER ATTENDED OR BEEN REFERRED TO ANY OTHER AGENCY: **YES / NO**

CHILD GUIDANCE CLINIC____   SOCIAL WORKER _____   SPECIAL SCHOOL ___
COUNSELLOR___   PSYCHOLOGIST___   PSYCHIATRIST_____   OTHER_____
IF SO, WHERE: _____WHEN: _____

WILL CLIENT RETURN THERE **YES / NO** Reason: _____

_____

TEEN'S NAME: _____ _____**AGE:** ____ **D.O.B**:_____
ADDRESS:_____NATIONALITY:_____
_____ LANGUAGE:_____
MOTHER'S NAME:_____**FATHER'S/other's NAME:**_____
address if diff:_____address if diff:_____
_____ _____
tel/mobile:_____ tel/mobile:_____
REFERRED BY:_____ tel: _____
SUGGESTED BY: _____ tel: _____
SCHOOL:_____YEAR: _____

IS MOTHER AWARE OF REFERRAL? _____   WILLING TO ATTEND? _____
IS FATHER AWARE OF REFERRAL? _____   WILLING TO ATTEND? _____
IS TEENAGER AWARE OF REFERRAL? _____   WILLING TO ATTEND? _____

(Before appointment can be given to clients whose parents are separated)

HAVE YOU INFORMED MOTHER / FATHER?   YES / NO

REASON FOR REFERRAL Cont:

_____
_____
_____
_____
_____
_____

INTAKE/CENTRE MEETING DATE:_____ _FOR OFFICE USE ONLY_

On Waiting List:_____ Date:_____

Not Accepted:_____ Date:_____

Referred On:_____ Date:_____

Awaiting Clarification:_____ Date:_____

Off Waiting List:_____ Date:_____Client ( )   Problem resolved ( )

Gone elsewhere ( )   Teen won't attend ( )   Don't know ( )   Other_____

PLAN OF ACTION:

_____
_____
_____
_____
_____

SOCIAL WORKER REFERRAL

Centre E-mail: Centre Fax:

Referrer Details

Referral Date: _____

Name:_____ Title: _____

Address:

_____

_____ Tel. No. _____

Teen Details

Teen's Name: _____

Address: _____

_____

D.O.B.: _____   School:_____   Year: _____

Other relevant addresses if parents are separated or teenager is living away from home:

Mother's Name_____ Father's Name_____

Address: _____   Address_____

_____   _____

Phone No. _____Phone No. _____

Contact details of person teen is living with if he/she is not living with parents

Name: _____   Phone No.:_____

Has this referral been discussed with *(please tick)*			Are Mother, Father and Adolescent willing to attend? *(please tick)*	
Mother	Yes ☐	No ☐ Mother	Yes ☐	No ☐
Father	Yes ☐	No ☐ Father	Yes ☐	No ☐
Teen	Yes ☐	No ☐ Teen	Yes ☐	No ☐
If no to any of the above, why?_____			If no to any of the above, why?	

Have you referred this teen to any other service?   Yes ☐   No ☐

If yes where?

_____

<u>you answered yes to this question please contact Teen Counselling before returning this form.</u>

1. What is your assessment of the problem?

_____

_____

_____

_____

_____

_____

_____

_____

_____

2. What are the specific issues you would like Teen Counselling to address with the family?

_____

_____

_____

_____

_____

_____

_____

_____

_____

_____

2a. How important do **you think** it is for *(teen)* _____ to come to Teen Counselling at this time?

0 - - - - - 1 - - - - - 2 - - - - - 3 - - - - - 4 - - - - - 5 - - - - - 6 - - - - - 7 - - - - - 8 - - - - - 9 - - - - - 10
    not at all important   *don't mind either way*   *really very important*

2b. How important do you think *(teen)* _____ **thinks it is for him/her to come** for counselling at this time.

0 - - - - - 1 - - - - - 2 - - - - - 3 - - - - - 4 - - - - - 5 - - - - - 6 - - - - - 7 - - - - - 8 - - - - - 9 - - - - - 10
    not at all important   *don't mind either way*   *really very important*

3. Describe the nature of the relationship and contact your client has with parent(s) living outside of the home.

_____

_____

_____

_____

_____

_____

4. Who does the teen live with? (specify) Describe the nature of the relationship.

_____
_____
_____
_____
_____
_____
_____
_____
_____
_____

5. What is your level of contact to date with this family?

_____
_____
_____
_____
_____
_____
_____
_____
_____
_____
_____

6. What is the nature of HSE contact with this family whilst they await an appointment with Teen Counselling?

_____
_____
_____
_____
_____
_____
_____
_____
_____

7. What HSE Social Worker will be working with this family while Teen Counselling is involved.

_____

_____

_____

8. Is the teen on any medication? (specify):

_____

_____

_____

Generally speaking we would expect a joint working approach between Teen Counselling and the HSE. Do you see this as appropriate in this case?

_____

_____

_____

_____

_____

If relevant reports are requested, will they be made available to us?

Yes ☐ No ☐

INTAKE MEETING DATE: _____ **FOR OFFICE USE ONLY**

PLAN OF ACTION:

Who should attend at the first appointment?

_____

_____

_____

_____

_____

_____

_____

_____

☐ CONFIDENTIALITY   **PARENTS**

DATE: _____   FILE NO: _____

AT FIRST VISIT

What do you see as the main problem now?...

1.   How severe is the problem?

            (1) Mild

            (2) Moderate

            (3) Serious

            (4) Very serious

            (5) Dangerous to self or others

2.   How difficult is this for you to cope with?

            (1) Cannot manage

            (2) Very difficult

            (3) Fairly difficult

            (4) Not difficult

Mother

Father

Other (specify) ....

AT CLOSURE

DATE: _____

1.   How severe is the problem now?

        (1) No problem

        (2) Mild

        (3) Moderate

        (4) Serious

        (5) Very serious

        (6) Dangerous to self or others

2.   Looking back to the first visit, would you say that the problem has:

        (1) Greatly Disimproved

        (2) Disimproved

        (3) No change

        (4) Improved

        (5) Greatly Improved

3.   How difficult is the situation for you now?

        (1) Cannot manage

        (2) Very difficult

        (3) Fairly difficult

        (4) Not difficult

4.   Looking back to the first visit, would you say that the situation for you has:

        (1) Greatly Disimproved

        (2) Disimproved

        (3) No change

        (4) Improved

        (5) Greatly Improved

TEENAGERS

☐ CONFIDENTIALITY

DATE: _____

FILE NO: _____

AT FIRST VISIT

What do you see as your main problem now? ....

How much of a problem is this?

Re:	School	Re:	Home	Re:	Friends	Re:	Self
(0)	No Problem	(0)	No Problem	(0)	No Problem	(0)	No Problem
(1)	Mild	(1)	Mild	(1)	Mild	(1)	Mild
(2)	Moderate	(2)	Moderate	(2)	Moderate	(2)	Moderate
(3)	Serious	(3)	Serious	(3)	Serious	(3)	Serious
(4)	Very Serious	(4)	Very Serious	(4)	Very Serious	(4)	Very Serious
(5)	A Danger to Self or Others	(5)	A Danger to Self or Others	(5)	A Danger to Self or Others	(5)	A Danger to Self or Others

AT CLOSURE

DATE: _____

1. Right now, how much of a problem is ....*(the initial main problem)*

Re:	School	Re:	Home	Re:	Friends	Re:	Self
(0)	No Problem	(0)	No Problem	(0)	No Problem	(0)	No Problem
(1)	Mild	(1)	Mild	(1)	Mild	(1)	Mild
(2)	Moderate	(2)	Moderate	(2)	Moderate	(2)	Moderate
(3)	Serious	(3)	Serious	(3)	Serious	(3)	Serious
(4)	Very Serious	(4)	Very Serious	(4)	Very Serious	(4)	Very Serious
(5)	A Danger to Self or Others	(5)	A Danger to Self or Others	(5)	A Danger to Self or Others	(5)	A Danger to Self or Others

2. Looking back at how you were at the first visit, what is the difference between how you were then and how you are now in relation to:

Re:	School	Re:	Home	Re:	Friends	Re:	Self
(1)	Greatly Disimproved	(1)	Greatly Disimproved	(1)	Greatly Disimproved	(1)	Greatly Disimproved
(2)	Disimproved	(2)	Disimproved	(2)	Disimproved	(2)	Disimproved
(3)	No Change	(3)	No Change	(3)	No Change	(3)	No Change
(4)	Improved	(4)	Improved	(4)	Improved	(4)	Improved
(5)	Greatly Improved	(5)	Greatly Improved	(5)	Greatly Improved	(5)	Greatly Improved

First session – Confidentiality

File Number: _____

Date: _____

☐ **THIS IS A VOLUNTARY SERVICE** – a space apart – you only come if you want to.

☐ **THIS IS A CONFIDENTIAL SERVICE** – which means that what you tell us is not discussed with anyone outside Teen Counselling unless you ask us to, or we all agree that it would be useful. Teen Counselling includes ourselves and other team members.

☐ **HOWEVER, THERE ARE SOME IMPORTANT LIMITATIONS TO CONFIDENTIALITY** which we tell everyone about before we start talking as we never know what information families will give us:
- when we hear that either adults or children are at risk of harming themselves or others, or are being harmed by others.
- when we hear that anyone is currently being abused or has been abused in the past.

When any of these situations occur we have to do something about it, but if we need to contact another agency we would usually discuss it with you first.

☐ **AFTER THE BREAK IF CLIENTS ARE TO RETURN AND INDIVIDUAL SESSIONS ARE PLANNED -** one of us will work with (**name of teen**) and the other will work with (**name of parents**) and we will meet separately as well as together, like today. We have separate sessions that are confidential and we do not:-
- tell a Teen what a Parent has said in a session.
- tell a Parent what a Teen has said in a session.
- carry messages from Parent to Teen or vice versa - unless there is concern about risk or where we decide with you that this is a useful thing to do. Counsellors, of course, share information to make sure that the support you get is relevant.

For referrals made on Social Worker's form

2c. How important do you (teen) think it is to come to Teen Counselling at this time?

0 - - - - - 1 - - - - - 2 - - - - - 3 - - - - - 4 - - - - - 5 - - - - - 6 - - - - - 7 - - - - - 8 - - - - - 9 - - - - - 10
   not at all important   *don't mind either way*   *really very important*

INTERVENTION PLAN

1. _____

_____

_____

2. _____

_____

_____

3. _____

_____

_____